Investigation of Fr
and Economic Crim

Investigation of Fraud and Economic Crime

Michael J Betts

With contributions from
Nick Court, Michael Dodge, Andrew Fyfe, Kerrie Gower, Nigel Howard,
Oliver Little, David Manley, Ian Sales, John Unsworth, Russell Wate
City of London Police

Consultant editor

David Clark

Head of Economic Crime Directorate
City of London Police

Foreword by

Commander Chris Greany

National Coordinator for Economic Crime

OXFORD

UNIVERSITY PRESS

Great Clarendon Street, Oxford, OX2 6DP,
United Kingdom

Oxford University Press is a department of the University of Oxford.
It furthers the University's objective of excellence in research, scholarship,
and education by publishing worldwide. Oxford is a registered trade mark of
Oxford University Press in the UK and in certain other countries

The moral rights of the authors have been asserted

First Edition published in 2017

Impression: 2

Published in the United States of America by Oxford University Press
198 Madison Avenue, New York, NY 10016, United States of America

British Library Cataloguing-in-Publication Data

Data available

Library of Congress Control Number: 2016953422

ISBN 978–0–19–879901–6

Printed and bound by
CPI Group (UK) Ltd, Croydon, CR0 4YY

Foreword

As the National Coordinator for Economic Crime I am delighted to be writing this foreword for *Investigation of Fraud and Economic Crime*.

I welcome this guide for practitioners which will be an asset to the law enforcement and counter-fraud community alike, providing clarity in the complex landscape of fraud investigation.

Fraud is growing both in reporting and the harm and loss it causes. The internet has created a place where criminals can both exploit technology to steal large sums of money and use it to attempt to evade the range of law enforcement agencies active across the UK.

Law enforcement has made great strides at targeting the most serious offenders and more cases are being investigated. However, the scale of the challenge is increasing and prevention (helping businesses and individuals protect themselves and designing out vulnerabilities) is the most effective long-term way of reducing the threat.

We are continually building partnerships nationally and internationally that will help reduce victimisation in the UK. To get to the root of fraud it is essential that all members of the police and wider counter-fraud community understand more about the structure, legislation and investigative methodologies of fraud crime and prevention. This book will introduce the reader to the Fraud Investigation Model. It is a framework that should be embedded in policing practice and provides a logical process for countering fraud.

The UK is in a good position to be at the forefront of tackling fraud. Law enforcement, government and the private sector are operating in ever closer alliance. If we are to reduce fraud we need to build upon the impressive work underway, drawing upon the expertise of one another and collaborating to provide a conjoined, consistent, proactive and reactive response to fraud crime and prevention.

This book will make a significant contribution to combating fraud; it covers a wide range of topics and makes the subject of fraud accessible to all. I know both the editors and many of the contributors; they have committed their knowledge and experience to this publication making it essential reading for those either tasked with or interested in countering fraud.

Commander Chris Greany
National Coordinator for Economic Crime
City of London Police
August 2016

Editor's note

The threat, harm and loss caused by fraud is one of the greatest challenges currently facing the police service. Indeed, as I prepare this note the BBC are reporting new figures detailing that one in ten UK citizens were victims of fraud in 2015/16. This is the volume and priority crime of the twenty-first century; it is being committed on an industrial scale. The use of the internet and widespread possession of digitally enabled devices have contributed to it being the most prevalent crime in the UK.

It is the intention of this book to provide a practitioner's view of countering fraud using prevention, disruption and good investigative practice. It is written by practitioners for practitioners and details how the investigator can effectively use the 4Ps—namely, Pursue, Protect, Prepare and Prevent—to combat fraud by implementing the framework provided by the Fraud Investigation Model (FIM). The FIM provides a logical process for those combating fraud to follow and is at the centre of the processes described in this book. Importantly, it places an emphasis on prevention and disruption in addition to investigation.

The range of authors who have contributed to this book brings a depth of personal experience and knowledge in countering fraud. All have two key skills in common that are required in fighting fraud: diligence and attention to detail. I am immensely grateful for their commitment to this project.

This book is designed to be a gateway to the world of fraud. It is hoped that it can make the terms used accessible, demystify the typologies and where necessary be a useful refresher to the key topics of material recovery and disclosure, and highlight the value of operational learning. Throughout the book there are signposts to further reading which will assist the reader to find more information about topics of interest.

This Blackstone's guide gathers together in one place a wide range of elements that contribute to combating fraud; it is not meant to be a weighty textbook but a useful guide. The attention to detail is critical as often the challenges made by defence teams are on procedural matters when the case is presented at court. The book looks at the available methods of recovery and disclosure. As a fraud investigation is often focused on following the money, there is a chapter on financial investigations, the powers available and the role of the financial investigator.

Key to countering fraud in both its investigation and prevention is the identification of the key enablers used to facilitate the fraud. In many cases these are the fraudsters' vulnerabilities—they have a need to communicate, move money and often use the internet, and these enablers present both investigative and disruption opportunities. The book examines enablers, their identification and the methods available to the investigator to deny the fraudster access to them.

Special thanks must go to all those who supported this project from inception through to publication. This has very much been a team effort and thanks should go to the consultant editor, Detective Chief Superintendent Dave Clark, who took the project forward with passion and encouraged the contributors throughout. I should also mention Kathy Hearn, who has given her full support to the project and was committed in making it a success.

I am grateful to all the members of the Strategic Development Unit at the City of London Police who assisted in the project. In particular, I would like to thank both Alison Harle and Lucy Grummell, who were key members of the project team. It was their continuous commitment, encouragement and perseverance that were instrumental in making this book happen.

Whilst every care has been taken to ensure that the contents of this book are accurate, neither the publisher nor the authors can accept any responsibility for any action taken, or not taken, on the basis of the information contained within the book.

Michael J Betts
Head of Training Delivery
Economic Crime Academy
City of London Police
August 2016

Preface

The increasing globalisation of fraud continues, driven by an enhanced international communications infrastructure, increased accessibility to the internet, poor levels of regulation and under-resourced law enforcement capabilities in some countries. The threat of fraud exists not just to individuals and organisations, but to UK national security, the economy and our infrastructure. Fraudsters continue to use new techniques to commit their crimes including the use of cyber technologies with risks extending into many aspects of social life.

Successful reduction of fraud criminality requires a holistic approach; no single government agency or private institution can tackle the wide range of threats from fraud overseas alone. The borderless nature of cyber-enabled and cyber-dependent crime means the UK can be targeted from jurisdictions across the world, introducing further complexity in investigation.

The growing scale of fraud places an increasing demand on UK police resources and the wider counter-fraud community, the challenge is increased as it is set against a backdrop of austerity. The ever increasing international dimensions in terms of money flow present further challenges to prosecution and asset recovery.

Recent years have seen a major shift in the police response to fraud; the National Fraud Reporting Centre—Action Fraud—created in 2010, is an effective mechanism to facilitate the reporting and dissemination of fraud crime amongst law enforcement. This facility feeds the National Fraud Intelligence Bureau, which harnesses the information available from the public and private sectors, forming a sound intelligence base on which the threat and associated harm can be assessed.

Unique challenges present themselves to officers and staff who are trying to negotiate their way through the volume of powers available to them, such as the complexity of fraud itself, the nature of the specialist roles involved and the political sensitivities when dealing with influential bodies in the private sector. This publication recognises these challenges and for the first time seeks to provide the police and wider counter-fraud community with a resource to address fraud criminality both reactively and proactively. It focuses on the application of the Fraud Investigation Model, which is a useful framework for use by the practitioner in countering fraud.

Fraud extends its reach to all types of policing: neighbourhood policing teams, specialist crime, response policing and specialist roles such as asset recovery. Police professionals will find this publication an excellent reference on a daily basis, an aid to inform training programmes or ongoing professional development. This publication will equally serve the vast counter-fraud community by providing a valuable insight into the law and investigative methodologies that can be applied in their own areas. Emphasis is placed upon the power of a collaborative approach and the benefits of pooling knowledge, resources and powers. This publication has been informed by a network of fraud investigation, prevention and disruption specialists.

It is imperative that the harm associated with fraud remains at the forefront of the minds of chief officers, Crime Commissioners, senior executives and government officials. The threat from fraud will only grow and present an ever increasing risk to UK citizens, the economy and infrastructure. It is recognised that knowledge gaps will exist within law enforcement and counter-fraud agencies; this publication seeks to fill those gaps by providing the reader with guidance and support through all aspects of fraud investigation, disruption and prevention.

Detective Chief Superintendent David Clark, MSt (Cantab)
Head of Economic Crime Directorate
City of London Police
August 2016

Acknowledgements

The editor is grateful to the following people for providing their expert opinions on a complex topic: David Aldous, Sanjay Andersen, Katie Balls, Stephen Barnett, Sean Bylinski-Gelder, Richie Carr, Fred Ellis, Paul Farley, Lesley Galpin, Richard Hanstock, Ian Havis, Kathy Hearn, Delia Heath, Dr Stephen Hill, Mark Johnson, Paul Jones, Leonie Lewis, Graham Mace, Steve Morran, John Munton, Alix Newbold, Peter Ratcliffe, Steve Taylor, Kerrie Wadmore, Jennifer Wilson and Lara Xenoudakis.

The editor would like to extend his thanks to the College of Policing for their kind permission to use the Fraud Investigation Model diagram.

Contents

Contents

Table of cases

Table of legislation

Abbreviations

4Ps	Pursue, protect, prepare and prevent
ABE	Achieving best evidence (in criminal proceedings)
ABI	Association of British Insurers
ACPO	Association of Chief Police Officers
AFI	Accredited financial investigator
AMC	Accident management company
AO	Authorising officer
APP	Authorised Professional Practice (College of Policing)
ATCSA	Anti-Terrorism, Crime and Security Act (2001)
ATM	Automated teller machine
BBA	British Bankers' Association
BIBA	British Insurance Brokers Association
BIM	Bribery Investigation Model
BIS	Department for Business, Innovation and Skills
BRP	Biometric residence permit
CACD	Court of Appeal Criminal Division
CCTV	Closed-circuit television
CFA	Company formation agent
CHIS	Covert human intelligence source
CIFAS	Credit Industry Fraud Avoidance System (UK)
CiSP	Cyber-security Information Sharing Partnership
CMA	Computer Misuse Act (1990)
CNP	Card not present
CPD	Continued professional development
CPIA	Criminal Procedures and Investigation Act (1996)
CPS	Crown Prosecution Service
CoLP	City of London Police
DBS	Disclosure and Barring Service
DCPCU	Dedicated Card and Payment Crime Unit
DDoS	Distributed denial-of-service attack
DTD	Dial through draft
DISA	Direct inward system access fraud
DMC	Digital media coordinator
DMD	Disclosure management document
DMI	Digital media investigator
DNS	Domain name system
DoS	Denial-of-service attack
DPA	Data Protection Act (1998)

DVD	Digital video disc
DWP	Department for Work and Pensions
EC3	European Cybercrime Centre
ECC	Economic Crime Command
ECP	Economic Crime Portfolio
ECPC	Economic and Cyber Crime Prevention Centre
EU	European Union
FACT	Federation Against Copyright Theft
FATF	Financial Action Task Force
FCA	Financial Conduct Authority (formerly the FSA)
FFA UK	Financial Fraud Action (UK)
FI	Financial investigator
FIM	Fraud Investigation Model
FIO	Financial intelligence officer
FIU	Financial investigation unit
FOG	Fraudulently obtained genuine (document)
FSA	Financial Services Authority (now the FCA)
FSMA	Financial Services and Markets Act (2000)
GPMS	Government Protective Marking Scheme
GSO	Get Safe Online
HM	Her Majesty's
HMCTS	Her Majesty's Courts and Tribunals Service
HMG	Her Majesty's Government
HMPO	Her Majesty's Passport Office
HMRC	Her Majesty's Revenue and Customs
HO	Home Office
HOCR	Home Office Counting Rules
HOLMES	Home Office Large Major Enquiry System
ICO	Information Commissioner's Office
IDA	Identity Documents Act (2010)
IFB	Insurance Fraud Bureau
IFED	Insurance Fraud Enforcement Department
IFIG	Insurance Fraud Investigators Group
IFR	Insurance Fraud Register
IO	Investigating Officer
IP	Intellectual property
IP	Internet protocol
IPO	Intellectual Property Office
ISA	Information-sharing agreement
IT	Information technology
JARD	Joint Asset Recovery Database
JIT	Joint investigation team
KDL	Key decision log
KVM	Keyboard, video, mouse

LPP	Legal professional privilege
MAP	Material assets people
MAPPA	Multi-Agency Public Protection Arrangements
MB	Megabytes
MIB	Motor Insurers Bureau
MIR	Major incident room
MIRSAP	Major Incident Room Standardised Administrative Procedures
MIT	Major investigation team
MiTM	Man-in-the-middle attack
MLAT	Mutual legal assistance treaties
MO	Modus operandi
MoJ	Ministry of Justice
MoU	Memorandum of understanding
MP	Member of Parliament
MPS	Metropolitan Police Service
NaVCIS	National Vehicle Crime Intelligence Service
NCA	National Crime Agency
NCA POCC	National Crime Agency Proceeds of Crime Centre
NCOCC	National Crime Operations Coordination Committee
NCSC	National Cyber Security Centre
NDFU	National Document Fraud Unit
NFA	National Fraud Authority
NFA	No further action
NFIB	National Fraud Intelligence Bureau
NHS	National Health Service
NI	Northern Ireland
NLF	National lead force
NPCC	National Police Chiefs' Council
OCG	Organised crime groups
OIC	Officer in the case
PA	Personal assistant
PACE	Police and Criminal Evidence Act (1984)
PAT	Problem analysis triangle
PBX	Private branch exchange
PC	Personal computer
PCC	Police and Crime Commissioner
PII	Public interest immunity
PII	Personally identifiable information
PIN	Personal identification number
PIPCU	Police Intellectual Property Crime Unit
PND	Police National Database
POCA	Proceeds of Crime Act (2002)
POLKA	Police OnLine Knowledge Area
POLSA	Police search adviser

PSAR	Private sector asset recovery
PSP	Payment service provider
RFT	Regional fraud team
RIPA	Regulation of Investigatory Powers Act (2000)
ROCU	Regional organised crime unit
ROI	Return on investment
SAR	Suspicious activity report
SARA	Scanning, analysis, response, assessment
SFO	Serious Fraud Office
SIO	Senior investigating officer
SLT	Senior leadership team
SME	Subject matter expert
SMS	Short message service
SOC	Serious organised crime
SOCA	Serious Organised Crime Agency (UK)
SOCPA	Serious Organised Crime and Police Act (2005)
SOP	Standard operating procedure
SPOC	Single point of contact
SRA	Solicitors Regulatory Authority
TCSP	Trust or company service provider
TLD	Top-level domain
ToR	Terms of reference
TUFF	Telephone UK Fraud Forum
UCO	Undercover officer
UK	United Kingdom
UKBA	United Kingdom Bribery Act (2010)
URL	Uniform resource locator (an internet address)
VoIP	Voice over internet protocol
VPN	Virtual private network

List of contributors

Michael J Betts Mike is an experienced and highly regarded officer with the City of London Police, who has developed a unique understanding of fraud and bribery. This is based on knowledge gained from undertaking both complex investigations and training delivery in this specialist area. His experience has been gained over 15 years serving as an operational detective and eight years as a specialist fraud trainer. He is currently the head of training delivery at the City of London's Police Economic Crime Academy and is the vice chair of the counter-fraud professional accreditations board.

Nick Court Nick is a City of London Police officer with 14 years' experience in law enforcement, having worked in fields including investigation and intelligence analysis. He is an experienced investigator of fraud, money laundering and counterfeiting offences, and has experience in counter-terrorism and acquisitive crime. In addition to his core policing role, Nick spent part of his career working within national law enforcement agencies and the Home Office. Nick led the National Fraud Intelligence Bureau (NFIB) cyber team until 2015, working with UK police forces, national agencies, government departments and colleagues to improve the national response to incidents of cyber crime.

Michael Dodge Michael is the deputy head of the Police Intellectual Property Crime Unit and manages the team's investigation and disruption capabilities, with a focus on continued delivery of unique and innovative strategies. In 2004 he joined the City of London Police's Economic Crime Directorate (ECD) as a financial investigator and has worked in asset recovery, money laundering and payment fraud teams, notably as part of the Dedicated Card and Payment Crime Unit (DCPCU). Michael has operational expertise in the investigation and disruption of serious and organised economic crime, in domestic and international environments, and in particular where offending is 'cyber-enabled'.

Andrew Fyfe Andrew is Head of Crime within the NFIB, leading the NFIB fraud and cyber crime teams. He ran fraud teams investigating serious and organised criminality, including setting up the London Regional Fraud Team, deploying proactive, covert evidence-gathering techniques to crack complex fraud cases. He ran the Police Intellectual Property Crime Unit, instigating groundbreaking techniques to disrupt web-based criminality in partnership with the advertising industry. Andrew set up the Economic Crime Academy, pioneering the police provision of training for the public and private sectors. He regularly presents as a subject matter expert at training courses and financial industry conferences.

Kerrie Gower Kerrie is the Head of the DCPCU, a national policing team which focuses on tackling organised payment crime affecting the UK card and banking industry. During her 18-year career within the City of London Police, Kerrie has gained extensive experience having worked in a number of policing commands including the Criminal Investigations Department, Covert and Undercover Policing Department and the ECD since 2008. Whilst in ECD, Kerrie specialised in money laundering and asset recovery investigation and was responsible for implementing the force criminal finances strategy.

Nigel Howard Nigel has worked in fraud investigation for many years, and has been involved in many successful prosecutions in major cases. As the City of London Police ECD lead for disclosure, he has researched and disseminated best practice across the department, plus delivered training in the subject at the Economic Crime Academy.

Oliver Little Oliver began his policing career in Surrey, where he worked in uniformed response and specialist operations. He moved to the City of London Police in 2003 and has served in a wide variety of units with a career anchor in complex case investigation. He moved into the ECD in 2010, and joined the Insurance Fraud Enforcement Department (IFED) in 2014 as lead for operations and was promoted in January 2016 to become the head of IFED.

David Manley David currently heads up fraud and financial investigation for the City of London Police, which includes its operational response as national lead force for fraud investigation. David has worked within the ECD for the past 18 years and his current role includes the management of the suspicious activity regime, confiscation and asset recovery. David is an experienced senior investigating officer in large-scale fraud and money laundering cases. He has qualified as a financial investigator and has recently achieved an International Compliance Training diploma in Anti-Money Laundering.

Ian Sales Ian studied law at university and has been in the City of London Police for over 20 years and has worked within the ECD for over five years; during his time at the academy, Ian travelled nationally and internationally training specialist investigators from the public and private sectors in the prevention, detection and investigation of complex financial crime. Ian has also played a major part in the writing and delivering of wider investigation training when he was an associate lecturer at the City of London University's Centre for Investigative Police Sciences.

John Unsworth John is the former head of the Economic and Cyber Crime Prevention Centre (ECPC), within the City of London Police. John has 20 years' experience in law enforcement, which has involved successfully leading national initiatives aimed at identifying, preventing and detecting criminal activities and targeting economic and cyber crime threats committed by organised crime groups. John has frequently been an ambassador for the UK at international crime forums, and has regularly briefed senior government officials on the criminal threats affecting the UK.

Russell Wate QPM Russell is a retired police officer, who for the last six years of his service was the Detective Chief Superintendent for the Cambridgeshire Constabulary. He has a strong operational and strategic understanding of fraud investigations having worked in the field for over 30 years as both an investigating officer and a senior investigating officer on major fraud investigations. In the 2008 birthday honours he was awarded the Queen's Police Medal for his work nationally as a detective. He has a doctorate and his thesis is on Investigating Child Deaths.

Other contributors to this publication: Matthew Andrews, Mahwish Anwar, Mark Baker, Kaitlan Billings, Matthew Bradford, Richard Butcher, Roger Cook, Simon Cordell, Paul Curtis, Victoria Davies, Robert Dawson, Carl Dempsey, John Ellis, Nicola-Jane Fairbairn, Christopher Felton, Tony Forte, Alan Gooden, Glenn Goodwin, Lucy Grummell, Alison Harle, Robert Haslam, Neil Jordan, Phillip Keating, Timothy Lee, Amanda Lowe, Mark Lugton, Richard Maynard, Daniel Medlycott, Melonie Moody, Craig Mullish, Donna Murdoch, Melissa Nimmons, Peter O'Doherty, Julian Page, Stephen Proffitt, David Robertson, Stephen Scarrott, Lauren Smith, Neil Taylor, Steven Taylor, Michael Wandel, Mark Warner, Glyn Whittick, Megan Wild.

Glossary

Account takeover fraud A type of fraud whereby the suspect poses as a genuine customer to gain control of an account and make unauthorised transactions.

Acquisitive crime An offence where the offender derives material gain from the crime, e.g. theft blackmail.

Action fraud A national centre for reporting of fraud and cyber crime.

Actus reus The action or conduct element of a crime, other than the guilty person's state of mind.

Administration (of a company) Designed to keep a company trading while a financial rescue plan is put together, or while plans are put in place to determine how best to sell the company and its assets in order to obtain the best result for creditors.

Administrative receivership The process initiated by creditors holding security over a company's assets, once they have become concerned about the company's ability to repay its debts to them. The receiver is appointed to sell the company and its assets in order to try and recover the money owed to the secured creditor(s).

Advance fee frauds Where the fraudster requests that a victim makes advance payment for goods or services that never appear.

Boiler room fraud Involves bogus stockbrokers cold-calling people to pressure them into buying shares promising high returns. In reality, the shares are either worthless or non-existent.

Bot A software application that runs automated tasks over the internet; normally these tasks are simple, repetitive and carried out at a high speed.

Botnet A network of private computers infected with malicious software and controlled as a group without the owner's knowledge.

Brute-force attack Consists of quickly and systematically testing many combinations to guess passwords in order to break a security system.

Business directory fraud Involves fraudsters duping businesses into purchasing advertising space and listings.

Call for service A report received directly by the police, when the offender is present or known to the victim.

Carbon credits Where the victim is sold credit certificates or given an opportunity to invest in green initiatives.

Case theory A specific approach to investigating complex fraud.

Charity fraud Fake charities that capture well-intended donations instead of sending them to the worthy causes they promote.

Civil recovery investigation An investigation into assets that are derived from or intended for use in unlawful conduct with the ultimate aim of forfeiting them in civil proceedings in the High Court.

Click fraud A type of fraud where online advertisers generate income by visitors clicking on their advertisement. The fraud occurs where automated script or computer programs are used to replicate consumers.

Cloud computing Enables users to store and access data and programs with third parties over the internet instead of via a computer's hard drive.

Collateral intrusion The risk of intrusion into the privacy of persons other than those who are directly the subjects of the investigation or operation.

Command and control server A server that controls a botnet by issuing instructions and taking on information.

Companies House Companies House incorporates and dissolves limited companies, registers the information companies are legally required to supply and makes that information available to the public.

Computer software service fraud Fraudsters inform victims that their computer security has been compromised and offer to fix it for a small fee. The fraudster can then go on to use the victims' bank details fraudulently or install a virus to help to commit further frauds.

Confiscation investigation An investigation into the extent and whereabouts of a person's benefit from their criminal conduct.

Confiscators Those who carry out confiscation investigations and any linked restraints.

Copyright A form of intellectual property, applicable to certain forms of creative work.

Counterfeit To counterfeit means to imitate something. Counterfeit products are fake replicas of real products.

Courier fraud When fraudsters phone and attempt to trick a potential victim into handing their cards and PIN numbers to a courier on their doorstep.

'Crash for cash' To stage or deliberately cause a road traffic collision solely for the purpose of financial gain.

Cuckoo smurfing The disposal of criminal cash through third-party cash deposits.

Cyber attack Can be thought of as a collection of criminal activities undertaken mostly via computers and computer networks in order to steal money, steal information or cause damage.

Cyber crime Crime that usually involves the use of a computer and/or digital network.

Dark web A term that refers specifically to a collection of websites which use the internet but which require specific software, configurations or authorisation to access (often containing information regarding/access to illegal scams).

Denial-of-service (DoS) attack A network layer attack. This is usually an attack on a website and it works by overloading the target with networked traffic.

Detained cash investigation Investigation into the origins and intended use of cash seized under Part 5 of the Proceeds of Crime Act (POCA) 2002.

Digital envelope A secure electronic data container that is used to protect a message through encryption and data authentication.

Digital footprint Describes the trail, traces or footprints that people leave online whilst using the internet.

Directed surveillance Covert but not intrusive surveillance undertaken for a specific operation but likely to result in private information about a person being obtained (RIPA 2000).

Disclosure management document Document setting out what has been done when and how regarding disclosure.

Disclosure officer Responsible for the day-to-day management of unused material and complying with all legal obligations.

Disclosure policy file Comprehensive audit trail detailing the day-to-day management of material.

Disclosure test Material that might reasonably be considered capable of undermining the case for the prosecution or assisting the case for the accused.

Disruption An alternative way of combating fraud, typically involving suspension of websites to prevent further criminality.

Distributed denial-of-service (DDoS) attack A DoS attack that distributes its traffic over a large number of infected computers. This makes it more difficult for the victim to distinguish between ordinary traffic and DDoS traffic.

Domain A subset of the internet with addresses showing a common suffix, or under the control of an individual or organisation.

Domain registrar A company that manages the use of internet addresses and names.

Domain tree A collection of domains that are grouped together.

Dumped The act of copying raw data from one place to another with little or no formatting for readability.

Economic and Cyber Crime Prevention Centre (ECPC) Works with policing and the counter-fraud community to develop prevention campaigns and activities, and share best practice and advice.

Exploit kit Used to exploit some vulnerability in a system. It is commonly used for a malicious purpose such as installing malware. Exploit kits are routinely sold by criminals to enable others to exploit a vulnerability.

Facilitation payments Low-level payments routinely solicited by low-ranking public officials to facilitate routine government actions.

Fast-track actions Any investigative actions that are likely to establish important facts, preserve evidence or lead to the early resolution of the investigation if pursued immediately.

Fiduciary relationship A legal or ethical relationship based on trust.

Financial enablers The methods and means by which fraud is committed using financial institutions, e.g. payment card fraud, money laundering.

Financial intelligence gateway Confidential communication channel between financial institutions and law enforcement.

Financial intelligence officers Able to identify and access financial intelligence through both open sources and specialist databases and gateways.

Financial investigators Able to exercise cash seizure and forfeiture powers and make appropriate court applications for this (can be police constables or accredited financial investigators).

Financial Services and Markets Act Introduced to make provision for the regulation of financial services and markets.

Firewall A program put on a computer to protect a network or computer system from unauthorised access.

Foreign exchange Conversion of one country's currency into that of another.

Fraud health check A proactive counter-fraud measure that examines how robust an organisation's ability is to identify and respond to a potential fraud threat.

Fraud Investigation Model A logical framework to assist the investigator to respond to fraud.

Fraud Prevention Network (FPN) Coordinated by the ECPC, the FPN harnesses all crime prevention resources and equips them for the delivery of economic and cyber-related crime prevention.

Fraud typologies Classification according to the general type of fraud crimes in relation to the characteristics or traits they have in common.

Gatekeepers People who control access to financial systems, such as bankers, accountants, solicitors, estate agents.

Get Safe Online A joint public–private sector partnership to provide advice on all types of fraud and cyber threats.

Ghost broker An illegal intermediary.

Ghost broking A type of fraud where an individual or group sets up insurance policies for members of the public.

Grand corruption Predominantly conducted by business people and involves large contracts or transactions.

Grey market goods Legal, non-counterfeit goods sold outside the normal distribution channels.

Hacktivist A person who gains unauthorised access to a computer file or computer network in order to further social or political ends.

Hajj **fraud** Type of fraud targeting those travelling to Mecca as part of the world's biggest annual gathering of people.

HOLMES Computer database designed to aid the investigation of large-scale inquiries.

Horizon scanning Describes the process by which organisations systematically investigate evidence about future threats, risks, emerging issues and opportunities.

Infringing items Items that may be in breach of certain copyrights, trade marks or other rights.

Insolvency When a company or person has insufficient assets to cover their debts and may be unable to pay creditors.

Integration Where the proceeds of the crime, having been suitable disguised, can now be spent or used openly without suspicion.

Intrusive surveillance Covert surveillance carried out relating to anything taking place on any residential premises or in any private vehicle (RIPA 2000).

Investigating officer The person conducting or assisting in the conduct of a criminal investigation.

IP rights holder A legal entity or person with exclusive rights to a protected copyright, trade mark or patent.

Joint Asset Recovery Database Database holding details of all detention and forfeiture orders, all confiscation, restraint and financial reporting orders and all civil recovery and criminal taxation cases.

Keylogger (also known as keystroke logging) A type of tool that has the capability to record information directly from the keyboard interface and send it directly to an attacker.

Keyword sampling Searching digital evidence to identify relevant material for disclosure schedules.

Know Fraud System used by the NFIB to ingest fraud reports.

Land banking Schemes that often involve land that is divided into smaller plots to be sold on, with the promise of a high-value return that never materialises.

Layering Changing the nature of the proceeds of the crime and disguising their origins (e.g. the process of moving funds from one account to another).

Legal privilege material Material subject to legal privilege, commonly confidential material exchanged between a lawyer and their client regarding legal advice or an existing civil litigation.

Logging The act of keeping a log. Occurs in an operating system or other software as it runs or sends messages between the different users of a piece of communication software.

Long firm fraud Involves fraudsters setting up a good relationship to gain a credit rating with a supplier, and then placing large orders and refusing to pay following delivery.

Malware Malicious computer software such as viruses.

Mandate fraud Where the fraudster gets account transaction details and changes them in order for future payments to be made to their account instead.

Man-in-the-middle (MiTM) attack When an attacker secretly intercepts and alters the communication between two systems that believe they are directly communicating with each other.

Material attrition The gradual wearing down of the available material.

Mens rea The guilty person's intention or knowledge that what they are doing is wrong and criminal.

MG12 List of exhibits.

MG9 List of witnesses.

Modus operandi A particular way or method of working or operating.

Money laundering The processes of converting the proceeds of crime into something that can be used without attracting suspicion and disguising their illicit origins.

Money laundering investigation Criminal investigation into a person(s) engaged in laundering the proceeds of crime.

Money mules Individuals recruited by criminals to receive the proceeds of crime into their bank accounts.

Money transfer agents A money transfer agent transfers monies between two separate parties; examples of money-transferring agencies include PayPal and Western Union.

Mortgage fraud Giving misleading information in mortgage applications in order to obtain a larger mortgage than should be allowable.

Mutual legal assistance treaty Method that allows information exchange between UK prosecuting agencies and overseas central authorities.

Official Receiver A civil servant who is also an officer of the court appointed to protect the public interest.

PAT A crime prevention tool used to provide a way of thinking about recurring problems of crime and disorder.

Patch Software that fixes or improves a computer program or supporting software.

PEACE model Method of interviewing—Preparation and planning, Engage, Account, Closure and Evaluation.

Petty corruption Small routine payments usually made to low-ranking public officials.

Phishing email An email purporting to come from a legitimate organisation (e.g. a bank) in an attempt to obtain sensitive information.

Placement The process whereby criminal property, in its rawest form, is placed into the financial system or converted into a form that can be used more easily.

Ponzi scheme Typically a word-of-mouth investment scam promising quick high-yield financial returns to investors that almost never materialise.

Private branch exchange Hardware designed to allow circuit switching within an organisation's telephone system.

Procurement fraud Can take many forms but commonly relates to the procurement or tender processes of an organisation not being followed.

Professional enablers Those who have specialist knowledge of weaknesses in the organisations and processes that allows crime to be committed, e.g. solicitors.

Proxy server Acts as an intermediary between an internet user and web-based services or connected resources that the user is seeking to access. It makes it difficult to trace a user's internet activity by providing a level of anonymity.

Pyramid scheme An unsustainable business model that recruits members with a promise of making money and obtaining rewards for enrolling others into the business.

Ransomware A type of malware that extorts money from the victim, either by locking up their important files and demanding a ransom or by using a social engineering attack.

Realisable property Any free property held by the defendant or any free property held by the recipient of a tainted gift (section 83 of POCA 2002).

Red flags Warning/indicators/signs of fraud.

Rental fraud When would-be tenants are tricked into paying an upfront fee to rent a property that in reality does not exist.

Romance fraud Where fraudsters use fake online profiles to trick victims into romantic cyber relationships that inevitably lead to requests for gifts and money from the victim.

Root access When a user attains administrative-level permissions.

SARA A crime prevention model used to design out vulnerabilities (Scanning, Analysis, Response and Assessment).

Senior investigating officer The person responsible for strategies and decision making from the beginning to the end of a case.

Share fraud (boiler room fraud) Where the victim is cold-called out of the blue by the fraudster, who offers investments that sound attractive but are often worthless, or even non-existent.

Short firm fraud Involves a business purchasing goods from a supplier on credit and getting them delivered to a third-party address. The business will collect the goods, selling them on quickly and disappearing without paying their supplier.

Skimming A device to capture the card and account information embedded in the card's magnetic strip for the purposes of counterfeiting.

Smishing A security attack in which the user is tricked into downloading a Trojan horse, virus or other malware on to a mobile device.

Social engineering A key enabler, as fraud relies on deceit. Criminals manipulate their victims in order to achieve an open line of communication and gain access to confidential personal information.

Spam email Can be sent to many recipients at the same time and recipients are often not personally targeted. This is a type of email that can include scripts containing malware or altered website links for seemingly genuine sites, which are actually phishing sites.

Spear phishing A targeted and focused phishing attack aimed at a specific person. This attack usually uses data about that person to launch the attack. An email typically arrives from an apparently genuine source requesting the recipient to visit a realistic-looking website, where the recipient would be asked to input personal information.

Special procedure material Journalistic material or material obtained in the course of a trade, profession or similar and which is held subject to a duty of confidence (PACE).

Spoofed website A hoax website designed with the intention of misleading visitors that the website has been created by a different person or organisation.

Spoofing When a person or a program is disguised as another system or user on a network, in order to launch attacks, steal data or bypass access controls. Email spoofing is when a message is forged so that it appears to come from somewhere other than the actual source.

Stand-alone terminal A computer or laptop computer that is used on its own without requiring a connection to a local area network or a wide area network.

Streaming Where content is delivered to a device and viewed as it is received, instead of a file being downloaded to a device so that it can be viewed offline.

Subject matter expert A person who is required to give or prepare expert evidence for the purpose of criminal proceedings.

Sucker list List of victims defrauded by previous scams.

Technical enablers Required to contact the victim, steal personal and financial data and disguise the offender's identity and location, e.g. malware, botnets.

Thematic A body of topics for study or discussion.

Third-party material Material held by organisations or people who are not part of the prosecution team.

Trojan (Trojan horse) Currently, a Trojan is a piece of malicious software designed to gain root access to a computer. It is usually used to bring other malware into the computer.

Trojan virus A computer virus disguised as genuine software.

Verification bias Where the investigator tries to prove their personal belief of what they consider has happened and limits investigations to their view at the cost of a more inclusive investigation strategy.

Victims Code Statutory document that sets out the services and information victims of crime are entitled to.

Virtual private network (VPN) Connects remote computers or offices on a private network across a public network like the internet. A VPN uses an encrypted connection offering security over a less secure network. A VPN can also be used to circumnavigate geographical restrictions and censorship on the internet. Additionally, VPNs can be used to connect to proxy servers to conceal identity and location.

Virus A malicious software program that infects computers by interfering with their operation. Unlike a Trojan horse, a virus replicates itself once it has been executed.

Vishing The act of using a telephone in an attempt to scam the user into surrendering private information that can be used for identity theft.

Voice over internet protocol (VoIP) Enables the user to use the internet to make telephone calls. It is sometimes referred to as Internet Telephony and can be at no charge or very low cost.

Volatile data Any data that is stored in memory, or exists in transit. This data will be lost when the computer's power is switched off.

Vulnerability A design flaw that can be exploited to make a program do what it is not designed to do, such as escalating user privileges or installing programs.

'WHOIS' An official listing of the full details of all .uk domain names.

Witness Charter Standards of care for witnesses in the criminal justice system.

Worms A stand-alone malware computer program that is self-replicating and does not need to attach itself to an existing program in a computer.

1

Fraud: scale, impact and response

1.1 **Introduction**

This chapter defines the terms 'fraud' and 'economic crime' and places them into context within the twenty-first century. It will help the investigator understand how profiles of fraudsters and knowledge of fraud indicators can be used to help prevent, disrupt and investigate cases. It details the organisations, structures and systems at the local, regional and national levels to tackle fraud. The final section looks at the Fraud Investigation Model (FIM). This is used to counter fraud through the application of a logical process that is focused on reducing the harm it causes, supporting victims and implementing operational learning. This model is referenced in the Policing Fraud document contained in the College of Policing's Authorised Professional Practice (APP) for investigations.

1.2 **Defining fraud**

The offence of fraud is defined in the Fraud Act 2006. In summary it consists of three key elements: false representation, financial gain or loss, and the element of dishonesty. In order to establish the facts of the case, investigators should keep these in sharp focus as they progress their investigation.

Definition of fraud

The definition of fraud in England, Wales and Northern Ireland is defined under the Fraud Act 2006 as:

(1) A person is guilty of fraud if he is in breach of any of the sections listed in subsection (2), which should provide for different ways of committing the offence.

(2) The sections are:

    (a) Section 2 (fraud by false representation);

    (b) Section 3 (fraud by failing to disclose information); and

    (c) Section 4 (fraud by abuse of position).

(See Chapter 2 for further information.)

Economic crime is a little more difficult to define, as it encompasses a wider range of offending. There should clearly be an element of the offence that relates to economic gain or loss.

The definition of 'economic' is rather wide, and in terms of economic crime tends to relate to offences involving direct or indirect financial gain or loss and can include the offences of money laundering, bribery, counterfeiting, computer misuse and other miscellaneous fraud offences. In addition, there are a number of organisations in law enforcement that use a range of specific powers in their fight against fraud and related offences. Examples of these include the Competitions and Markets Authority (CMA) utilising the Enterprise Act 2002 for criminal enforcement and the Competition Act 1998 for civil proceedings.

The Serious Fraud Office (SFO) has compulsory powers, under section 2 of the Criminal Justice Act 1987, which require any person (or company/bank) to provide them with relevant documents, including confidential documents.

1.2.1 **The challenge for the investigator**

Fraud and economic crimes are made more complex by the range of enablers and mechanisms used to conceal both the movement of money and the true nature of the fraud. Historically, the fraudster had to rely on personal interaction or use of the written word on manuscript, which, to some degree, limited the reach of the fraudster. However, today their reach is extended by the use of modern communication methods, primarily the development, accessibility and widespread use of the internet, as accessed through a range of digital devices. This, combined with the perpetually increasing speed and accessibility of moving money, often across jurisdictions, has increased the scale of the harm caused to society. Indeed, all the ingredients for a 'perfect storm' of motive, opportunity and capability are ever present in the twenty-first century. Never before has the challenge been greater for those tasked with countering fraud. The investigation of these offences requires a diligent and logical approach and the investigator should utilise the extensive network of skilled professionals available in the counter-fraud world.

1.2.2 **Historical context**

Fraud and deceit have been part of the interactions between people throughout history, and the investigator can learn a great deal by analysing previous cases. The features of fraudulent activity that are described in Figure 1.1 still have relevance today. It is true to say that although the nature of the fraudster perhaps hasn't changed very much, their reach and impact has. History shows us that the fraudster often holds or purports to hold a position of authority and power. This also adds to the complications of identifying fraud and undertaking any subsequent investigation, as the fraudster can be shielded by their cloak of respectability.

1.2.3 **Literature, mythology and infamous fraudsters**

There is an interesting mix of literature, mythology and art that refers to deception and those who perpetrate this crime. Fraud is often connected with the themes of evil and hell, which is quite apt. History and literature inform us that fraudsters are drawn to opportunities to make money; they are capable of manipulating victims, who are often motivated by the prospect of making a significant financial gain on their investments. Victims frequently find it difficult to differentiate between fraudulent and lawful schemes, as the fraudster is often highly convincing, which lends them an air of credibility.

Figure 1.1 Timeline of fraud throughout history

900/800 BC	Greek mythology presents us with one of the first representations of fraud in the goddess 'Apate'—the personification of deceit, fraud and guile
360 BC	First reported attempted fraud by Greek merchant Hegestratos
1265	Birth of Dante. Part one of his *Divine Comedy—Inferno*—follows the journey of Dante through the nine descending circles of hell, the eighth circle being fraud
1700s	South Sea Bubble, which was synonymous with the development of fraudulent schemes
1820s	Prince of Poyais fraud
1840s	Industrialisation and expansion of the railway network in the UK is open to fraudulent activity by chief officers
1919	Carlo Ponzi sets up the first Ponzi scheme involving postal reply coupons
2006	Jeffrey Skilling convicted of insider trading at collapsed energy giant Enron
2009	Bernie Madoff convicted of Ponzi scheme involving Wall Street wealth management company

The timeline in Figure 1.1 details some of the more significant and infamous fraud events throughout history.

1.3 Scale and impact

1.3.1 The scale of fraud

Fraud and economic crime are significant threats to society as a whole and to the vulnerable in particular. They take many forms and there have been numerous attempts to measure the financial losses across various sectors. In 2016, the estimated loss attributable to fraud across the United Kingdom (UK), as detailed in the Annual Fraud Indicator 2016 (*Annual Fraud Indicator 2016*, Experian, PKF Littlejohn LLP (PKF) and Portsmouth University, 2016) was £193 billion.

It is estimated that businesses and organisations around the world are losing an average of 5.6 per cent of their annual expenditure due to fraud and error. This equates to a global loss of £2.78 trillion each year (*The Financial Cost of Fraud 2015*, PKF, 2015).

KEY POINTS—SOURCES OF RESEARCH REGARDING FRAUD LOSS

A sample of sources identifying losses attributable to fraud and similar offences:

- *Annual Fraud Indicator 2016*, Experian, PKF and Portsmouth University, 2016;
- *The Financial Cost of Fraud 2015*, PKF, 2015;
- *Fraud the Facts 2015: The definitive overview of payment industry fraud and measures to prevent it*, Financial Fraud Action UK, 2015;

- *FraudTrack Report: February 2016*, BDO LLP, 2016;
- *Global Economic Crime Survey 2016: UK Report*, PricewaterhouseCoopers, 2016;
- Office for National Statistics.

There are significant challenges in obtaining the actual level of offending for fraud and related offences, as it is difficult to assess those crimes that go undetected. This is particularly pertinent to fraud, as the most successful fraudsters tend to be those who go unnoticed. The number of actual reported fraud offences in England and Wales for the year ending December 2015 totalled 385,398 (Action Fraud's Know Fraud database). This is equivalent to six offences per every 1,000 UK residents. (See Tables 1.1 and 1.2.)

For the first time, the Office for National Statistics used the British Crime Survey to measure the number of fraud and cyber incidents for the year ending June 2015. It identified that there were 5,110,000 incidents of fraud and 2,460,000 incidents of computer misuse in England and Wales.

Further reading

- The Office for National Statistics' interpretation of fraud and computer misuse, as reported in the British Crime Survey, can be viewed at: http://webarchive.nationalarchives.gov.uk/20160105160709/http://www.ons.gov.uk/ons/rel/crime-stats/crime-statistics/year-ending-june-2015/sty-fraud.html

Table 1.1 Action Fraud figures for 2015 fraud type—top 10 reported by volume

National Fraud Intelligence Bureau (NFIB) fraud category	No of reports
NFIB5A—cheque, plastic card and online bank accounts (not payment service provider (PSP))	57,973
NFIB90—uncategorised elsewhere	49,145
NFIB3A—online shopping and auctions	42,385
NFIB5B—application fraud (excluding mortgages)	31,713
NFIB3E—computer software service fraud	30,705
NFIB3B—consumer phone fraud	25,390
NFIB1H—other advance fee fraud	24,939
NFIB3D—other consumer non-investment fraud	16,137
NFIB7—telecom industry fraud (misuse of contracts)	15,862
NFIB3G—retail fraud	9,475
Total	**303,724**
Total no of reports for 2015	**385,398**

Table 1.2 Action Fraud data for 2015 fraud type—top 10 by reported loss

NFIB fraud category
NFIB90—uncategorised fraud
NFIB2E—other financial investment
NFIB9—business trading fraud
NFIB1D—dating scam
NFIB5D—mandate fraud
NFIB5A—cheque, plastic card and online bank accounts (not PSP)
NFIB5AI—cheque, plastic card and online bank accounts (not PSP)—information
NFIB19—fraud by abuse of position of trust
NFIB8A—corporate employee fraud
NFIB3D—other consumer non-investment fraud

1.3.2 The impact of fraud

Fraud and economic crime have an impact across society. They harm individuals and organisations through financial loss, take life savings from the vulnerable and, if left unchecked, can destabilise the economy.

KEY POINTS—THE IMPACT OF FRAUD

Organisations:
- reputational damage;
- lack of public confidence;
- product failure;
- business failure.

State:
- lack of public confidence;
- loss of money to invest in services;
- failure of the state.

Charity sector:
- funds are not reaching those in need;
- lack of confidence to donate.

Individual victims:
- significant impact on the vulnerable within our society;
- personal trauma;
- loss of savings/pension;
- reliance on the state for funds.

1.4 **Local, regional and national structures and responsibilities**

1.4.1 **Introduction**

The Attorney General and Chief Secretaries' review of fraud was commissioned in 2005, and it examined the impact of fraud in England and Wales. The review was reported in 2006 and made 62 recommendations, a number of which significantly affected the police service. The review placed the importance of fraud on the national government's agenda and instigated collaboration across the public and private sectors to combat both the economic impact and harm to society.

One of the recommendations was to create a national fraud reporting centre. Subsequently, Action Fraud (administered by the then National Fraud Authority (NFA)) and the National Fraud Intelligence Bureau (NFIB) were established to provide a mechanism to report, assess and disseminate information on fraud. With national reporting accessible through phone and online services, there has been a significant increase in the volume of fraud reporting.

The current counter-fraud community is complex and involves many different organisations across the public, private and third sectors. The NFIB referral landscape is shown in Figure 1.2.

Figure 1.2 Dissemination of referrals for investigation by the NFIB

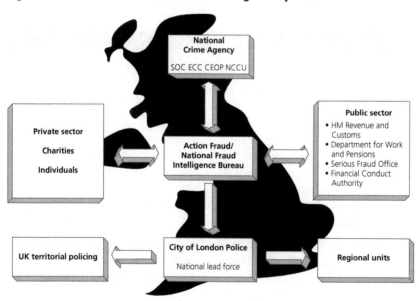

1.4.2 **Economic crime portfolio and the '4Ps' structure**

Chief police officers support the work of the National Police Chiefs' Council (NPCC) by taking responsibility for crime and policing issues from a national operational perspective, through the National Crime Operations Coordination Committee (NCOCC). The NCOCC is divided, on a thematic basis, into 12 separate portfolios, each having a chief officer appointed as the lead. One of these is the Economic Crime Portfolio (ECP), chaired by the City of London Police Commander responsible for economic crime.

The ECP is divided into five sub-groups, one for each of the '4Ps'—pursue, protect, prepare and prevent—and one focusing on victims. Each group has a programme of work that seeks to improve the police service's response to fraud.

1.4.3 **National Crime Agency (NCA)**

The NCA targets the criminals and groups posing the biggest risks to the UK. It does this in three ways by:

- conducting its own operations;
- providing operational and specialist support to its partners' operations;
- providing clear national leadership that ensures UK law enforcement makes the best use of its collective resources and targets these in the most effective way possible.

The NCA has a wide remit to tackle serious and organised crime, including the fight against fraud and cyber crime, which sits within its own Economic Crime Command (ECC).

KEY POINTS—NCA ECC PRIORITIES

The ECC focuses its activity in four priority areas:

1 **Tackling money laundering and criminal assets** by:
   - leading multi-agency action to understand and combat national and international-scale money laundering;
   - working with law enforcement, regulators, banks and professional bodies to disrupt criminal access to those with professional skills (e.g. solicitors, accountants);
   - increasing the impact of the NCA's operational capabilities in financial investigation, civil recovery and taxation.
2 **Leading the UK law enforcement response to domestic and international bribery, corruption and sanctions.**
3 **Ensuring that the NCA's proactive investigation capabilities are deployed against high-priority economic crime threats in support of partner agencies**, such as the Serious Fraud Office (SFO), the Financial Conduct Authority (FCA) and the Competition and Markets Authority (CMA).
4 **Leveraging change in the economic crime operating environment**, particularly the law enforcement/financial sector relationship, through:
   - leading (together with the Home Office and the British Bankers' Association) the new Financial Sector Forum;

- identifying and making the case for legislative changes or changes to government policy;
- the Joint Money Laundering Intelligence Taskforce (JMLIT);
- developing intelligence-led prevention activities to support individuals and the private sector;
- leading work across law enforcement to identify and respond to changes in the economic crime threat—particularly the emergence of new types of threat.

The ECC has responsibility for the UK Financial Intelligence Unit and the Proceeds of Crime Centre. It also works alongside the NCA Intelligence Hub to maintain an accurate picture of the economic crime threat and use that picture to identify the highest priority targets and agree on a shared national strategy. (See www.nationalcrimeagency.gov.uk/about-us/what-we-do/economic-crime)

1.4.4 **National lead force (NLF)**

The City of London Police (CoLP) assumed the role of NLF for fraud on 1 April 2008 in response to the 2006 Fraud Review's recommendation for the creation of this role, along with a Centre of Excellence. The NLF was created to provide specialist support and guidance regarding fraud education and investigation to:

- police forces;
- other law enforcement bodies;
- industry.

KEY POINTS—ROLE OF THE NLF

The 2006 review identified the following responsibilities for the NLF:

- Investigate, on behalf of UK policing, those frauds that impact the UK and cause the greatest harm.
- Accept inquiries and provide appropriate guidance as an authority on fraud crime.
- Receive requests for assistance or guidance from, and offer and provide assistance to, UK regional police forces, UK business and industry, the NFIB and the NCA.
- Liaise and develop mutually beneficial and cooperative relationships, wherever practicable, with foreign law enforcement agencies and services involved in the fight against fraud crime.
- Implement a centre of excellence that educates and upskills individuals and businesses across the public and private sectors, enabling them to identify and combat fraud.

The NLF considers the referral of fraud offences where these crimes meet defined case acceptance criteria. The NLF conducts certain investigations on behalf of other police forces when these cases prove to be complicated and protracted.

1.4.5 National Fraud Intelligence Bureau (NFIB)

Like the NLF, the NFIB was formed as a result of recommendations emanating from the Fraud Review of 2006.

KEY POINTS—ROLE OF THE NFIB

- Harvesting, processing and analysing fraud data to provide actionable intelligence to the UK counter-fraud community, promoting a better understanding of fraud, including themes and trends, in order to inform more focused and collaborative prevention and disruption.
- Developing and allocating crime packages to facilitate local, regional and national police functions and other law enforcement agencies' investigations into the most harmful instances of fraud-linked criminal activity.
- Achieving an improved and effective response to organised fraudsters by adding value to the knowledge and understanding of organised crime groups (OCGs) directly and indirectly related to fraud through its connectivity with the Organised Crime Coordination Centre.
- Making effective use of intelligence from fraud victims across the UK (be they individuals, businesses or the public purse). This information should be exploited to help alert, educate and protect, find new and effective ways to engineer out the threat from fraud and positively influence the UK's limited enforcement resources for tackling fraud.

The NFIB's outputs include the production of crime and intelligence products, such as:

- subject profiles;
- problem profiles;
- strategic and tactical assessments;
- information on current and emerging trends;
- crime report packages;
- identification of organised crime and associated OCGs.

1.4.6 Regional fraud teams (RFTs)

These are embedded within the existing national regional organised crime unit (ROCU) structure to improve the quality of fraud investigations across England and Wales. RFTs initiate proactive and reactive investigations in order to combat organised fraud, and initiate investigations into the links between fraud and other areas of crime in the region in which they operate.

1.4.7 Force-level economic crime and fraud capability

Most forces across England and Wales have developed a specialist capability to combat fraud. For the forces that have not established dedicated fraud teams, the majority of specialist fraud investigators are embedded within either their serious and organised crime teams or their mainstream criminal investigation teams.

1.4.8 Government departments

In addition to the response from law enforcement, other government departments have a statutory responsibility to investigate certain fraud types.

> **KEY POINTS—HER MAJESTY'S GOVERNMENT (HMG) COUNTER-FRAUD ORGANISATIONS**
>
> - **Department for Work and Pensions (DWP)**: the UK government's department responsible for welfare and pension policy. The DWP Fraud Investigation Service investigates benefit fraud in cases where it is suspected that claimants have provided incorrect or misleading information.
> - **Single Fraud Investigation Service (SFIS)**: works with the DWP, Her Majesty's Revenue and Customs (HMRC) and local authorities to investigate and prosecute welfare benefit fraud and tax credit fraud.
> - **Her Majesty's Revenue and Customs (HMRC)**: the UK's tax, payments and customs authority, responsible for the administration and collection of tax. HMRC is responsible for investigating serious organised fiscal crime and suspected tax fraud.
> - **Serious Fraud Office (SFO)**: an independent government department, operating under the superintendence of the Attorney General. Its purpose is to protect society by investigating and, if appropriate, prosecuting those who commit serious or complex fraud, bribery and corruption and pursuing them and others for the proceeds of their crime. The SFO, although an independent investigative body, does not have the full range of powers that are available to police officers, so in many cases they will call upon the support of the police to assist, where necessary, with procedures requiring police powers. The SFO has jurisdiction in England, Wales and Northern Ireland. It does not have jurisdiction over Scotland, the Isle of Man or the Channel Islands.
> - **Charity Commission**: raises awareness of fraud among trustees and the wider public; specifically the risks and vulnerabilities that charities face, as well as their ability to protect and safeguard their funds and assets. They provide alerts and warnings to raise awareness of specific frauds and other risks, and publish wider lessons from their investigatory work.
> - **Insolvency Service**: the government agency responsible for administering and investigating companies that have gone into compulsory liquidation or have received bankruptcy or debt relief orders. The agency also investigates allegations of misconduct in live companies.
> - **NHS Protect**: part of the NHS Business Service Authority. It investigates fraud, bribery, corruption and other unlawful actions within the National Health Service (NHS). Counter-fraud work ranges from investigations into falsely claimed prescription charges to alleged drug price-fixing.

- **UK Intellectual Property Office (IPO)**: intellectual property (IP) is created when an idea takes some tangible form. IP can include a copyright, design, patent or trade mark that others cannot manufacture, use, sell or import without prior permission. The unauthorised use of IP is a criminal offence in some instances and can lead to prosecution under section 94 of the Trade Marks Act 1994 in relation to trade mark infringement, and sections 107A and 198 of the Copyright, Designs and Patents Act 1988 in relation to copyright infringement.
- **Her Majesty's Passport Office (HMPO)**: the sole issuer of passports to UK nationals. The office is responsible for investigating fraudulent passport applications, and offers a passport validation service for businesses and government departments.
- **Cabinet Office Fraud, Error, Debt and Grant Function**: this service is responsible for setting government-wide standards for fraud and error, and providing strategic leadership in these matters.

1.4.9 Non-government departments

Non-government departments also have the capability and capacity to investigate fraud, particularly where the offence is a civil rather than a criminal matter. They can provide a useful resource to assist in investigations and also hold intelligence.

KEY POINTS—NON-HMG FRAUD-RELATED ORGANISATIONS

There are many organisations focused on countering fraud. The list below is a representative sample:

- **Financial Conduct Authority (FCA)**: this regulates the financial services industry in the UK. Its aim is to protect consumers, ensure the industry remains stable and promotes healthy competition between financial services providers. The FCA has rule-making, investigative and enforcement powers that it uses to protect and regulate the financial services industry.
- **Fraud Advisory Panel (FAP)**: a registered charity and membership organisation that seeks to develop best practice in fraud prevention, detection, investigation and prosecution. Its charitable objectives are set out in its articles of association: to protect life and property by the prevention, detection, investigation, prosecution and deterrence of fraud, in particular through the promotion of advice, education, collaboration and research.
- **British Bankers' Association (BBA)**: the voice of the banking industry for all banks that operate in the UK. The BBA is the leading association for the UK banking and financial services sector and has a focus on countering financial crime.
- **Financial Fraud Action UK (FFA UK)**: raises awareness about all types of financial fraud in the UK. The FFA UK website includes information about different types of payment fraud and useful downloads, including bank and building society contact details, as well as bank identification numbers (BINs) that will assist with fraud investigations.

- **UK Payments**: the UK trade association for payments and for those institutions that deliver payment services to customers. One of its key responsibilities is coordinating a range of activities to tackle payment-related fraud. At the heart of its role is the need to ensure that the UK payments industry operates to the highest international standards and that payments are safe, reliable and resilient.
- **Credit Industry Fraud Avoidance System (CIFAS)**: a non-profit membership association dedicated to the prevention of financial crime and staff fraud. CIFAS provides a range of fraud prevention services to its members, including a fraud avoidance system used by the UK's financial services companies and public authorities. Members share information about identified frauds in the fight to prevent further fraud. Following specification by the Home Office under the Serious Crime Act 2007, public authorities are able to join CIFAS and share information reciprocally to prevent fraud.
- **Chartered Institute of Public Finance & Accounting (CIPFA)**: a professional body for people in public finance and has a counter-fraud centre which works collaboratively to combat fraud and corruption across government and related sectors.
- **Federation Against Copyright Theft (FACT)**: its primary purpose is to protect the UK's film and broadcasting industry against counterfeiting, copyright and trade mark infringements. FACT works closely with police services and other government and enforcement bodies across the UK.
- **British Phonographic Industry (BPI)**: a trade body representing the UK's recorded music industry. The organisation aims to raise awareness of fraud among the wider public and help its members and the music industry by leading action against illegal downloading and piracy.
- **UK Interactive Entertainment (UKIE)**: a not-for-profit trade body for the UK's game and interactive entertainment industry. The organisation's primary aim is to support and raise the profile of the industry.
- **Anti-Counterfeiting Group (ACG)**: a not-for-profit trade association aiming to raise awareness among the public of the widespread counterfeiting of products.
- **Motion Picture Association of America (MPAA)**: the US trade association representing the six major Hollywood studios. The association is involved in a number of initiatives to combat the unauthorised distribution and piracy of film, using both publicity campaigns and legal action.
- **PRS for Music**: a UK copyright collection society made up of 118,000 members. Members can license their performance and mechanical rights through the organisation, handing it their administration duties. PRS aims to ensure that royalties are paid whenever their members' music is played, performed or reproduced, taking action against breaches in regulation.
- **Get Safe Online**: provides a source of unbiased, user-friendly advice about online safety to UK consumers and micro-businesses, making sure that internet users are aware of key risks and have the right information to protect themselves. It is a joint initiative between HMG, the NCA and private sponsors from retail, technology, finance and communications companies.

- **Insurance Fraud Investigators Group (IFIG)**: a non-profit members' organisation dedicated to the detection and prevention of insurance fraud. Counter-insurance fraud professionals can apply to the IFIG for membership.

1.5 **Offender and victim profiles**

1.5.1 **Victim profiles**

It is estimated that approximately 90 per cent of fraud goes unreported every year (Crime Survey of England & Wales, October 2015), which leaves a considerable intelligence gap in our understanding of fraud victimology. The reasons for this under-reporting range from a lack of awareness (victims do not realise they have been victims of fraud), to a reluctance to report a fraud due to embarrassment or shame, or (in the case of businesses) the potential risk of damage to their reputation. Available data, including that taken from Action Fraud, paints a complex picture of fraud victims; when looking at different types of fraud, the demographic profiles of victims, the initial contact method and the transfer type, the methods vary considerably.

KEY POINTS—CHARACTERISTICS OF FRAUD VICTIMS

- **Volume crime fraud**—victims are more likely to be:
  aged between 21 and 40, male, contacted initially on a website.
- **Mass marketing fraud**—victims are more likely to be:
  aged 51 or over, female, contacted initially by phone/text.
- **Banking and corporate fraud**—victims are more likely to be:
  aged between 21 and 50, male, contacted initially in person.
- **Cyber crime**—victims are more likely to be:
  aged between 31 and 60, male, contacted initially by email.
- **Investment fraud**—victims are more likely to be:
  Aged 51 or over, male, contacted initially by phone.

Source: Victimology Report 2014/2015, NFIB, October 2015.

The variety of methods used by fraudsters to obtain personal details and/or money from their victims is often supported by sophisticated technology and carried out on a large scale using the anonymity of the internet. Large-scale phishing/vishing scams, whereby fraudsters use social-engineering techniques to steal sensitive information, can target many people at once, meaning that anyone can become a victim of fraud.

Using data from the NFIB and interviews with victims, the Home Office's 'Serious and Organised Crime Protection: Public Interventions Model' identifies traits and habits that put people at risk of becoming a victim of fraud. According to their report, 'people's protective or "risky" actions are determined by a range of factors: their own personality; personal circumstances (e.g. lack of time), perception of risk (e.g. likelihood and £ value) and general awareness (e.g. previous experience)'. As an example, people who scored highly in 'confidence' and 'readiness' and took precautions—such as destroying documents, never sharing their personal identification number (PIN), using credit rather than debit cards to pay online, and regularly checking their transactions—were considered the lowest risk segment. Those who scored highly in 'trusting' and 'malleability' and did not often exhibit protective behaviours—such as refusing to engage with strangers on the street, cold-callers, and door-to-door salesmen—were considered higher risk.

Targeted prevention campaigns from both the public and private sectors have been launched to reduce the risk of members of the public falling victim to fraud. As more people gain an awareness of cyber security and the basic measures they can take to protect themselves from fraud, it is hoped that the number of victims will fall. However, fraudsters are constantly adapting and evolving their tactics, which necessitates a vigorous and proactive approach to identifying emerging trends and communicating these to the public.

1.5.2 Fraudster methodologies

Profiling fraudsters can be difficult, as accurate information regarding the suspects in many fraud reports is not available via victim reporting due to the nature of the offence (false representation) and the lack of face-to-face contact between the suspect and victim. Reports from Action Fraud tell us that 74 per cent of fraud suspects are male, and the majority fall into the 22–40 age bracket. Apart from that, their commonalities appear to lie in a creative approach to finding ways of convincing people to part with their personal data and money. Sophisticated techniques designed to steal data (vishing, phishing and data hacks) mean that identity crime is a constant risk, and continues to act as a key enabler across all fraud types. For an example, see the following case study, which is based on an alert produced by the NFIB's Proactive Intelligence Team.

....

Case study—fraudsters target senior executives

Fraudsters are targeting residential premises, specifically in affluent areas of London, that lack security and closed-circuit television (CCTV) with the aim of stealing post (specifically banking documentation) to identify senior executives within companies and organisations. Once the fraudster has stolen the mail, open-source research is conducted to identify whether the victim works in a suitable position to ultimately become a target. The fraudster uses social engineering to gather information on them and their employer and then contacts the organisation (purporting to be the victim) to carry out mandate and payment diversion fraud on the company.

....

15

1.6 **Fraud indicators (red flags)**

1.6.1 **Introduction**

Historically, substantial research has been undertaken into the nature of the occupational fraudster. In the early twentieth century, Donald Cressey, an American criminologist, studied the so-called 'white collar criminal'. He created the 'Cressey fraud triangle', which is a highly useful concept for those countering fraud. Not only does it identify the component elements required for the internal fraudster to operate, but it also offers the investigator three clear lines of inquiry (see Figure 1.3).

Figure 1.3 Cressey's fraud triangle

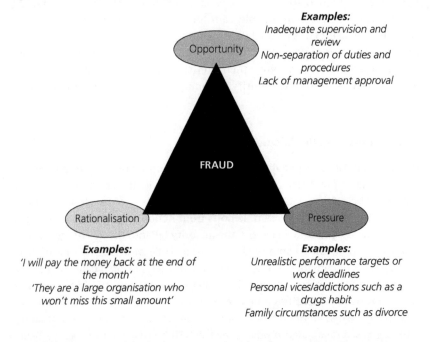

Examples:
Inadequate supervision and review
Non-separation of duties and procedures
Lack of management approval

Examples:
'I will pay the money back at the end of the month'
'They are a large organisation who won't miss this small amount'

Examples:
Unrealistic performance targets or work deadlines
Personal vices/addictions such as a drugs habit
Family circumstances such as divorce

KEY POINTS—THE THREE CRESSEY ELEMENTS

- **Opportunity**: circumstances exist that provide the opportunity for fraud to be perpetrated, for example there may be the opportunity to manipulate or falsify records to gain a financial advantage. This may relate to claims for travel or directing payments to personal accounts.
- **Situational pressures**: situational pressures can occur when an employee is financially exposed or has habits, such as gambling, that require funding via a flow of money.
- **Rationalisation**: internal fraudsters will justify their behaviour by convincing themselves that what they are doing is not fraud: they may consider it payment in kind, or the pay rise they never received.

Understanding the 'indicators' of fraud is helpful in its detection and investigation. An indicator of fraud can be defined as a condition that is directly attributable to dishonest or fraudulent activity and may manifest itself as an observable indicator. The indicator could result from the fraud itself, or could emerge from the attempt to conceal it.

1.6.2 Fraud indicators (red flags)

Fraud indicators are often referred to as red flags and are very prevalent in insider fraud. These occur when there is an unusual occurrence or feature that varies from the norm; this is not only an indicator of fraud, since it can also signify investigative opportunities.

Rarely is an act of fraud a one-off. Red flags are often present, but are either not recognised or not acted upon, thus giving the fraudster a licence to carry on operating. By responding appropriately to a red flag, fraud can be detected sooner and in some cases prevented.

Red flags may be present around the main entities:

- the individual offender;
- the victim (organisation).

KEY POINTS—PERSONAL RED FLAGS

- **Offender lifestyle changes**: purchase of expensive cars, jewellery, homes and clothes. Fraudsters will often be living beyond their means. Some fraudsters will be secretive and careful about their spending, but others will share their joy by bragging about significant new purchases.
- **Offender experiencing financial difficulties**: significant personal debt and credit problems could be the result of a variety of factors, such as a spouse losing their job or separation from a partner.
- **Offender displaying behavioural changes**: someone who is dependent on alcohol, drugs or gambling may experience financial pressures and therefore needs to steal funds to ease the dilemma. Addictions can often be hard to spot, as many addicts are able to function as normal; however, patterns in absenteeism, ill health, family problems and creative explanations could raise concerns. Someone who is keen to conceal their fraudulent activity may be reluctant to take leave and be resistant to allowing other employees access to their clients, files and accounts.

Case study—Insider X

Insider X worked for four years at a well-known City company in London, one of the world's richest investment banks, and was employed as a secretary/personal assistant (PA) to a number of managing directors of the firm. Prior to the fraud, after a number of administrative jobs, they signed with a temping agency and in 1998 were sent to the company.

Insider X started by embezzling small amounts into their own accounts, but after realising that they had got away with it, they continued issuing forged cheques and siphoning larger amounts. Insider X rationalised their actions by convincing themselves that they had earned the money. Insider X:

- deceived individuals within the company rather than the company itself;
- was not in a senior position.

Red flags and warnings

- They enjoyed a lavish lifestyle that included a luxury car, villas and designer gems—they effectively lived beyond their perceived/legitimate means. They felt they had been treated as little more than a servant and a second-class citizen in a company culture that disrespected support staff.
- They were put in a position of trust and held in high regard, making themselves indispensable on both business and personal fronts.
- Policies and procedures were in place, but were often circumvented in order to 'get things done'; for example, it was common for secretaries working for partner-directors to forge signatures.
- They regularly settled the directors' household bills, paying for travel and family holidays, so had open access to their personal chequebooks.

Insider X was convicted of a £4.3 million bank fraud and received a seven-year prison sentence.

....

There are many factors that enable internal fraud to occur. These include:

- poor tone set from the top of the organisation;
- little or no training or communication of counter-fraud controls;
- failure to undertake a fraud risk assessment;
- weak and ineffective internal controls;
- poor vetting and/or due diligence;
- lack of management oversight and effective audit.

All organisations are at risk of fraud and many put in place policies, procedures and training in order to counter fraud.

Checklist—example indicators of fraudulent activities

- **Unusual transactions**: in time, date, frequency, place and amount.

- **Conflicting or missing evidential matters and original documents**: check sequences, anomalies or gaps. If something is frequently occurring or if there are gaps in reconciled numbers, this would suggest that further investigation is needed.

- **Close association with suppliers and other stakeholders**: unusual relationships with clients, lavishing them with or receiving expensive gifts and hospitality; retaining a monopoly on liaisons with these clients in order to prevent detection.

- **Excessive voids and regular price overrides**: lack of significant internal controls and enforcement of them due to weaknesses in management.

- **Invoices just under approval amounts**: employees may be aware of the management threshold and create invoices just below the level that requires authority.

KEY POINTS—EXAMPLES OF ORGANISATIONAL RED FLAGS

Structural: occurs when organisational structures are weak or broken. Indicators include:

- poor organisational controls;
- lack of segregation of responsibilities;
- poor security of information;
- poor physical security;
- lack of scrutiny;
- lack of monitoring;
- circumventing tendering or contracting procedures;
- poor record keeping;
- lack of proper authorisation;
- lack of records;
- overriding of controls;
- unusual transactions.

Quality

- product substitution;
- product failure;
- increase in product-related complaints.

Further reading

- Fraud Advisory Panel, 'An Introduction to Fraud Indicators', *Fraud Facts*, Issue 14, 2011: www.fraudadvisorypanel.org/wp-content/uploads/2015/04/Fraud-Facts-14B-Fraud-Indicators-Nov11.pdf
- Chartered Institute of Management Accountants (CIMA), *Fraud Risk Management: A Guide to Good Practice*, 2008: www.cimaglobal.com/Documents/Thought_leadership_docs/cid_techguide_fraud_risk_management_feb09.pdf.pdf

1.7 **Reporting fraud**

In 2009, under the governance of the NFA, Action Fraud was created with an initial remit to receive reports of fraud crime and information from members of the public and businesses. It later expanded in 2012 to assume responsibility for the escalating and overlapping threat presented by financially motivated internet crime.

Parallel to the formation of Action Fraud was the creation of the NFIB. This saw the CoLP working with Action Fraud to provide victim-focused help, guidance and reporting channels. On 1 April 2014, ownership of the national reporting side moved to the CoLP, combining both reporting and response under one organisation. This approach is the route to encouraging greater reporting of crime and intelligence, captured in high detail to inform the response.

The NFIB aggregates confirmed reports of fraud and cyber crime and intelligence to inform a more effective strategic and tactical response, and to make that response intelligence-led. See Figure 1.4.

KEY POINTS—ACTION FRAUD AND NFIB SERVICES

Since its inception, the Action Fraud and NFIB services have evolved to:

- provide an accessible, effective and consolidated means for members of the public and businesses to report instances of fraud and cyber crime committed in the UK;
- provide all members of the public and businesses with an effective, efficient and professional level of customer service;
- identify, develop and disseminate crime reports for investigation to UK law enforcement agencies operating locally, regionally and nationally in the pursuit of visible justice for victims;
- proactively identify, target and disrupt the enablers used in the preparation and commission of fraud and cyber crimes, in order to prevent and reduce harm;
- provide education and awareness, through the enrichment of the national fraud and cyber crime threat assessment and intelligence picture, in order to help protect and prepare members of the public and businesses;
- work with partners across the counter-fraud and cyber landscape to protect the UK from, and pursue, serious and organised fraud and cyber crime;
- provide the above in a way that is committed to service delivery and that gives the UK public value for money.

Since the adoption of Action Fraud by all forces in England and Wales in April 2014, the service, to the end of March 2016, has:

- responded to 2,236,874 phone calls;
- received 5,584,384 unique website visitors;
- recorded 707,141 crime reports; the NFIB has reviewed these reports and disseminated intelligence on 189,249 networks of crimes for enforcement action;
- submitted 411,947 entities for disruption.

Figure 1.4 Reporting, assessment and investigation process

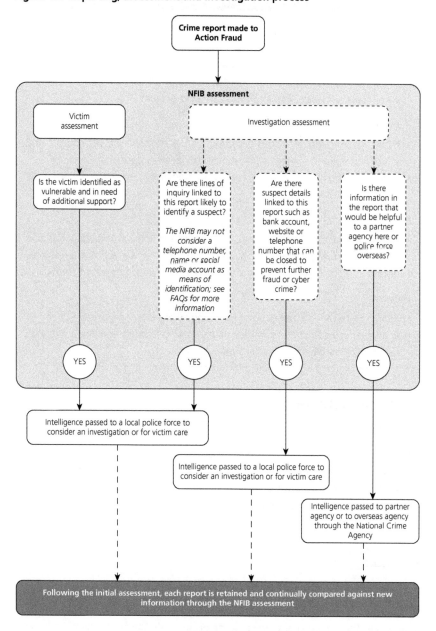

In August 2015, a new contract was awarded for the design, development and implementation of the infrastructure for the above services. This will enable Action Fraud and the NFIB to deliver a service that achieves consumer confidence and meets the 4Ps (pursue, protect, prepare and prevent) that are currently used to define the activities used to counter fraud across law enforcement.

KEY POINTS—4PS APPROACH TO COUNTERING FRAUD

Pursue

- Enable tactical enforcement through the aggregation and enhancement of reports with intelligence, through to delivery at the local, regional and national levels.
- Disrupt criminal behaviour through the sharing of intelligence on risk entities with service providers, regulators and law enforcement.

Protect

- By providing insight into the trends and themes of fraud, we will educate and inform communities at risk, working with key delivery partners.
- Analysis of the mechanics of offending will underpin partnership opportunities to design out threats.

Prepare

- Enable a rapid response to high-volume or high-loss criminal offending, bringing together key law enforcement partners to ensure effective tactical intervention.
- Provide the public with advice and guidance on the changing threat.

Prevent

- Support intervention programmes by raising awareness and illustrating harm.
- Enable effective lifetime offender management through Serious Crime Prevention Orders via intelligence sharing.

1.8 **Fraud enablers**

1.8.1 **Introduction**

There are a range of enablers that are used by those who perpetrate fraud. It is useful to understand the nature of these enablers, as they present the investigator with opportunities for disruption, prevention and investigation. The key enablers are grouped into three categories, namely:

- professional;
- technical;
- financial.

1.8.2 **Professional enablers**

Enablers in this category include a range of professionals with specialist knowledge of organisations and their processes, allowing them to use their professional status to facilitate fraud-related offending. They include:

- **Solicitors**: the large sums of money handled confidentially by solicitors offer opportunities for serious and organised criminals to launder significant amounts of money. The law firm can provide legitimacy to transactions through its professional and legal standing.

- **Trust or company service providers (TCSPs)/company formation agents (CFAs)**: these agents can provide a mechanism whereby the actual directors and owners of a company can effectively be hidden. The degree of anonymity provided offers significant opportunities for organised criminals to launder money.

Other professionals, such as accountants and mortgage brokers, have also been identified as enablers of fraud. The involvement of a qualified and/or trusted individual adds a degree of credibility to a transaction, while their expert knowledge, skills and access to information can facilitate a range of criminal activities, including fraud.

There is no universal definition of a professional enabler, or agreement on how they differ from insiders. Some definitions of professional enablers centre on individuals who are qualified to perform their role and facilitate crime in the course of executing their duties, such as solicitors or doctors. These definitions exclude individuals who commit or facilitate crime while working in non-accredited roles—for example, legal assistants, conveyance clerks or bank cashiers. These roles may not require formal qualifications, but are generally recognised as working in a professional capacity.

1.8.3 Technical enablers

Technical enablers are required to contact the victim(s), steal personal and financial data, and disguise identity and location. These include:

- use of malware (malicious software);
- use of botnets (network of infected devices controlled by cyber criminals for malicious gain, without the consent or knowledge of the owner);
- phishing;
- websites;
- virtual currencies;
- use of voice over internet protocol (VoIP);
- data compromise.

KEY POINTS—MOST COMMON ENABLERS FOR FRAUD REPORTED TO NFIB

The most common enablers for fraud reported to the NFIB:

- 28.5 per cent phone;
- 16.7 per cent online sales (websites);
- 14.3 per cent email.

Source: Fraud Force Profile, NFIB, June 2016.

1.8.4 **Financial enablers**

Financial enablers are the methods and means by which fraud is committed using financial institutions. They include the use of:

- digital currencies;
- money laundering.

Money laundering is the process by which criminal proceeds are sanitised to disguise their illicit origins. Acquisitive criminals will attempt to distance themselves from their crimes by finding safe havens for their profits where they can avoid confiscation orders and where those proceeds can be made to appear legitimate.

Money laundering schemes can be very simple or highly sophisticated. More sophisticated money laundering schemes involve three stages:

- **Placement**: the process of getting criminal money into the financial system.
- **Layering**: the process of moving money in the financial system through complex webs of transactions, often via offshore companies, to disguise the audit trail.
- **Integration**: the process by which criminal money ultimately becomes absorbed into the economy, for example through investment in real estate.

KEY POINTS—METHODS OF LAUNDERING MONEY

- **Cuckoo smurfing** is the disposal of criminal cash through third-party cash deposits. The technique exploits a criminal money launderer's ability to pay cash into any bank account over the counter of any branch of a bank as long as they know the appropriate sort code, account number and account name. Individual money laundering groups operating in this way in the UK have been identified after successfully laundering approximately £100 million in criminally derived cash (NCA, June 2015, *JMLIT Red Alert—Cuckoo Smurfing—A0151-ECC*).
- **The Money Service Business (MSB)** sector is diverse, with participants ranging from large international corporations, which operate worldwide, to local corner shops offering remittance services to their community. MSBs offer an important service to those who do not use, for a variety of reasons, the traditional banking sector. They can exchange currency, cash cheques and transfer money, making it attractive to criminals seeking to conceal the origins of criminal proceeds by, for example, remitting the funds overseas or converting them into high-denomination foreign notes.
- **Money mules** are individuals recruited by criminals to receive the proceeds of crime into their bank accounts. It can often be accessed easily and remotely, and funds can be transferred quickly. This can enable criminality and therefore leave a bank vulnerable to use as a conduit for the proceeds of a crime. A money mule can be complicit, negligent and/or unwittingly involved in illegal activity. The cumulative nature of money mule activity means that significant sums can be laundered. Retail banks in the UK can accept thousands of new customers every month and this can

---

> make it challenging for banks to apply adequate risk-sensitive controls, particularly in terms of ongoing monitoring of account activity and business activity.

Further reading

- CPS, 'Introduction to Money Laundering': www.cps.gov.uk/legal/p_to_r/ proceeds_of_crime_money_laundering/#Introduction_to_Money.

1.9 Other methods used to facilitate fraud

There are a range of other methods frequently used by fraudsters to facilitate fraud. These include:

- social engineering;
- data compromise;
- identity related.

1.9.1 Social engineering

The psychological manipulation of the victim is another method used by the fraudster. They manipulate their victims in order to gain access to information and/or convince them to send funds. Social engineering frequently involves the criminal piecing together information from various sources, such as social media and intercepted correspondence, in order to appear convincing and trustworthy, with the eventual aim being to defraud the victim.

The first step for a fraudster is to persuade the potential victim to engage with them. Techniques for this include spoofing telephone numbers, short message service (SMS), emails or websites in order to appear as a recognised company or brand. During the introduction, the criminal may also fraudulently assert their identity in order to gain the trust of the victim. For example, they may purport to be a bank employee or an authority figure.

The extent and method of interaction between the criminal and the victim depends on the fraud type, complexity and the potential for criminal gain. Some advanced fee fraud types require no further communication between the criminal and victim beyond an initial email, text or letter. For example, a lottery fraud may involve the victim receiving an email instructing them to send a fee in order to release their fictitious winnings. The criminal simply has to send the emails and then wait for payments to be received into their account. More complex fraud types often require a conversation between the criminal and the victim. This can be face to face, via telephone or via messaging services. For example, in some investment fraud cases the fraudster will cold-call victims in order to initiate real-time conversations. This allows the fraudster to sell the bogus investment opportunity using a carefully worded script, overcome any of the victim's objections and apply pressure to the victim to make payments.

1.9.2 Data compromise

Personally identifiable information (PII) is used to assert identity and authenticate customers across many service platforms and payment channels. Examples include:

- use of usernames and passwords in order to log on to online banking;
- use of credit card details to make remote purchases via the telephone.

Therefore, PII is valuable to the fraudster, who may wish to use the information to commit fraud, or to a criminal, who may wish to sell the information to those who would use it to commit fraud.

Typically, criminals will research organisations in order to gain access to a database containing PII. This can be low tech (e.g. conducting open-source research to identify company employees who may be susceptible to corrupt practices), or high tech (e.g. scanning for network vulnerabilities such as open ports, out-of-date software and a lack of encryption). Third-party database compromises/hacks are also a threat to organisations. These occur when an organisation has outsourced business processes, therefore entrusting a third party with the security of their data.

During recent years, there have been several high-profile incidents of data breaches. This has contributed to an enormous volume of compromised PII being readily available to criminals via the open web, dark web or social media. The ability to make money from breaking into virtual data vaults has never been higher. This compromised PII is used to facilitate criminality such as account takeover fraud, remote payment fraud and counterfeit card fraud.

Data compromise impacts on both individuals and organisations. Individuals may become victims of fraud and suffer financial or psychological harm, while victim organisations that suffer a breach may incur reputational damage resulting in a negative impact on their businesses. The extent of data compromise can be exacerbated by poor business practices, such as storing PII for unnecessarily long periods.

1.9.3 Identity-related crime

Identity is a collection of PII/attributes that uniquely define a person or organisation. Authentication and verification are essential for determining a level of confidence in an identity in order to establish that someone is who they claim to be, therefore confirming their right to conduct an action or to receive goods and services that are restricted.

Identity-related crime refers to the misuse of false personal data (as defined in section 8 of the Identity Documents Act 2010, usernames, passwords, etc) or corporate identity data (company names, names of company directors, company websites, etc) in the commission of any crime. Criminals know the value of an identity and use compromised or synthetic PII/attributes as a facilitator.

Two examples of identity-related crimes are identity fraud and facility takeover fraud.

- Identity fraud is the use of a stolen identity in criminal activity in order to obtain money, credit, goods or services by deception. Stealing an individual's identity details does not, on its own, constitute identity fraud.
- Facility takeover fraud involves a person (facility hijacker) unlawfully obtaining access to the details of the 'victim of takeover', namely an existing account holder or police holder, and fraudulently operating the account or policy for their own benefit.

While these two fraud types are dependent on identity-related crime, identity-related crime also enables other fraud types. For example, the fraudster may impersonate a company employee in order to convince the victim to change the payment details on a mandate.

Identity-related crime also helps the criminal to evade detection by law enforcement. Suspects rarely assert their genuine identity when committing fraud, which complicates any subsequent law enforcement investigation.

Further reading

- For more information around the definitions of identity fraud, see: www.actionfraud.police.uk/fraud_protection/identity_fraud

---

1.10 **The Fraud Investigation Model (FIM)**

1.10.1 **Introduction**

Over the last few years, the police service has done much to professionalise the investigative process. This saw the development of a 'model' of investigation that was placed at the heart of the ACPO's 2005 publication, 'Practice Advice on Core Investigative Doctrine', and is used extensively in the national detective training programme.

Though this core model of investigation was highly effective in most crime types, it did not take into account the unique nature of fraud. As a result, the CoLP developed the model further to improve the response to fraud-related offences. It was intended that this newly developed model should bring a structured and logical approach to the investigative process and build on the concepts detailed in the Core Investigative Doctrine. The culmination of this was the introduction of the FIM; this model adds a number of additional elements to the original Core Investigative Doctrine. The FIM can be used effectively by all those involved in countering fraud-related offences, from instigation through to prosecution.

Throughout this publication, the FIM is referenced and its practical application is highlighted. The model should be at the heart of all fraud-related investigations. This section looks at the development of the model and introduces the reader to its elements, which are described in more depth.

1.10.2 Why fraud requires a different response

The need for the new model to counter fraud was driven by the growing impact of fraud on society and the requirement to counter both its growth and the ever-increasing diversity of fraud types. When fraud is compared to traditional crime types, there are some very significant differences. The traditional response to crime is illustrated in Figure 1.5.

Figure 1.5 Traditional response to crime

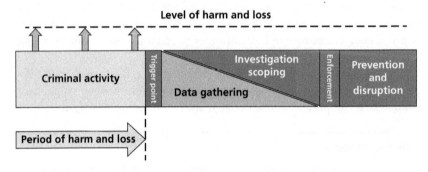

As can be seen in the traditional response to non-fraud crime, the criminal activity occurs and the offence is subsequently reported. Following the report there is a period of data gathering and investigation scoping that results in enforcement action. Once the case has been investigated, prevention and disruption opportunities may be considered. In many crime types this is an effective response, as the period of harm and loss is limited to the period of criminal activity and does not increase over time. A useful example of this is an assault that occurs at a night club—the offence occurs, the victim reports the assault and the period of scoping commences to identify the offender. Meanwhile, the offender has fled and is residing with an associate; no further offences are committed during this time. However, with fraud offences the dynamics of the offence type are quite different, as illustrated in Figure 1.6.

With fraud-type offences, the initial fraudulent activity takes place and the offence is reported. While the data gathering and investigation scoping are being undertaken, due to the nature of the fraudster, further offences are committed. This increases both the level and period of harm; in many cases, if left unchecked, the fraudster will develop new types and styles of fraudulent activity. The reach of and harm caused by the fraudster are perpetually increasing and are aided by the use of cyber-enabled devices, many of which are portable. This has created conditions that accelerate the scale of the harm being caused to both society and individual victims, who are, in many cases, among the most

Figure 1.6 Fraud crime types

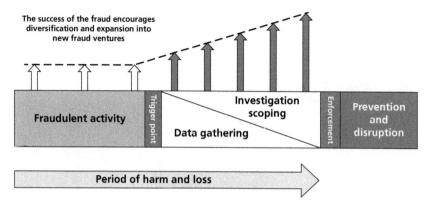

vulnerable in society. In addition, there are many examples of how fraudsters develop the range of their frauds over a period of time, increasing the level of offending and harm. This is commonly seen in romance fraud, boiler room fraud and Ponzi scams (see Chapter 3).

There is, therefore, a need to limit the period of harm and loss by stopping the fraudster at the earliest opportunity. As such, following the instigation of the case, emphasis is placed upon opportunities for early disruption and prevention, as shown in Figure 1.7.

Figure 1.7 How the FIM changes the fraud landscape

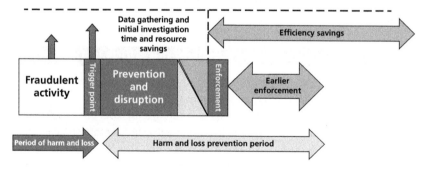

The effective use of the FIM will reduce the potential period of harm caused by the fraudster. Subsequently, the loss caused is significantly mitigated by reducing the enablers and vulnerabilities that the fraudster uses to perpetrate their crimes.

1.10.3 **The FIM**

A flow diagram displaying the elements of the FIM is shown in Figure 1.8. It is a very logical framework that gives the investigator a structure to follow when considering how to respond to allegations of fraud.

Figure 1.8 Flow chart of the FIM (reproduced under licence from the College of Policing)

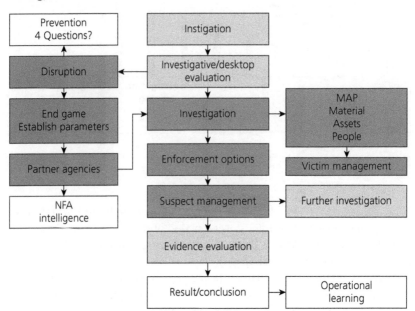

The dark grey sections represent activities requiring investigative strategies or policy decisions. The light grey sections represent the main decision points and the white sections are the outcomes that can be achieved and post-investigative considerations.

KEY POINTS—FOUR FRAUD PREVENTION QUESTIONS IN THE FIM

- What were the principal enablers that allowed this fraud to be perpetrated?
- Who else could be at risk from this or a similar fraud?
- What could have been done to remove or reduce the risk from this fraud?
- How can the lessons learnt be used to prevent others from becoming victims of a similar fraud?

The FIM brings disruption, prevention and partner agencies to the forefront of the response to fraud. This process is not fixed and the investigator can take their own investigative route.

1.10.4 Instigation

Allegations of fraud can be instigated in a number of different ways; most individual victims report their cases through the Action Fraud national reporting process. The information is then analysed by the NFIB, and where there is a viable line of inquiry they send analytical packages out for investigation. A report may be received directly by the police (this is often when it is a 'call for service' offence, where the offender is present or known to the victim), and in these cases Action Fraud will be updated. Reports of fraud from businesses may be received internally through confidential reporting processes. Other methods for instigating fraud inquiries can be through liaison with other law enforcement partners. Once the report has been received, an initial evaluation should take place.

1.10.5 Investigation/desktop evaluation

Once the case has been reported, it is important that an assessment/evaluation takes place. In the NFIB, this process is normally automated; following this, a crime reviewer will analyse the findings. Factors that should be considered when undertaking the evaluation should follow the development of an initial case theory (hypothesis). The development of this hypothesis should be based upon the information presented to identify what may have happened.

Checklist—investigation/desktop evaluation

- Identify status against case acceptance criteria;
- offence type;
- linked offences;
- vulnerability of victims/witnesses;
- location of relevant material;
- identification of suspects;
- connections to other offending;
- scale of the criminal activity;
- level of loss;
- proceeds of crime opportunities (restraint/confiscation);
- scale and geographical spread of victims;
- identification of jurisdictional issues;
- identification of any enablers;
- identification of partner agencies;
- prevention opportunities;
- disruption opportunities.

1.10.6 **Disruption**

Disrupting the fraudster, by denying them the enablers required to perpetrate their offending, is highly effective, particularly when an investigation is not likely to result in a successful prosecution. Fraudsters often rely on enablers such as use of the internet, communications systems and money movement methods. The identification of these enablers provides the investigator with useful lines of inquiry, as well as the opportunity to limit the ability of the fraudster to use these enablers. Disruption relies on confidence and trust between law enforcement and those overseeing those processes, as they are often the ones who withdraw the right to use the enabler (see Chapter 5 for more information).

1.10.7 **Prevention**

Fraud prevention is now accepted as a vital component of fraud reduction and involves targeting hardened individuals, organisations and indeed society as a whole; it is an integral part of the FIM. The prevention considerations when fraud is reported are informed by four questions, namely:

- What were the principal enablers that allowed this fraud to be perpetrated?
- Who else could be at risk from this or a similar fraud?
- What could have been done to remove or reduce the risk from this fraud?
- How can the lessons learnt be used to prevent others from becoming a victim of a similar fraud?

The answers to these four questions will shape the prevention response. If others are at risk of the fraud, then action should be taken to inform that particular group (see Chapter 5 for more information). Often, the prevention response is made most effective by partnering with other agencies, organisations and the media, who have the capacity to reach those who may be future victims of fraud.

1.10.8 **Partner agencies**

The multi-agency approach to tackling fraud is essential to effectively combating this crime type. Other law enforcement or regulatory bodies often have differing powers and skills that are better suited to the fraud type reported. There is an extensive range of organisations involved in countering fraud across all sectors, including the public, private and third sectors. Intelligence held by these organisations may be relevant to a case being investigated by another. A decision should be made as to which is the best agency to take the investigation forward, or which combination of organisations should undertake the inquiry.

1.10.9 **End-game investigation parameters**

When setting investigative parameters, it is useful to consider the 'end game', which will differ for each case; there are a number of sanctions that can be considered in fraud-related offences, including criminal and civil prosecution and regulatory sanctions. On occasion, dual criminal and civil investigations may take place. When this happens, careful consideration needs to be given to the implications for each inquiry, particularly in relation to the disclosure of material.

1.10.10 Material recovery

A key element of the FIM is the mnemonic MAP, which stands for material, assets and people. This is really useful for the investigator, as it highlights the areas for consideration in an investigation and helps to map the inquiry.

Checklist—MAP considerations

Material

- What offence(s) may have been committed?
- What is the material relevant to the investigation?
- Where is the material located?
- When should the material be recovered (prioritisation)?
- How should the material be recovered (what power)?
- Record your rationale for the decisions made.

Assets

- Consider restraint of assets that could be dissipated from the start of the investigation.
- Engage an accredited financial investigator re use of powers under the Proceeds of Crime Act (POCA) 2002.

People

- Identify the suspect(s).
- Manage the suspect.
- Identify witnesses.
- Classify witnesses (vulnerable, key or significant).
- Manage witnesses.

1.10.11 Victim management

Victim management can be challenging, in fraud cases particularly, especially when there are multiple victims who are spread over a large geographical area. These cases can often be prolonged and can affect the most vulnerable in society. A strategy for managing victims is of paramount importance and is a key consideration for the investigator (see Chapter 6 for more information).

1.10.12 Operational learning

In fraud cases, operational learning is important in order to identify what went well, what didn't go so well, what could be done differently next time and what advice should be given to those investigating similar offences (see Chapter 9 for more information).

1.10.13 Summary

In summary, the FIM adds a logical framework to the investigation of fraud. It is a highly practical model that can be used as a checklist for the investigator when dealing with fraud-related offences. The role of the investigator in countering fraud is shown in Figure 1.9.

Figure 1.9 Role of the investigating officer in fraud cases

The advantages of the FIM are that it limits the period of harm and loss, encourages disruption and multi-agency working, and focuses on prevention to stop further loss and harm. It provides a logical approach to countering fraud, with a significant focus on supporting the victim.

2

Legislation

2.1 **Introduction**

It is important that investigators stay up to date with the current law and understand how this impacts on their investigations and decisions. Changes to the law are made so that it does not become outdated and remains relevant in the face of emerging threats. This also provides the ability to react to society's demand for tougher sanctions.

Keeping up to date with changes to the law is not always as easy as it might at first appear. Changes can be subtle, and are sometimes buried deep within case law; the headline might bear no hint of its significance to the investigator. However, the impact of such subtlety should never be underestimated. The investigator who seeks to ensure that their investigations are both lawful and ethical ignores such changes at their peril. What follows is an explanation of some of the legislation that the investigator is most likely to encounter. It should be noted that the majority of the law applicable to England and Wales will also cover Northern Ireland (NI); however, there are subtle differences, and the investigator operating within NI will need to refer to the appropriate statute to check its nuances.

2.2 **The Fraud Act 2006**

The Fraud Act 2006, which came into effect on 15 January 2007, replaced all the deception offences under the Theft Acts 1968 and 1978 and was a game changer for the investigation and prosecution of fraud-related offences. The introduction of this legislation assisted investigators greatly, as there was no longer a need to show that a deception had been operated upon the victim's mind. This has enabled the investigator to concentrate on gathering evidence in a way that focuses on the suspect's intentions and actions rather than evidencing that a victim has been deceived. Additionally, the law encompasses cases in which a fraud is perpetrated without any human interaction, meaning that many new frauds carried out using or exploiting technology, particularly digital technology, can now be prosecuted far more easily. The offence of going equipped to cheat, previously defined by section 25 of the Theft Act 1968, has been abolished and is now covered in section 6 of the Fraud Act.

KEY POINTS—FRAUD OFFENCES

Section 1(1) of the Fraud Act has sought to simplify fraud by creating an offence of criminal fraud, which can be committed in three ways:

- section 2—fraud by false representation;
- section 3—fraud by failure to disclose information;
- section 4—fraud by abuse of a position of trust.

2.2.1 Defining gain and loss

Although the Fraud Act no longer requires the prosecution to show that a fraud operated on the mind of a victim, it is necessary to show that the offender intended to bring about some gain or loss in money or other property, even if no gain or loss was in fact caused.

Checklist—key points regarding gain and loss

Section 5 of the Fraud Act provides that 'gain' and 'loss':

- extend only to money or other property;
- include temporary as well as permanent gains and losses;
- include:
  - keeping what one already has;
  - not getting what one might get;
- as well as:
  - getting what one does not have;
  - parting with what one does have.

Note that a defendant can intend to make a 'gain' without making an overall profit from the fraud.

2.2.2 Fraud by false representation—section 2

Checklist—key points regarding fraud by false representation

The key parts to this offence are that:

- a person makes a false representation;
- dishonestly;
- knowing that the representation was, or might be, untrue or misleading.

Intending either:

- to make a gain for himself or another; or
- to cause loss to another person or to expose another person to the risk of loss.

If we break this section down, we can start to understand the finer points of the offence. This will assist us greatly with not only trying to determine if the offence is complete, but also informing the direction of our investigation.

False representation can be expressed or implied and can be either untrue or misleading. The use of the word 'misleading' makes the law more flexible in nature. In this way, the Crown is in a better position to prosecute those who close their eyes to the possibility that what they are doing amounts to fraud.

The Fraud Act does not define dishonesty, preferring to import the test for dishonesty as defined in *R v Ghosh* and successfully used in cases of theft. This test is a combination of both an objective and subjective test.

Case study—*R v Ghosh* [1982] EWCA Crim 2

In 1982 Dr Ghosh was a surgeon who was said to have made false claims for payment for operations. At his appeal, Dr Ghosh claimed that he had not acted dishonestly, as he had believed that he was entitled to the sums claimed. Dr Ghosh was convicted at trial, and appealed on the basis that the judge had directed the jury to use their common sense to decide whether his conduct had been dishonest or not (an objective test) rather than whether he had himself felt that his behaviour had been dishonest (a subjective test). The Court of Appeal dismissed the appeal, but reformulated the test of dishonesty into a hybrid objective/subjective test.

Further reading

- *R v Ghosh* [1982] EWCA Crim 2: www.bailii.org/ew/cases/EWCA/Crim/1982/2.html

---

First, the jury is asked to consider whether by the standards of an ordinary and reasonable person they would consider the acts of the accused to be dishonest (the objective test). If the answer is no, then that is the end of the matter and dishonesty will not be proved. However, if the answer is yes, the jury is then asked to consider whether the accused must have realised that what they were doing was, by those standards, dishonest (the subjective test).

It is worth noting that the offence can be complete once the false representation is made with the requisite intent. This means that the full offence can still be made out even if there is no resulting gain or loss; such conduct might have previously been prosecuted as an attempt.

The investigator should always keep in their mind the three key points to be proved in offences contrary to this section, as shown in Figure 2.1.

Figure 2.1 Fraud by false representation—key elements

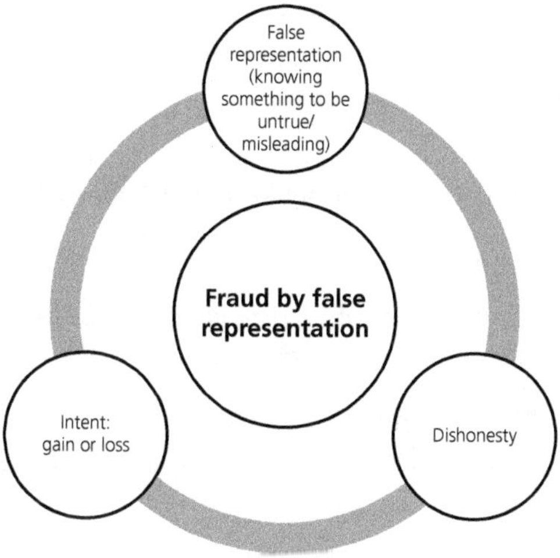

2.2.3 **Fraud by failing to disclose information—section 3**

Fraud by failing to disclose information recognises that a person can dishonestly gain, or dishonestly cause a person a loss, by failing to disclose certain information when under a legal duty to do so.

KEY POINTS—FRAUD BY FAILING TO DISCLOSE INFORMATION

The key parts to this offence are:

- the defendant failed to disclose information to another person;
- when he was under a legal duty to disclose that information;
- dishonestly intending, by that failure;
- to make a gain, cause a loss or expose another to a risk of loss.

Like the previous offence, there will need to be a dishonest intention to make a gain, cause a loss or expose another to a risk of loss. Investigators also need to show that there was a legal duty to disclose such information; for example, through the existence of a fiduciary relationship, in applications for insurance, or through the express or implied terms of a contract.

KEY POINTS—FAILING TO DISCLOSE INFORMATION CONSIDERATIONS

This offence is not intended for situations that might raise a moral duty to disclose the information.

2.2.4 **Fraud by abuse of position—section 4**

Those that offend under this section are in a position of trust with a responsibility to safeguard another's financial interest; this often gives the offender an opportunity to conceal their offending.

Checklist—key points of fraud by abuse of a position

The key parts of this offence are:

- the defendant occupies a position in which he is expected to safeguard, or not to act against, the financial interests of another person;

- but dishonestly abuses that position;

- intending to make a gain, cause a loss, or expose another to a risk of loss.

The investigator will need to be mindful that the trusted point of contact, appointed by the victim, might actually be the offender. This is where looking carefully at the weaknesses in processes and systems or at fraud indicators (red flags, see Chapter 1) might narrow down the list of potential suspects.

KEY POINTS—FRAUD BY ABUSE OF A POSITION

When considering an offence of 'fraud by abuse of a position':

- this offence can be committed by either an act or an omission by those in a position of trust;
- a position of trust is not defined and will largely come down to the facts of the matter. Examples may include:
  - trustee/beneficiary;
  - director/company;
  - professional/client;
  - agent/principal;
  - employee/employer;
  - partners or family members;
- the judge will determine if a particular relationship is *capable* of falling within the definition;
- the jury will determine whether the relationship *did* fall within the definition.

2.2.5 **Possession of articles for use in fraud—section 6**

The key element of this offending is that the suspect had possession or control of an article for use in the course of, or in connection with, any fraud. This offence has modelled itself on the previous law of going equipped to cheat under section 25 of the Theft Act 1968.

As an investigator, you will have to show that the person had within his posses-sion or control an article for use in the course of, or in connection with, any fraud (as defined by section 1 of the Fraud Act 2006). You will not need to show that the suspect had any specific fraud in mind, but they should have had a general intention to have the article to commit fraud, whether by themselves or others.

The offence includes computer programs or data held electronically for use in fraud. The word 'article' is defined in section 8 of the Fraud Act. However, the offender must know that they are in possession or control of the article, and must have the technical know-how to retrieve it.

The offence under this section is wider than the previous law of 'going equipped' as, under the Fraud Act, items found at a place of residence can also be included.

KEY POINTS—POSSESSION OF ARTICLES FOR USE IN FRAUD

When considering an offence 'possession of articles for use in fraud':

- there is no defence of reasonable excuse and any suspect would have to rely on a lack of intention to possess the article for use in the course of or in connection with any fraud;
- the term 'article' is wide and could include most items if it is possessed for use in fraud.

2.2.6 Making or supplying articles for use in fraud—section 7

The key parts to this offence are that the person makes, adapts, supplies or offers to supply any article for use in the course of or in connection with fraud, know-ing it is designed or adapted for use in the course of or in connection with fraud, or intending for it to be used to commit or assist in the commission of fraud.

KEY POINTS—SUPPLYING ARTICLES FOR USE IN FRAUD

When considering an offence of making or supplying an article for use in fraud:

- knowledge under this offence is a strict *mens rea* requirement.

2.2.7 Obtaining services dishonestly—section 11

Checklist—key points of obtaining services dishonestly

The key parts to this offence are:

- that the person obtains services;
- by a dishonest act;
- for himself or another;

- knowing that the services are or might be made available on the basis that payment has been, is being or will be made;

- but intending to avoid payment in full or in part.

An example of this type of offending is when someone might download software without payment, use the services of a private members' club without being a member, obtain banking or other financial or commercial services or enter into a hire-purchase agreement.

KEY POINTS—CONSIDERATIONS OF OBTAINING SERVICES DISHONESTLY

When considering an offence of 'obtaining services dishonestly':

- the person must have the intention not to pay at the point that the service is obtained;
- this is a result crime and requires the actual obtainment of the service;
- this offence will sometimes involve a false representation having been made and it will be for the prosecutor to decide which charge best fits the offence;
- this offence did not repeal the offence of 'making off without payment' (section 3 of the Theft Act 1978).

Checklist—CPS fraud charging practice (overlap with theft and other offences)

In many cases, fraud will also be theft. Prosecutors should bear in mind that:

- theft carries a lower minimum sentence;

- the *actus reus* requirement for fraud is far less;

- the credit/debit status of any bank accounts debited is irrelevant to the Fraud Act offences. All that is in issue is the defendant's right to use the account;

- it is not necessary to prove or demonstrate any consequences of fraud (though they will clearly be material to sentence, compensation and confiscation). 'Preddy'-type difficulties will not arise (where the property obtained had not belonged to another);

- Fraud Act offences do not require an intent to permanently deprive;

- a charge should describe what actually happened and reflect the true criminality;

- the indictment should be as simple as is reasonably possible.

In some cases, there will be other possible offences, such as false accounting (section 17 of the Theft Act 1968), making off without payment (section 3 of the Theft Act 1978) and obtaining services dishonestly (section 11 of the Fraud Act 2006). There are also offences under the Computer Misuse Act (CMA) 1990, the Forgery and Counterfeiting Act 1981, the Identity Cards Act (ICA) 2006, the Proceeds of Crime Act (POCA) 2002 and the Financial Services and Markets Act (FSMA) 2000.

Prosecutors must decide which offence properly reflects the criminality concerned.

Source: www.cps.gov.uk/legal/d_to_g/fraud_act/

Further reading

- Fraud Act: www.legislation.gov.uk/ukpga/2006/35/pdfs/ukpga_20060035_en.pdf
- CPS Fraud Act Legal Guidance: www.cps.gov.uk/legal/d_to_g/fraud_act/
- Fraud, bribery and money laundering offences sentencing guidelines: www.sentencingcouncil.org.uk/wp-content/uploads/Fraud_bribery_and_money_laundering_offences_-_Definitive_guideline.pdf

---

2.3 Conspiracy to defraud

The common law offence of 'conspiracy to defraud' was not abolished during the passing of the Fraud Act. This was due to acknowledgement that there may be occasions when the interests of justice can only be served by presenting the jury with an overall picture of the offence, particularly if the fraud is complex, with the involvement of many offenders, all carrying out different roles within the criminal enterprise.

Checklist—key points for conspiracy

Where there is an agreement by two or more people in crime involving fraud or dishonesty, this may be both a:

- statutory conspiracy (section 1(1) of the Criminal Law Act 1977);

- common law conspiracy to defraud.

It will be for the prosecutor to decide which conspiracy should be charged in accordance with the Code for Crown Prosecutors, section 6.

However, it should always be the priority to use statute law where possible, so prosecutors will need to specify a reason why this charge is being preferred.

KEY POINTS—ATTORNEY GENERAL'S GUIDELINES RE CONSPIRACY

Extract from Attorney General's guidelines:

A—Conduct that can more effectively be prosecuted as conspiracy to defraud

12—There may be cases where the interests of justice can only be served by presenting to a court an overall picture that cannot be achieved by charging a series of substantive offences or statutory conspiracies. Typically, such cases will involve some, but not necessarily all, of the following:

- evidence of several significant but different kinds of criminality;
- several jurisdictions;
- different types of victims, e.g. individuals, banks, website administrators, credit card companies;
- organised crime networks.

13—The proper presentation of such cases as statutory conspiracies could lead to:

- large numbers of separate counts to reflect the different conspiracies;
- severed trials for single or discrete groups of conspiracies;
- evidence in one severed trial being deemed inadmissible in another.

14—If so, the consequences might be that no single court would receive a cohesive picture of the whole case that would allow sentencing on a proper basis. In contrast, a single count of common law conspiracy to defraud might, in such circumstances, reflect the nature and extent of criminal conduct in a way that prosecuting the underlying statutory offences or conspiracies would fail to achieve.

B—Conduct that can only be prosecuted as conspiracy to defraud

15—Examples of such conduct might include but are not restricted to agreements to the following courses of action:

- the dishonest obtainment of land and other property that cannot be stolen, such as intellectual property not protected by the Copyright, Designs and Patents Act 1988 and the Trademarks Act 1994, and other confidential information. The Fraud Act will bite where there is intent to make a gain or cause a loss through false representation, failure to disclose information where there is a legal obligation to do so, or abuse of position;
- dishonestly infringing another's rights (for example, the dishonest exploitation of another's patent in the absence of a legal duty to disclose information about its existence);
- where it is intended that the final offence be committed by someone outside the conspiracy;
- cases where the accused cannot be proved to have had the necessary degree of knowledge of the substantive offence to be perpetrated.

Source: www.gov.uk/guidance/use-of-the-common-law-offence-of-conspiracy-to-defraud--6 (accessed 25 April 2016).

2.4 **The Bribery Act 2010**

2.4.1 **Introduction**

This section is designed to give the investigator an insight into the main offences of the UK Bribery Act (UKBA) 2010.

The UKBA came into force on 1 July 2011. The UKBA itself is not retrospective; therefore, despite the change in the law some investigations will be undertaken using the points to prove from the previous legislation to deal with corruption which was repealed, this included:

- Public Bodies Corrupt Practices Act 1889;
- Prevention of Corruption Act 1906;
- Prevention of Corruption Act 1916;
- Anti-terrorism, Crime and Security Act 2001.

KEY POINTS—UKBA

The UKBA introduced the following:

- defences to bribery (intelligence services and armed forces)—section 13;
- an offence of bribing a foreign public official—section 6;
- increased the sentence to ten years and/or an unlimited fine   section 11;
- a new corporate offence of 'failing to prevent bribery'—section 7;
- defence to section 7 re adequate procedures—section 7;
- consent to prosecute Director of Public Prosecutions, Director of SFO or Director of Revenue and Customs Prosecutions—section 10.

Bribery has a number of unique features, which increases the challenge facing the investigator; it takes many forms and is widely referred to as being either petty or grand corruption. Petty corruption is often defined as small routine payments made to low-ranking public officials. Grand corruption is predominantly conducted by business people and involves large contracts or transactions.

By its very nature, corruption is often based on a secretive relationship involving very few individuals or selected and trusted third parties. The two parties involved in bribery are often referred to as the 'happy parties', as each party involved benefits from the crime. Historically, this has on occasion been described as a 'victimless crime'; however, this crime has consequences for individuals, organisations and society that can be devastating and far-reaching.

2.4.2 **Who is covered by the UKBA?**

An offence may be committed under the UKBA by:

- a British citizen;
- a British company;
- an overseas citizen ordinarily resident in the UK;
- a body incorporated under the law of any part of the UK.

2.4.3 The Bribery Investigation Model (BIM)

The BIM is a very useful model that can be used to identify the appropriate legalisation to use in an investigation. Following the report (instigation) of the suspected bribery, the case should be assessed and consideration given to working with, or referring the investigation to, another agency. The two key organisations that have specialist capability in the bribery field are the National Crime Agency (NCA) International Corruption Unit and the Serious Fraud Office (SFO). The offence date is the trigger for selecting the legislative framework to operate within: before 1 July 2011, it will be the legislation pre-UKBA. If it is on or after this date there are a number of additional considerations for the investigator including that of a section 7 offence, for the commercial organisations (if they feature in the case), that is failing to prevent bribery. See Figure 2.2.

Figure 2.2 Bribery Investigation Model

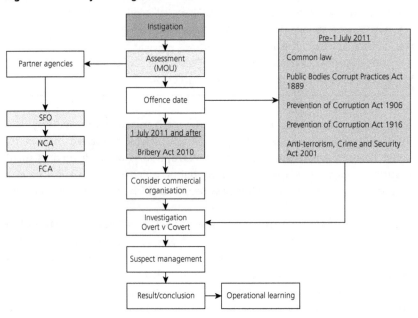

2.4.4 Offences of bribing another person—section 1

If a person promises, offers or gives a financial or other advantage to another person and intends for that advantage to induce a person to perform a relevant function or activity improperly, or to reward a person for the improper performance of such a function or activity, then they commit an offence under the Act.

The advantage does not have to be money, and could be any 'reward', including gifts or hospitality (e.g. concert tickets, theatre tickets and offers of employment). The mere offer of the advantage or reward is sufficient to trigger the offence. The advantage can be passed to an associate of the person who promises to undertake the improper performance.

Section 1(3) deals with the offer or giving of an advantage where the person offering or giving knows or believes it is improper for the other party to accept the advantage.

2.4.5 Offences related to being bribed—section 2

The offence under section 2 relates to where a person requests, agrees to receive or accepts a financial or other advantage, intending that, in consequence, a relevant function or activity should be performed improperly by themselves or another person.

Section 2(3) includes where a person requests or accepts an advantage, which is in itself improper. This could be where the request or receipt of an advantage is against the job rules to accept.

2.4.6 Function or activity to which the bribe relates—section 3

A relevant function or activity for the purpose of the UKBA is:

- any function of a public nature;
- any activity connected with a business;
- any activity performed in the course of a person's employment;
- any activity performed by or on behalf of a body of persons (whether corporate or unincorporated).

In addition, a person performing the function or activity is expected to perform their function in one or up to all three of the following conditions:

A good faith;
B impartially;
C a position of trust.

2.4.7 Improper performance to which the bribe relates—section 4

Improper performance simply means if it is performed in breach of a relevant expectation A, B and or C as defined in section 3 above.

2.4.8 Expectation test—section 5

The expectation test would be what a reasonable person in the UK would expect. It should be noted that any local custom or practice outside the UK is to be disregarded unless it is permitted or required by the law of the relevant country.

2.4.9 **Bribery of foreign public officials—section 6**

A person who bribes a foreign public official is guilty of an offence if their intention is to influence the official in their capacity as a foreign public official.

The briber must also intend to obtain or retain business or an advantage in the conduct of business. The bribe can be done directly or through a third party, or to another person that the foreign public official requests.

KEY POINTS—FOREIGN PUBLIC OFFICIAL

Means an individual who holds one of the following positions outside the UK:

- legislative position;
- administrative position;
- judicial position.

2.4.10 **Failure of a commercial organisation to prevent bribery—section 7**

The introduction of the section 7 offence of failing to prevent bribery by a commercial organisation was designed to improve corporate governance and encourage the use of effective measures to counter bribery. The maximum punishment under section 7 is an unlimited fine.

KEY POINTS—SECTION 7 OFFENCE

- A commercial organisation is guilty of this offence if a person associated with the organisation bribes another person, intending to:
  - obtain or retain business;
  - obtain or retain an advantage in the business for the organisation.
- This is a strict liability offence, though there is a defence if the organisation can demonstrate, on the balance of probabilities, that they had in place adequate procedures to prevent the person paying a bribe.
- This offence is triggered by sections 1 and 6, that is where the person bribes another person.

The section provides organisations with a defence if they can prove that they 'had in place adequate procedures designed to prevent persons associated with them from undertaking such conduct'. 'Adequate procedures' is something that will be tested in court; however, the Ministry of Justice has provided 'six principles' to help organisations wishing to prevent bribery being committed on their behalf.

In domestic (UK) cases, the section 7 corporate offence can be triggered as shown in Figure 2.3. If Mr Jones, the sales director, offers or gives an advantage to Mr Parker, the NHS buyer, to induce or reward improper performance, the section 1 offence is committed.

Figure 2.3 UKBA—domestic corruption section 1 offence

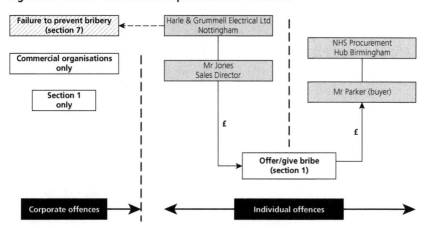

It the bribe was to obtain or retain a business advantage then Harle & Grummell Electrical may have committed the section 7 offence. The investigation should then consider whether Harle & Grummell Electrical had adequate procedures to prevent the bribery from taking place, if so this is a defence. If Mr Parker asks for the advantage, the section 2 offence is committed; this offence alone does not trigger the corporate liability under section 7 (Figure 2.4).

Figure 2.4 UKBA—domestic corruption section 2 offence

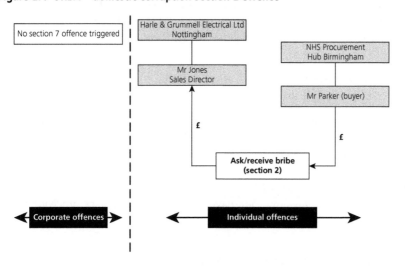

In cases involving an international perspective, the section 6 offence can trigger the commercial organisation's liability. In the example in Figure 2.5, if Mr Jones pays a bribe to Mr West, the foreign public official, consideration could be given to both a section 1 offence and a section 6 offence, both of which trigger the commercial organisation's (Harle & Grummell Electrical Ltd) liability under section 7.

Figure 2.5 UKBA 2010—overseas corruption triggering the bribery offences

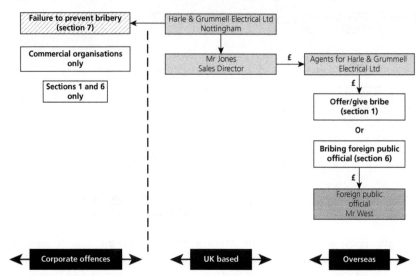

2.4.11 Meaning of associated person—section 8

A 'person associated' includes a person who works for, or is an agent or a subsidiary of, the organisation. Organisations that use third parties should ensure that those parties are aware of their responsibilities under the UKBA (regardless of where they are in the world) and they understand the impact their actions can have on the organisation they are working for.

2.4.12 Guidance to commercial organisations to prevent bribery—section 9

The Ministry of Justice (MoJ) has provided a guidance document on how to prevent bribery for commercial organisations. This guidance is based on six principles which are interlinked and offer an important and sound framework for organisations to build upon.

Organisations that wish to avail themselves of the section 7(2) defence will need to demonstrate how they have implemented adequate procedures. See Table 2.1.

2.4.13 Consent to prosecute—section 10

No prosecution may be brought unless consent has been sought from either the Director of Public Prosecutions (or the equivalent) or the Director of the SFO.

Table 2.1 Adequate procedures—The six principles

Proportionate procedures	The organisation should ensure that the procedures it has put in place are proportionate to the risk. The risk to an organisation will change with the environment it is operating in; therefore, any procedures should be flexible and link directly to the organisational risk assessment.
Top-level commitment	Senior management should be committed to developing an anti-bribery culture within their organisation. This should be communicated both internally, to members of the organisation, and externally, to those that the organisation does business with. The top-level management should ensure that the anti-bribery measures within their organisation are appropriately resourced.
Risk assessment	The organisation needs to assess the nature and extent of its exposure to the bribery risks, both internally and externally. This will vary depending on the sector the organisation operates in and where it is based. There will also be other factors—such as type of contract and value—that may also increase the risks and mitigation required
	The risk assessment may be undertaken by a suitably qualified person and the methodology and risks identified should be recorded. The assessment should be ongoing and, where possible, embedded into the organisational policies and procedures. A risk manager should be appointed to coordinate the risk assessment activities. Evidence of risk mitigation and the level of acceptable risk should be recorded.
Due diligence	This is something that all organisations should do and can form part of their wider governance procedures. Due diligence checks should be undertaken on those the organisation does business with and engages to do business on its behalf. It should ensure that all parties it engages with are not likely to have been or have been engaged in bribery. This can be done through undertaking a series of checks, both through open-source inquiries and by making use of existing networks.
Communication (including training)	This is an essential element of adequate procedures and will take a number of different forms within an organisation based primarily on the risk assessment. The training plan for the organisation in relation to bribery should be comprehensive and ensure all associated personnel are aware of the bribery risks, and the mitigation and reporting procedures. Each role within the organisation should be assessed to identify its vulnerability to bribery, and training should be scaled appropriately.
	Where possible, bribery training should be embedded throughout organisational processes.
	Communicating the anti-bribery message should be a continuous process and would normally be seen throughout the following:
	• organisational intranet and website;
	• staff handbooks;
	• induction training material;
	• regular updates/bulletins.

(continued)

Table 2.1 *continued*

	Organisations should have effective methods for those associated with the organisation to report any concerns they may have regarding bribery. This should include the ability to report anonymously.
Monitoring and review	The person or team with responsibility for monitoring the anti-bribery controls should ensure this is undertaken throughout the organisation on a regular basis. Each department within the organisation may own the risks associated with bribery and conduct their own monitoring of these risks.
	If, while monitoring, suspicions of bribery are identified, these should be escalated to the appropriate level.
	There should be policies and procedures that document how the monitoring should be implemented throughout the organisation. A review process should be built into these policies.

2.4.14 Penalties—section 11

The maximum sentence for an individual guilty of an offence under sections 1, 2 and 6 would be ten years and/or an unlimited fine.

2.4.15 Defences for certain bribery offences—section 13

There are defences available for individuals; however, they are limited to:

- the intelligence services;
- the Armed Forces when engaged on active service (meaning an action or operation against an enemy, an operation outside the British Islands for the protection of life or property or military occupation of a foreign country or territory).

Each case would be reviewed and arrangements, which satisfied the Secretary of State, would need to be put in place.

2.4.16 Facilitation payments

These are low-level payments routinely solicited by low-ranking public officials to facilitate routine government action; these are referred to as 'facilitation payments'. The receipt and payment of these are an offence under the UKBA.

Further reading—bribery and corruption

Pre-1 July 2011 bribery and corruption offences

- Public Bodies Corrupt Practices Act 1889: www.legislation.gov.uk/ukpga/ Vict/52-53/69/contents/enacted

---

- Prevention of Corruption Act 1906: www.legislation.gov.uk/ukpga/Edw7/6/34/contents/enacted
- Prevention of Corruption Act 1916: www.legislation.gov.uk/ukpga/Geo5/6-7/64/contents/enacted
- Anti-terrorism, Crime and Security Act 2001 (sections 108–110): www.legislation.gov.uk/ukpga/2001/24/contents/enacted

UKBA

- Full list of who is covered by the UKBA 2010: www.legislation.gov.uk/ukpga/2010/23/section/12/data.pdf
- MoJ, 'The Bribery Act 2010: Guidance': www.justice.gov.uk/downloads/legislation/bribery-act-2010-guidance.pdf
- Bribery Act 2010: www.legislation.gov.uk/ukpga/2010/23/contents

2.5 The Proceeds of Crime Act 2002 (money laundering offences)

2.5.1 Introduction

The laundering process is often referred to as 'washing', since the ultimate aim is for 'dirty' money to be converted into 'clean' money. It is also referred to as a 'cycle' because the process can be repeated as many times as necessary. Broadly speaking, the mechanics of the process comprise three main stages: placement, layering and integration.

There are three main money laundering offences that were introduced in the money laundering provisions in Part 7 of the POCA 2002, which came into effect on 24 February 2003. These three offences are covered in detail later in the section, and each is based on the understanding that the property to be laundered constitutes benefit from criminal conduct.

Checklist—related money laundering offences—POCA

- section 327—concealing criminal property, etc;
- section 328—arrangements;
- section 329—acquisition, use and possession;
- section 330—failure to disclose offence: regulated sector;
- section 331—failure to disclose offence: nominated officers in the regulated sector;
- section 332—failure to disclose: other nominated officers;
- section 333—tipping off.

The predicate offence may be investigated in tandem with the linked money laundering offence; so, for example, an investigation into a fraud (the predicate offence) will be linked to a money laundering investigation to identify what subsequently happened to the monies generated by that fraud. It is not always possible, however, to identify the predicate offence or even the predicate type of offence. In these circumstances, all the evidence can be weighed up and considered when deciding whether the criminal property is indeed the proceeds of crime.

Case study—*R v Anwoir* [2008] EWCA Crim 1354

Lord Justice Latham states at paragraph 21 of this case that 'We consider that in the present case the Crown are correct in their submission that there are two ways in which the Crown can prove the property derives from crime, (a) by showing that it derives from conduct of a specific kind or kinds and that conduct of that kind or those kinds is unlawful, or (b) by evidence of the circumstances in which the property is handled which are such as to give rise to the irresistible inference that it can only be derived from crime.'

Paragraph 22 of the same case then quotes from the judge's comments to the jury, saying 'you will note from the definition of criminal conduct that you do not have to be satisfied what conduct it was that produced a financial benefit for the other person. While it could be the proceeds of theft or fraud it could equally be the proceeds of unlawful gambling, prostitution, revenue or any other kind of dishonesty. The useful test, you may think, is to ask yourselves whether the financial benefit was honestly derived from legitimate business or commercial activity.'

2.5.2 Criminal property

Although the offences are referred to as 'money laundering offences', there is actually no mention of money in any of the offences. Instead, the legislation refers to 'criminal property'. This is property that constitutes a person's benefit from their criminal conduct, either in whole or in part, directly or indirectly; the alleged offender should know or suspect that the property constitutes or represents such a benefit. This can range from cash, to funds in a bank account, to other financial instruments (e.g. shares), to art and antiques, jewellery, vehicles, properties and livestock. It can also include intangible items, such as intellectual property or a pecuniary advantage.

2.5.3 Criminal conduct

Criminal conduct is conduct that constitutes an offence in any part of the UK or, if the conduct occurred elsewhere and was an offence in that jurisdiction, would also constitute an offence in any part of the UK if it occurred there. In relation to overseas offences, there is a defence where the defendant knew or believed that the offence was not unlawful under the criminal law then applicable in the overseas jurisdiction. The exception to this is if the criminal conduct would have received a maximum sentence of 12 months or more were the conduct to have occurred in the UK.

It does not matter who carried out the conduct, who benefited from it or when it occurred as long as the actual laundering took place after February 2003. If it took place beforehand, then the previous legislation will need to be utilised.

2.5.4 Concealing, disguising, converting and transferring criminal property—section 327 of POCA 2002

The first offence is where a person commits an offence if he:

- conceals criminal property;
- disguises criminal property;
- converts criminal property;
- transfers criminal property;
- removes it from England and Wales, Scotland or NI.

In relation to this offence, concealing or disguising property relates to concealing or disguising its nature, source, location, disposition, movement, ownership or any rights with respect to it.

Examples of activity that could be covered by this section might include:

- keeping valuables in a hidden compartment under the floorboards;
- having false documentation suggesting that a work of art came from an inheritance;
- changing a large quantity of low-denomination bank notes into high-denomination ones to make them less bulky and more portable;
- moving funds from one account to another;
- driving a high-value car from London to Paris.

As long as the property is criminal property (see 2.5.2) and the requisite knowledge or suspicion is present, then the offence is complete.

2.5.5 Arrangements—section 328 of POCA 2002

The second offence is where a person commits an offence if they enter into or are otherwise involved in an arrangement to facilitate another person (by whatever means) acquiring, retaining, using or controlling criminal property. It must be established that they had knowledge or suspicion that the property constituted or represented benefit from criminal conduct.

This is usually a third-party offence, as the offender is facilitating another to acquire, retain, etc; however, they may be making some profit on the transaction themselves.

Those considered for this offence usually fall into two broad categories.

1 The first comprises the family or friends of the person involved in the predicate offence. Monies are frequently transferred into their accounts, and property put into their names or their businesses may be used to disguise the source of the criminal property. This category would also potentially include others such as business partners.
2 Those in the second category are sometimes called 'gatekeepers'. These are people who control access to the financial systems, such as bankers, accountants, solicitors, estate agents, financial advisers and insurance brokers, to name but a few. Many of these people have or should have a professional understanding of anti-money laundering legislation and procedures, and they are used not only to smooth entry to the financial systems but also to circumvent these controls. Their threshold access is what leads them to be termed gatekeepers. Another term often used is 'professional enablers'.

Something to remember about this second category of offenders is that they are often regulated by entities such as the Financial Conduct Authority (FCA), Her Majesty's Revenue and Customs (HMRC), the Law Society and other professional bodies. These bodies are a useful source of information and assistance to the investigator, as they can advise as to the level of training such a person would have had in anti-money laundering legislation and procedures, as well as the extent of their requirement to adhere to the money laundering regulations. This will potentially lend significant weight to the 'knowledge/suspicion' aspect of the offence. In appropriate cases, regulatory intervention by one of these professional bodies could be an alternative to criminal prosecution.

2.5.6 Acquisition, use and possession—section 329 of POCA 2002

This is the simplest, and often the easiest, to prove of the three offences. As a consequence, it often carries less weight when it comes to subsequent confiscation proceedings.

A person commits an offence if they acquire, use or possess criminal property and have the necessary knowledge or suspicion that the property represented a benefit from criminal conduct. Possession means having physical custody of criminal property, but can be passive in nature.

2.5.7 Penalties

The penalties for all three offences are:

• summary conviction up to six months' imprisonment, a fine or both; or
• on conviction on indictment a term of up to 14 years' imprisonment, a fine or both.

Conviction of offences under either section 327 or section 328 is classed as a 'criminal lifestyle' conviction and will have a significant impact on any subsequent confiscation.

2.5.8 Statutory defences

All three offences have the following statutory defences.

- The person made an authorised disclosure or they had a reasonable excuse for not making an authorised disclosure. An authorised disclosure is where a member of the regulated sector (e.g. a bank) can pass information on to law enforcement (usually via a gateway with the NCA) informing them of a transaction that they deem to be suspicious. These are also known as suspicious activity reports (SARs) or suspicious transaction reports (STRs). Where a transaction has not yet taken place, a request for consent to carry out the transaction can also be submitted in the same manner. If permission is actually granted (or implied due to a lack of response after a period of time), the institution has a defence to a subsequent charge of money laundering.
- The person was engaged in an act undertaken whilst carrying out a function relating to the enforcement of any provision of the Act. For law enforcement, this is very important as it is the statutory defence that allows them to be in possession of criminal property, even though they know or suspect it to be someone's benefit from their criminal conduct.
- In addition, section 329 has an additional defence: that the defendant acquired, used or had possession of the property for adequate consideration. For example, a person in possession of a painting that had been obtained by way of fraud would, therefore, have a defence to the charge of possession of criminal property if they could show that they had paid the full market price for the painting.

2.5.9 Knowledge

The prosecution will need to prove the defendant's knowledge from the circumstances in which they came into possession of the property. It will not be necessary to prove the identity of the person who committed the crime that gave rise to the creation of the criminal property. What is necessary is to show, by reference to the circumstances, that the property was 'dirty money'.

2.5.10 Suspicion

Suspicion is not defined in the Act, and traditionally the dictionary definition has been considered. Although dealing with a matter under pre-POCA

2002 legislation, the case of *R v Da Silva* [2006] EWCA Crim 1654 states at paragraph 16:

> It seems to us that the essential element in the word 'suspect' and its affiliates, in this context, is that the defendant must think that there is a possibility, which is more than fanciful, that the relevant facts exist. A vague feeling of unease would not suffice. ... We consider therefore that, for the purpose of a conviction ... the prosecution must prove that the defendant's acts of facilitating another person's retention or control of the proceeds of criminal conduct were done by a defendant who thought that there was a possibility, which was more than fanciful, that the other person was or had been engaged in or had benefited from criminal conduct.

Further reading—money laundering

- The CPS guidance on money laundering: www.cps.gov.uk/legal/p_to_r/proceeds_of_crime_money_laundering/#The_new_principle
- Legislation: www.legislation.gov.uk/uksi/2007/2157/contents/made
- *R v Anwoir* [2008] EWCA Crim 1354: www.bailii.org/ew/cases/EWCA/Crim/2008/1354.html
- The Law Society provides practice advice on money laundering: www.lawsociety.org.uk/support-services/advice/practice-notes/aml/
- The Joint Money Laundering Steering Group comprises the main trade associations in the UK financial services industry and provides advice and guidance in relation to money laundering issues: www.jmlsg.org.uk/
- The Financial Action Task Force recommendations for governments to follow: www.fatf-gafi.org/
- *R v Da Silva* [2006] EWCA Crim 1654: www.bailii.org/ew/cases/EWCA/Crim/2006/1654.html

---

2.6 The Theft Act 1968 (false accounting, section 17)

The key parts to this offence are:

(1) Where a person dishonestly, with a view to a gain for himself or another or with intent to cause loss to another—

    (a) destroys, defaces, conceals or falsifies any account or any record or document made or required for any accounting purpose; or

    (b) in furnishing information for any purpose produces or makes use of any account, or any such record or document as aforesaid, to which his knowledge is or may be misleading, false or deceptive in a material particular.

KEY POINTS—WHEN CONSIDERING AN OFFENCE OF FALSE ACCOUNTING

- A falsification can be made by making a false entry but also by omitting material particulars.
- The record or document 'must be made or required for any accounting purpose'. This will usually be a question of fact for the prosecution to show and it has been stated that a reasonable jury should be able to decide that the documents were required for an accounting purpose.
- Maximum sentence on indictment is seven years.

2.7 The Computer Misuse Act (CMA) 1990

2.7.1 Introduction

In 1990 the CMA introduced a range of offences to criminalise the misuse of computers. More recently there was pressure to update the legislation from the European Union (EU). The EU required the adoption of a set of minimum rules on offences and sanctions to deal with large-scale cyber attacks.

Further reading

- EU Directive 2013/40 on attacks against information systems.

This Directive was implemented by amendments to the 1990 Act made in Part 2 of the Serious Crime Act 2015, which also increased the sentences for attacks on computers to better reflect the serious damage that can be caused. For example, a maximum sentence of life imprisonment is now possible for cyber attacks that result in loss of life, serious illness or injury, or serious damage to national security. A sentence of up to 14 years is possible for attacks causing, or creating, a significant risk of severe economic or environmental damage or social disruption.

The amendments extended the existing extra-territorial jurisdiction to prosecute a UK national who commits any offence under the CMA while outside the UK. While there must be a 'significant link' with the domestic jurisdiction, the CMA provides that there is such a link where a UK national commits an offence abroad, provided that the foreign jurisdiction also criminalises the offence in question (see section 43(4) of the Serious Crime Act 2015).

KEY POINTS—WHEN CONSIDERING AN OFFENCE UNDER THE CMA

- The CMA does not provide a definition of a computer; this is because there was concern that any definition would soon become out of date.
- Definition is therefore left to the courts. Lord Hoffmann, in *DPP v McKeown, DPP v Jones* [1997] 2 Cr App R 155 at 163 defined a computer as 'a device for storing, processing and retrieving information'.

Further reading

- Home Office, 'Serious Crime Act 2015 Fact Sheet (Part 2: Computer misuse)', March 2015: www.gov.uk/government/uploads/system/uploads/attachment_data/file/415953/Factsheet_-_Computer_Misuse_-_Act.pdf.

2.7.2 Unauthorised access to computer material—section 1

The key part of this offence is that the person causes a computer to perform any function with an intention to secure unauthorised access to any program or data held in any computer. The person must know at the time that his access is unauthorised.

Section 17(2) provides that a person accesses a program or data if, by causing the computer to perform any function, he outputs, displays, copies, uses, modifies or deletes the program or data. Section 17(5) provides that access is unauthorised if the person does not have consent to the particular kind of access to the particular data, and the person is not himself entitled to control access of the kind in question.

An example of an offence under section 1 would include logging into a computer system using somebody else's password without proper authority in order to access a program or data.

2.7.3 Unauthorised access with intent to commit or facilitate commission of further offences—section 2

This is a more serious offence than that under section 1 as, in this case, the authorised access has been made with intent to commit or facilitate commission of a further offence.

KEY POINTS—WHEN CONSIDERING AN OFFENCE OF UNAUTHORISED ACCESS WITH INTENT TO COMMIT OR FACILITATE COMMISSION OF FURTHER OFFENCES

- It is immaterial if the intended further offence is committed at the same time or on a future occasion;
- additionally, a person can be guilty of an offence under this section even if the facts make the committing of the further offence impossible.

2.7.4 Unauthorised acts with intent to impair, or with recklessness as to impairing the operation of a computer—section 3

The key parts of this offence are that the person knowingly gains unauthorised access to the computer with an additional intention (or being reckless) that the computer will be impaired or access to it hindered. This offence is aimed at those who seek to carry out acts of sabotage or denial-of-service attacks.

In *DPP v Lennon* [2006] EWHC 1201 (Admin), the Divisional Court ruled that even where a computer system is designed to handle a particular kind of traffic, such as email, there is an implied limit to the level of that traffic, such that flooding an email server with unwanted email traffic in order to overwhelm that system constitutes unauthorised use, even if the computer system could have been configured to exclude such emails.

2.7.5 Making, supplying or obtaining articles for use in the above offences—section 3A

This part of the Act has been amended to include an offence of 'obtain to use' to cover the situation where tools are obtained for personal use to commit offences under the Act (an offence under section 1, 3 or 3ZA). This means that the requirement for the involvement of a third party has now been removed and now catches those acting alone (section 42 of the Serious Crime Act 2015).

KEY POINTS—SECTION 3A OF THE CMA

Section 3A creates three offences, which differ in the mental element necessary:

- section 3A(1) creates the offence of making, adapting, supplying or offering to supply any article, intending it be used to commit or assist in the commission of an offence under section 1, 3 or 3ZA;
- section 3A(2) creates the offence of supplying or offering to supply any article believing that it is likely to be used to commit or assist in the commission of an offence under section 1, 3 or 3ZA;
- section 3A(3) creates the offence of obtaining any article, either (i) intending to use it to commit or to assist in the commission of an offence under section 1, 3 or 3ZA or (ii) with a view to its being supplied for use to commit or to assist in the commission of an offence under section 1, 3 or 3ZA.

2.8 The Financial Services and Markets Act (FSMA) 2000

2.8.1 Introduction

The FSMA was introduced to make provision for the regulation of financial services and markets. Some of the offences contained within FSMA will be relevant to the investigator, these include:

- carrying out a regulated activity without authorisation (sections 19 and 23);
- making false claims to be authorised or exempt (section 24);
- misleading statements and practices (section 397);
- misleading the authority (section 398);
- communicating an invitation or inducement to engage in an investment activity (sections 21 and 25).

KEY POINTS—TWO AUTHORITIES FOR FINANCIAL REGULATION

- Originally, the Financial Services Authority (FSA) was primarily responsible for the regulation of the financial market. However, the financial crisis prompted a rethink and a decision was made to divide the responsibilities for financial regulation between two authorities.
- The two authorities are now:
  - the FCA, formerly the FSA, now responsible for maintaining and ensuring the integrity and competitiveness of the financial market, as well as the regulation of those providing financial services;
  - the Prudential Regulation Authority (PRA), responsible for the prudential supervision and regulation of banks, building societies, credit unions, insurers and investment firms.

Further reading

- The Financial Services and Markets Act 2000: www.legislation.gov.uk/ukpga/2000/8/contents
- The Financial Services Act 2012: www.legislation.gov.uk/ukpga/2012/21/pdfs/ukpga_20120021_en.pdf
- The Financial Conduct Authority: www.fca.org.uk
- The Prudential Regulation Authority: www.bankofengland.co.uk/pra/Pages/default.aspx

2.9 The Insolvency Act 1986

KEY POINTS—DEFINING INSOLVENCY

- Insolvency is when a company or person has insufficient assets to cover their debts; this also means that the company or person might be unable to pay their creditors when payment is due.

2.9.1 Purpose of the Insolvency Act 1986

The Insolvency Act 1986, which has been modified by the Enterprise Act 2002, is key legislation designed to protect creditors and assist with the rescue and recovery of a struggling company, but also has important provisions that can be used to punish directors who continue to trade when knowingly insolvent (an offence of wrongful trading). It is the statutory framework for insolvency in England and Wales.

2.9.2 What procedures are available to an insolvent company

There are five main processes available to an insolvent company. The first three procedures provide potential to rescue the company or its business. A rescue plan for the company (if possible) can be a preferable option for creditors, as this might help to maintain the value of the company, as well as its customers.

1 administration (explained below);
2 company voluntary arrangements (renegotiating an acceptable repayment term);
3 compulsory liquidations (wound up by the court following the application of one or more of its creditors);
4 members and creditors' voluntary liquidations (shareholders/directors decide to liquidate the company);
5 administrative receivership.

2.9.3 Difference between administration and receivership

Administration

A company can go into administration through the company directors or one or more of the creditors making an application to the court and providing evidence of the company's impending insolvency.

The administration of a company is designed to keep a company trading while a financial rescue plan is put together, or while plans are put in place to determine how best to sell the company and its assets in order to obtain the best result for the creditors.

The administration process is handled by an insolvency practitioner (who has a duty to the court), who will take over the management of the company and present the creditors with the best possible future options available to them. During the administration process, creditors will be unable to recover any assets or take actions against the company, without the prior permission of the administrator or court.

Administrative receivership

Receivership is the process initiated by creditors holding security over the company's assets who have become concerned about the company's ability to repay its debts to them. The receiver is appointed to sell the company and its assets in order to try and recover the money owed to the secured creditor(s). The primary duty of a receiver is to the holder of the charge who made the appointment.

These days, administrative receivership has been overtaken as an insolvency remedy by administration.

There will be occasions when the reason for a company's failure, as well as the need to ensure its successful administration/liquidation, will be of public interest. In these cases, the services of the Official Receiver from the Insolvency Service (an agency of the Department for Business, Innovation and Skills) will be appointed to investigate the company's affairs.

KEY POINTS—WHAT ARE THE ROLES IN INSOLVENCY?

- The **Official Receiver** is a civil servant who is also an officer of the court appointed to protect the public interest.
- An **insolvency practitioner** is someone in private practice, usually an accountant or sometimes a solicitor, who specialises in insolvency work and is authorised to undertake such work.

2.9.4 Disqualification of a director

The Insolvency Service has the power to apply to the court to have a person disqualified from being a company director, if it thinks the director has failed to meet their legal responsibilities. It is possible for a person to be banned from operating as a company director for up to 15 years. This will mean that, during the period of disqualification, the person will not be permitted to be a director of any company registered in the UK or an overseas company that has connections with the UK, and neither will the person be allowed to be involved in the forming, marketing or running of a company.

KEY POINTS—DIRECTOR DISQUALIFIED

Other bodies that are involved in director disqualification:

- Companies House;
- the Competition and Markets Authority;
- the courts.

Further reading—insolvency

- Company director disqualification: www.gov.uk/company-director-disqualification
- The Competition and Markets Authority: www.gov.uk/cma
- Companies House: www.gov.uk/government/organisations/companies-house
- Company insolvency practitioner: www.icaew.com/en
- The Insolvency Service: www.gov.uk/government/organisations/insolvency-service

---

2.10 **Identity crime-related legislation**

Unlike in other countries, there is no substantive offence of identity theft. With the exception of the Identity Documents Act 2010, and legislation created in 2015 to prevent the supply of specialist printing equipment for use in criminal activity (Specialist Printing Equipment and Materials (Offences) Act 2015), the investigation of offending relating to the criminal misuse of identity generally forms part of the investigation into fraud offences.

KEY POINTS—LEGISLATION FOR IDENTITY CRIME OFFENCES

Where the offence is committed by the creation or possession of a false document that could be used to fraudulently assert identity. This is predominantly categorised under the following legislation:

- Forgery and Counterfeiting Act 1981;
- Identity Documents Act 2010;
- Immigration and Asylum Act 1999.

Where the false identity is used to commit another offence, this mainly relates to the following legislation:

- Fraud Act 2006;
- section 25 of the Immigration Act 1971;
- National Immigration and Asylum Act 2002;
- section 4 of the Asylum and Immigration (Treatment of Claimants, etc.) Act 2004.

The prosecution of UK fraudulently obtained genuine (FOG) passports is dependent on when the passport was issued, evidence of its use and where in the world it was used:

- pre-6 June 2006-issued FOGs should be dealt with under section 15 of the Theft Act 1968 (obtaining property by deception), section 1(1) of the Criminal Attempts Act 1981 or section 36 of the Criminal Justice Act 1925;
- FOGs issued between June 2006 and January 2011 are dealt with under the Identity Cards Act (ICA) 2006.
- since 20 September 2009, by virtue of section 30 of the ICA 2006, a FOG used outside England and Wales (where a constituent element of the offence occurred in England and Wales) can be charged;
- the prosecution of a counter-signatory would take place using section 2 of the Fraud Act 2006 (false representation).

Types of fraud

3.1 **Introduction**

This chapter provides an introduction to the most common types and styles of fraud recorded by Action Fraud; it details both volume fraud and the more complex fraud types. It provides clear information and covers the following elements (where applicable):

- explanation of the fraud type;
- case studies;
- fraud prevention advice;
- signposts to further guidance.

The chapter also explains identity theft, which is a key enabler to fraud; it describes how it occurs, the prevention advice to be given and who can assist in the investigation of this crime.

There are many different types and categories of fraud; the National Fraud Intelligence Bureau (NFIB) records 56 types (as of July 2016). It is important for the investigator to understand the fraud typology, as this assists in the investigation; by aiding understanding of the method used by the fraudster to perpetrate the fraud and indicating where material relevant to the case may typically be located.

3.2 **Volume frauds**

3.2.1 **Online shopping and auctions fraud**

The internet has changed the way we live and has influenced consumers' shopping habits. As a result, many people now buy products through the convenience of clicking a button rather than purchasing items from the high street in a face-to-face transaction. These changing habits have resulted in an increase in online shopping fraud. Although this fraud tends to be associated with relatively inexpensive products, it does tend to be conducted at a high frequency and as such it impacts a significant number of victims. The fraud can be committed by organised crime groups (OCGs) or lone opportunistic offenders.

There is rarely physical contact between the offender and victim, and the internet enables the fraudster to easily disguise their identity.

This fraud type can involve a range of scenarios, but the most common are the following:

- The buyer (victim) responds to an advert and communicates with the seller (fraudster) via a legitimate auction site platform. The fraudster gives the impression that the sale is legitimate, and the buyer subsequently makes a payment for the goods; however, the goods are never received.
- Same as above and, in addition, the victim's financial information is compromised and used by the fraudster to commit other offences.

Figure 3.1 Diagrammatical representation of online shopping fraud

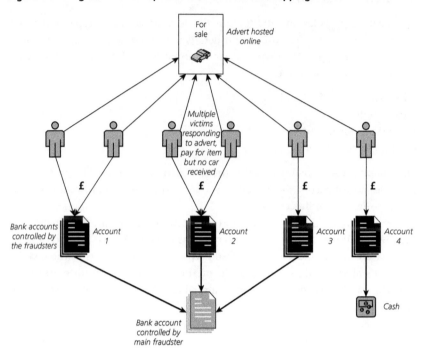

- The buyer (victim) responds and communicates with the seller (fraudster) via the auction site platform. The buyer pays for the goods, but when they are received they are not to the value of those advertised or of the quality of the description on the online platform.
- The seller (fraudster) creates a fake auction site platform/fake advert and gives the impression that the site is legitimate. The buyer (victim) responds and communicates with the seller via the spoof auction site platform. The buyer sends payment for the goods, but they are never received and/or the victim's personal and banking information is compromised.

See Figure 3.1.

> **KEY POINTS—INVESTIGATIVE OPPORTUNITIES (ONLINE SHOPPING FRAUD)**
>
> **Case management:**
>
> - Contact the online auction site via your force's/organisation's single point of contact and recover relevant material.
> - Secure online transaction records, including correspondence from the victim.
> - Obtain records of all financial transactions.

- Identify the holder account where monies have been sent by the victim.
- Identify the online account holder who advertised the article and corresponded with the victim.

Consultation:

- Consider contacting and seeking advice and guidance from your force's/organisation's experts (e.g. on digital evidence gathering) to ensure evidence is secured and seized in line with the force's/organisation's standard operating procedure (SOP).
- Financial investigators tasked to assist with tracing the money and/or assets.

Checklist—fraud prevention advice for online shopping fraud

- Recommend the use of well-known reputable payment methods to make online transactions.

- Warn that other payment services (e.g. virtual currencies) offer more anonymity for fraudulent practices and are harder to trace if fraud occurs.

- Recommend the use of legitimate online platforms and advise that individuals follow the site's guidance when trading with buyers and sellers. Advise that if you trade outside legitimate websites, this makes you more vulnerable to unnecessary risk.

- Recommend the use of website functionalities to research buyers/sellers. Review their ratings, how long they have been on the website, comments and positive and negative feedback. This will help decide whether they are genuine.

- Check the uniform resource locator (URL) certificate; look for the 'https' and the closed padlock.

- Ensure anti-virus software is up to date.

- Advise that even though the website may say '.co.uk', this does not necessarily mean that it is UK based.

- Advise the application of common sense. If a deal or product sounds too good to be true, it probably is.

- If purchasing a high-value product (e.g. a vehicle), inspect the item in person.

Further reading
- Get Safe Online (GSO): www.getsafeonline.org
- Action Fraud: www.actionfraud.police.uk/types_of_fraud
- Home Office Accounting Rules: www.gov.uk/government/uploads/system/uploads/attachment_data/file/515640/count-fraud-april-2016.pdf

3.2.2 **Computer software service fraud**

Fraudsters, employed in a call centre, call numbers they have obtained (often legitimately via a marketing list or from an online telephone directory). The fraudster informs the victim that their computer security has been compromised. The fraudsters making the initial contact are often very confident and use a well-rehearsed script to pretend to be a trustworthy source, for example they might claim to be an employee of a large, reputable and familiar organisation. Another method of contact is via the internet, where the victim receives an unsolicited email with security updates, which in turn directs the victim to the fraudster's website.

Once the contact has been made, the fraudster then agrees to fix the issues in one of the following ways:

- the victim paying a small fee to the fraudster to fix it, with the victim providing the fraudster with their banking, debit or credit card details. These are then used to either obtain routine payments or random additional larger withdrawals, without the victim's consent;
- by accessing the email and website, the victim gives the fraudster access to the victim's computer. This is done by directing the victim to a website that allows the fraudster to control the computer and install programs/viruses, giving them unlimited access to the computer, often without the victim's knowledge. The software downloaded allows further illegal activity to be conducted by the fraudster, including using the personal information obtained during the fraud to commit further offences.

In both cases, there is in fact no issue with the computer and no fix occurs. The call centre operators often reveal the victim's vulnerability by exposing them to high-pressure sales techniques. Another method involves informing the victim that their computer has been hacked and used to access restricted sites containing inappropriate material to make the fraud seem more convincing. See Figure 3.2.

Another method used by the fraudster is to infect the victim's digital device with malware, which is the abbreviation of 'malicious software'. The software is dropped onto the victim's computer solely to damage or disrupt the computer so that sensitive information can be stolen.

....

Case study—computer software service fraud

The victim was contacted by a suspect claiming that their computer was infected with a Trojan virus, and as a result their copy of Windows had become corrupt. The victim was reluctant, but allowed the suspect remote access to her computer. The suspect did several things, and then said that she would need to pay for a new Microsoft Windows licence. To pay for this, the victim provided her card details and payment was taken.

....

Figure 3.2 Diagrammatical representation of computer software service fraud

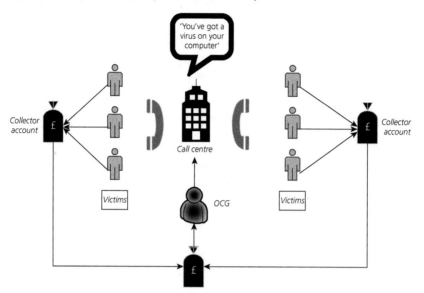

Checklist—fraud prevention advice—computer software fraud

Advice

- Rarely would a legitimate IT company make direct contact and inform potential victims that their computer is infected. If any such phone call or email is received, it should be advised that the call is not answered or the email should be deleted without opening it.

- Just because a caller may know some personal details, don't assume they are official or from the organisation they say they are representing.

- Do not give out personal information. If potential victims require further assurance, contact the organisation directly using a number obtained from a trusted source, for example a latest paper bill or the official website of the organisation. When contact is made with the company to check their details, consider using another phone or wait three minutes before making the call to ensure that the previous call has been terminated. Phone calls do not automatically end and fraudsters can clone telephone numbers and impersonate them, which tricks the victim into thinking they are contacting the legitimate organisation.

- Never allow an unsolicited caller to help install new computer software.

- If the victim has already been a victim of this type of fraud, fraudsters often retarget the victim claiming to be lawyers or police working to recover their money. Make victims aware of this secondary scam and advise them on what checks they should conduct.

- The victim will need to take their computer to a reputable high-street provider to get it cleaned.

- Ensure that the victim contacts their bank immediately and informs them of the fraud, so that the bank can cancel their cards/accounts and prevent further losses. Victims should also regularly check their bank statements for fraudulent transactions.

- Victims should ensure that their computer is installed with up-to-date software that protects it from viruses and unwanted programs.

- Ensure the firewall is switched on.

- Advise the victim not to open any emails from unknown sources and do not open any suspicious-looking attachments, as they may contain a virus.

- Advise the victim to opt out of cold calls by registering for free with the Telephone Preference Service on 0845 070 0707. Continue to be vigilant, even after such a registration.

3.2.3 Advance fee frauds

This is where a fraudster requests that a victim makes an advance payment for goods, services or financial gains that never appear. These scams often target the elderly or those in need.

Examples of advance fee frauds (this list is by no means exhaustive) are:

- job or employment opportunities requiring official checks, such as Disclosure and Barring Service (DBS) or visa applications;
- cheque overpayment fraud;
- lottery fraud;
- work from home scams;
- loan fraud and Payment Protection Insurance (PPI) claims;
- inheritance fraud.

Job or employment opportunities

These are also known as recruitment scams. The fraudster will often post an advert for a job in a local newspaper, on the high street, on the internet or on social media, offering the benefits of working from home and flexible hours; this often appeals to the most in need, enticing them with the promise that they can earn an additional income and make what is suggested to be 'easy money'. The job opportunity is usually bogus, as is the company doing the recruiting. It usually relies on the victim responding to the advertisement; there is then some communication between both parties, followed by an application process or initial consultation and telephone interview. The victim is then offered the job by the fraudster, but before this can be confirmed the fraudster

Figure 3.3 Diagrammatical representation of job scam fraud

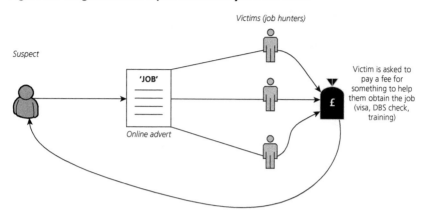

indicates that they will require an upfront payment to cover any arrangements and security checks. The payment is usually requested via money transfer agents, but once paid by the victim the job never materialises and the money is lost. See Figure 3.3.

Cheque overpayment fraud

This is where the fraudster makes a payment for goods or services by a fraudulent cheque and with a deliberate overpayment. The goods and services are usually advertised in classified ads. Some communication then normally takes place between the fraudster and the seller (victim). The fraudster persuades the victim to reimburse the excess money paid and distribute the goods prior to the cheques being cleared. Usually some days later, the victim realises that the cheque has not been honoured and the cheque is returned by the bank. The victim in this type of fraud not only loses the goods they have already forwarded on, but also the excess money they have reimbursed to the fraudster.

Fraud recovery fraud

This type of fraud typically occurs when a former victim of fraud is contacted by fraudsters claiming that they can recover part of their losses. The main premise of this fraud starts with a list of victims (sometimes called a 'sucker list') who have been defrauded by previous scams. Typically, fraudsters operating from what is commonly known as a boiler room, which is the location of a high-pressure sales team, carry out the fraud, target vulnerable victims and pose as legitimate organisations. To reinforce this notion of legitimacy, they sometimes claim to be an agency working with the government in order to recover fraud losses.

Once contact is made with the victim, a variety of subterfuge techniques are used to extract money from the victim. This normally involves an advance fee of around 10 per cent of the money that the victim is owed. The fraudsters may also ask for subsequent fees for a variety of reasons; for example, administration or release fees, legal costs or taxes. In some cases, if the victim asks for the fee to be taken from the recovered amount, they will give reasons as to why this is not possible. A commonly cited example is that the money is under the control of the court.

Case study—fraud recovery fraud

The victim had previously reported to Action Fraud a carbon credit investment fraud. In these cases the victim is either sold credit certificates or given an opportunity to invest in green initiatives. They were targeted for recovery fraud, having received a cold call from the suspects claiming that the company that sold them the original carbon credits had gone into liquidation, supposedly meaning the victim would be entitled to recover their losses (amounting to approximately £80,000). The victim was asked for an upfront payment to cover the cost of the suspect company's fee, and made this payment via bank transfer. The suspects then returned asking for another—this time much larger—payment to cover further fees. At this point, the victim realised that it was another scam.

Checklist—fraud prevention advice—fraud recovery fraud

Fraud prevention advice is the key to preventing this type of fraud. Victims are often repeat victims and are on a target list for fraudsters:

- Law enforcement or government agencies will never charge fees to return recovered money and they will not guarantee that monies will be returned.

- Similarly, they will not make contact via telephone or email requesting money.

Impersonation of officials

Fraudsters impersonate officials to make false promises about tax rebates or to demand fees, 'customs payments' or 'VAT payments'.

Another common variant of this type of fraud involves fraudsters setting up websites purporting to be Her Majesty's Revenue and Customs (HMRC), offering to assist people in completing their tax returns. Instead of offering genuine help, these websites are used as a means of extracting personal data, financial information and fraudulent payments from victims.

In a similar manner, fraudulent websites have been seen that purport to be official sites assisting people to obtain travel visas for countries such as the USA. These sites attract victims by offering a cheaper, quicker service than the real website, and rely on the fact that travel visas are often 'awarded' electronically to the would-be traveller, without any tangible document being delivered. The victim pays the fraudster, but no visa is provided.

Inheritance fraud

The fraudster contacts potential victims and suggests that someone with the same family name has died, explaining that they could be a beneficiary of an inheritance as no other family members can be traced; this prevents the money being transferred automatically to the government. The fraudster suggests that the inheritance could be split, but instructs that the victim should not speak openly about the deal. The fraudster normally claims to be a lawyer or legal official and sends the victim a letter or email on headed paper, but asks for an upfront payment to cover various fees required to release the inheritance, such as legal fees or inheritance tax. There is, in fact, no inheritance. The fraudster often uses delay tactics to extract more money from the victim.

Case study—inheritance fraud

The victim received an email from a suspect claiming to be an FBI agent based in Nigeria. The email stated that the victim was one of a number of beneficiaries to an inheritance and asked them to contact the sender urgently to discuss the matter. On doing so, the victim was advised that a fee of £175 was required in order to release the money to the UK. The victim paid this amount via Western Union. The victim was then told that the inheritance was at UK Customs and that a fee of £250 was required. The victim found this plausible, as he had been provided with a tracking number, which apparently indicated that the money had arrived in the UK from Nigeria. They therefore made this payment, again via Western Union. The victim was then told that he needed a 'non-residency permit' to receive the money and was sent an email with a form to complete and return along with a payment of £1,000. When the victim told the suspect he did not have this amount of money, the suspect said they would cover half the payment so the victim would owe only £500. The victim was unable to get this amount of money and, after researching further online, discovered that this was a scam.

Loans and PPI claims frauds

In this scam, the fraudster claims to be calling from or working for a loan provider or PPI claims company. The fraudster suggests to the victim that they are entitled to make a claim and that all they need to do is to provide personal details, including bank details, on a website. The victim is often then directed to a fake broker's website address. The fraudster then contacts the victim again to indicate that the PPI claim or loan cannot be processed until a fee is paid to cover the costs of administration and the necessary checks.

Case study—loans and PPI claims

The victim has been making loan inquiries online and shortly after was contacted by phone and congratulated on being successful in her application. The victim was asked to make an administrative payment of £60 via Ukash in order to secure the loan, which she did. Ukash was a UK-based electronic money system that allowed users to exchange their cash for a secure code to make payments online; it no longer exists. She was subsequently asked for other similar payments for a variety of reasons, which she continued to make in the same way up to the total sum of £510, until she realised that this was a scam.

Lottery fraud

The fraudster purports to be from an official lottery company and contacts the victim informing them that they have won a large sum of money, but they need to respond quickly. Prior to any winnings being released, the victim is instructed to provide the fraudster with personal information and documentation as proof of identification. This information is often then compromised and sold on by the fraudster. The fraudster will then insist that the victim pay upfront for various fees, such as banking fees and taxes, so that funds can be released. The winnings don't actually exist and are never released. The victims have often made several payments before it becomes clear that this is in fact a scam.

Case study—lottery fraud

The victim has been involved in an email conversation revolving around a supposed lottery win of £750,000. The emails suggested that they were from the UK National Lottery and Inland Revenue. Having provided personal information in response, the victim has also been telephoned and encouraged to make various administrative payments in order to receive their prize.

Rental fraud

Rental fraud happens when would-be tenants are tricked into paying an upfront fee to rent a property. In reality, the property does not exist, has already been rented out or has been rented to multiple victims at the same time. Rental fraudsters often target students looking for university accommodation. Many reports made to Action Fraud feature overseas victims who were seeking accommodation in the UK for their impending university course.

Case study—rental fraud

The victim was making inquiries to rent a flat and was contacted by the suspect, who purported to be the owner. The victim agreed to the rental terms over the phone and transferred a deposit as requested by the suspect. The victim can no longer get a response from the suspect and, having visited the address of the supposed flat, has discovered it to be a privately occupied house.

West African letter or 419 frauds

Historically one of the most common methods of advanced fee fraud is the West African letter, which is also known as 419 fraud (419 relates to the Nigerian criminal code used to deal with this style of fraud).

The victim will receive an email (or, on occasion, a letter) purporting to be from someone of importance—such as a lawyer or government employee—in a West African country. The email or letter will be sent out to multiple recipients. While the majority of people will ignore these emails, a handful will respond and fall victim to the fraud. The fraudsters say they have access to a substantial amount of money. The fraudsters will then offer the victim a substantial share of the money or goods (up to 40 per cent in some cases). In order to help the fraudster retrieve the full amount of money, the victim is required to pay a fee substantially less than the share they will receive.

If the victim does fall foul of this initial scam, the fraudster will then often invent further fees for the victim to pay, exploiting them further and continuing the promise of the fictitious large reward in the end.

Victims are often advised that assisting the fraudster is against local laws, this increases the pressure to make the payment and may result in the victim being reluctant to contact the police. See Figure 3.4.

Figure 3.4 Diagrammatical representation of advance fee fraud

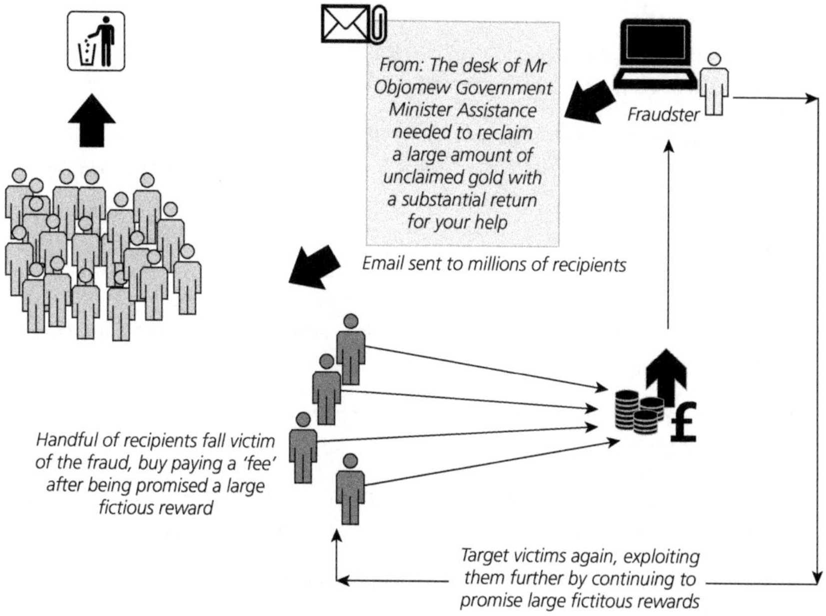

From: The desk of Mr Objomew Government Minister Assistance needed to reclaim a large amount of unclaimed gold with a substantial return for your help

Fraudster

Email sent to millions of recipients

Handful of recipients fall victim of the fraud, buy paying a 'fee' after being promised a large fictious reward

Target victims again, exploiting them further by continuing to promise large fictitous rewards

Work from home scams

The victim usually responds to an advert suggesting they can make easy money working from home and fitting it around other commitments they may have, while being their own boss. The victim releases some money to the fraudster upfront in order to register on the scheme, buy links to potential customers, set up a website and receive products to sell on. These products or goods are often non-sellable or the fraudster finds fault in the work delivered by the victim and fails to make any payments. These schemes often develop into pyramid schemes, where victims are offered a financial incentive to introduce other people to the scheme.

There is often a delay in the victims reporting this type of fraud, as they are tricked into believing that the profit will not be instant, but will come with work and time. They are often given some small returns to make the story more believable and to entice them into investing more into the scheme. The full returns never materialise and the monies invested are never returned.

Checklist—fraud prevention advice for other advance fee frauds

Fraud prevention advice will differ depending on the type of advance fee fraud that the victim encounters, but below are some possible suggestions:

- Don't be tempted by easy fast cash.

- If you have responded to an email/letter scam, break contact as soon as you realise it is a fraud.

- If you believe you have given the fraudster your bank account details, contact your bank immediately and carry out a credit check.

- Look out for adverts that only give mobile numbers or email addresses with domains such as @hotmail or @yahoo, as authentic businesses rarely use these types of web-based email accounts.

- Check the grammar/spelling of the advert: is it professional? If in doubt, run it via a trusted friend.

- Do research online into the company, reading customer reviews, customer complaints, relevant blogs and online forums.

- Don't be pressured to make a quick decision or be fooled by glossy brochures, plush office buildings or bogus websites.

- Question whether you actually entered a lottery or prize draw. If you have won a legitimate prize, it is not normal to have to pay a fee upfront to claim it.

- Never send money, personal details or banking information to people you don't know/trust or abroad.

- Be wary of requests for payment using unusual payment methods. Never send money via money transfer agents as, although the sender of the money has to provide identification documents, the person that collects the money does not, so the fraudsters are able to hide their identity. Paying by credit card offers the buyer more protection.

- Research addresses where you are asked to send correspondence. Fraudsters often use 'virtual offices' to avoid being identified and trick the victim into thinking they are dealing with a well-established professional company. These addresses are often rented using false identification.

- Don't trust the appearance of a telephone number. Fraudsters often purchase numbers and use these to divert to unregistered pay-as-you-go mobiles.

3.2.4 ATM (cash machine) fraud

A fraudster uses a magnetic recording device and carefully secreted pinhole cameras to capture card information as the victim is withdrawing money from an ATM. The fraudster then uses this information to take money from accounts in shops, online or from an ATM.

A recent variant of this occurred across the UK in 2014, when criminals uploaded computer malware to ATM machines, allowing the operatives to continuously withdraw cash without it registering on the machine. The entire cash contents of the 50 ATM machines attacked were obtained in this way, leading to the loss of approximately £1.6 million over the course of one bank holiday weekend. See Chapter 9 for further information.

3.2.5 Counterfeit cards

A fraudster counterfeits bank cards by using a device to capture the card and account information embedded in the card's magnetic strip. This is often known as 'skimming'. The fraudster then uses this information to carry out fraudulent transactions, particularly in countries where chip-and-PIN technology is not supported.

The fraudster may also use this information in transactions where the card doesn't have to be physically seen by the retailer or merchant (known as card-not-present fraud); for example, when shopping online, buying goods by telephone or mail order, or using cardholder-activated terminals (e.g. ticket machines). See Chapter 9 for further information.

3.2.6 Cheque fraud

Cheque fraud operates in a number of ways. For example, a fraudster pays the victim for goods or services using a stolen cheque, or deposits a fraudulent or stolen cheque into an account, or steals individual cheques or a cheque book from the victim.

Checklist—fraud prevention advice for cheque, plastic card and online bank accounts

Offer the following advice to victims of this type of fraud:

- Immediately report lost or stolen cards or suspected fraudulent use of the compromised card to the insurer (card company).

- Report lost or stolen cheque books or any missing cheques.

- Banks and companies have 24-hour emergency numbers printed on account statements.

- If the theft of the cards or cheques involved another crime—for example, if a bag was also stolen—this should be reported to the police.

- If a fraudulent account has been set up in the victim's name and they don't have a relationship with that bank or card company, they should report this directly to Action Fraud.

- Ask the victim to keep a record of all communications.

- Recommend that the victim obtains a copy of their personal credit report from one of the credit reference agencies.

- Advise contacting a credit reference agency or similar body to obtain a 'protective registration'. Protective registration requires further checking to be undertaken when an individual applies for a bank account, loan or credit, making the process more difficult for a fraudster.

Further reading
- Further advice on plastic card or cheque fraud can be obtained from: Dedicated Card and Payment Crime Unit (DCPCU) via dcpcu@dcpcu.pnn. police.uk

---

3.2.7 Retail fraud

Retail fraud encompasses a number of offences that can be described as using 'trickery' to obtain goods, rather than conventional stealing. This typology of fraud typically includes fraudsters going into shops with fake or copied receipts in order to try and get some kind of cash or voucher return.

Other examples:

- changing the labels on goods;
- gift card scams (where the details of a voucher are quickly copied before purchase can take place and are then used fraudulently to make online purchases);
- confusing the cashier by asking for different change/swapping bank notes.

Petrol stations are also typical victims of retail fraud. The offender will fill up their vehicle with no means of payment, but will provide false details or identity documents as security with a promise to return.

....

Case study—retail fraud

The suspect entered various fuel retail sites, on various dates, knowing that they had no means to pay and never intending to pay, and had drawn fuel. They then told the cashier that they had no means to pay, when this was in fact untrue and therefore dishonest and fraudulent. They completed a signed undertaking to pay on each occasion, but all subsequent attempts to contact the suspect to settle the matter have been ignored.

....

3.2.8 Retail distribution fraud

Retail distribution fraud entails fraudsters pretending to be a reputable UK store or business by setting up a fake domain or email address to contact overseas distributors and place an order of goods. The fraudster will specify delivery of the goods to a particular warehouse or location, where they will be received by the offender and typically sold on. The fraud is usually uncovered when the supplier tries to get payment from the UK store or business. See Figure 3.5.

Figure 3.5 Diagrammatical representation of retail distribution fraud

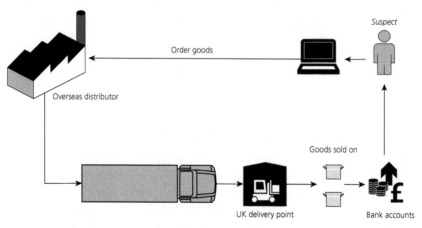

3.2.9 Lender loan fraud

Victims of lender loan fraud have typically entered their details into a loan comparison site to retrieve relevant quotes. They will then receive a phone call from what they believe to be a genuine call centre and are informed that they have been pre-approved for a loan—all they need to do to complete the transaction is to electronically pay the company an advance fee. The fraudster will typically call the victim again to ask for further money to ensure that the loan is secured. The victim will never receive the amount promised.

3.2.10 Ticket fraud

This fraud type usually involves music and sporting events or flight tickets. Fraudsters will typically create websites, social media or auction sites specifically to entice people to pay money for tickets. These websites appear to be legitimate, and the victim may only realise that they have been defrauded just before the event when the tickets fail to materialise and when they attempt to contact the seller only to find that the website or email address no longer exists. Victims of airline ticket fraud may arrive at the airport to find that their tickets are not genuine.

....

Case study—ticket fraud

The victim was looking to buy tickets for himself and his family to an ice hockey match in Canada. He searched online and found an advert to which he responded. The suspect emailed back and a price was eventually agreed. The suspect told the victim that Royal Mail had a service where he could leave the tickets with them and they would contact the victim to confirm their legitimacy and take payment before sending the tickets. The victim was advised that his money would only be transferred once the tickets were received. This sounded plausible, so the victim agreed. The next day, the victim received an email stating that they had the tickets and providing a package number. He was told to transfer money to a specific account under the name Royal Mail and provide a verification of the money transfer, which he did. He then heard nothing more despite making further contact with the suspect and 'Royal Mail'. The victim then looked online and found an alternative contact for Royal Mail, who advised that this was a scam.

....

3.2.11 Door-to-door sales and bogus tradesmen

This is a more 'traditional' type of fraud, typically involving home repairs and improvements that target those who could be considered more vulnerable. These frauds can involve offenders over-inflating prices for often sub-standard work or charging victims for work they didn't ask for. Door-to-door sales tricksters can use high-pressure tactics to force victims to purchase something they didn't want or need or that isn't worth the money paid. Any payments that may be made by victims will typically be in cash, so evidence of financial transactions can be limited.

....

Case study—bogus tradesmen

A male claiming to be a court bailiff attended the victim's house claiming he was there to collect £630 that the victim owed to a well-known water supplier for drainage works. The victim, feeling pressured, gave a sum of money to the suspect. The suspect left his calling card, which stated that he was a director of a collections company and that he was a court bailiff. The victim contacted the genuine water supplier the following day and they confirmed that there were no monies owed and they had not employed a bailiff.

3.2.12 Hacking—social media and email

Perpetrators of this offence gain unauthorised access to either the victim's email or social media accounts for malicious purposes. Typical examples of this type of fraud would include an offender hacking into a victim's email account and sending an email to their contacts list, stating that, for example, the victim was stranded in a foreign country and requesting that money be transferred to a named account to ensure their release and safe return home.

There may be personal as well as financial motivations for this fraud type. An ex-partner of the victim may unlawfully access social media or email accounts to send out abusive or slanderous messages to the victim's contacts or to send photographs intended to embarrass the victim. Hacking, social media and email offences can be enablers to subsequent frauds—for example, mandate fraud or phishing.

3.2.13 Mandate fraud

Mandate fraud occurs when the fraudster gets account transaction details (usually relating to direct debits or standing orders of a business) and changes them in order for future payments to be made into their account instead.

In the business world, mandate fraud typically involves an organisation receiving a spoofed email from a fraudster purporting to be a business that they have recently been dealing with. The email may use an almost identical email address and is likely to feature copied artwork and logos from the company to make it appear genuine at first glance. The fraudster, posing as a business, informs the company that their account details have changed and that the next payment should be made into the new account. The fraud is usually only uncovered when the genuine business doesn't receive payment as expected. See Figure 3.6.

Case study—mandate fraud

The victim business has received notification from several of its suppliers to advise that they have not received their payments, which were previously being paid via standing order. It has been established that there has been fraudulent use of the victim's online banking, and the beneficiary bank account details have been changed so that the regular payments are diverted to suspect accounts.

Figure 3.6 Diagrammatical representation of mandate fraud

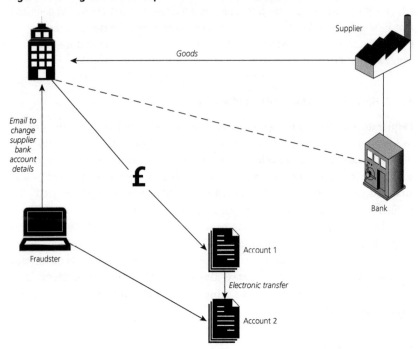

3.2.14 **Payment fraud**

This can take a number of forms, including:

- creating bogus customer records and bank accounts so that false payments can be generated;
- intercepting and altering payee details and amounts on cheques and payable orders, then attempting to cash them;
- creating false payment and financial information to support fraudulent claims for benefits;
- processing false claims by accomplices for benefits, grants or repayments;
- self-authorising payments to oneself;
- impersonating a senior officer of the business (e.g. the chief executive officer) and giving instructions to junior staff to make a payment to a 'new', but fictitious, supplier.

....

Case study—payment fraud

The victim regularly paid a supplier in arrears for products they sold to them. The victim received an email from the usual email address of the supplier suggesting that they had changed their bank details and requiring the next payment to be sent to the new bank account. This was actioned. The victim was surprised when the supplier chased them for payment a week later and it became clear that the supplier's email address had been hacked and that payment had been sent to a suspect bank account.

3.3 Other frauds

3.3.1 Financial investments fraud

Financial investment fraud scams often look and sound like plausible investments. The reason they often look like genuine investments is because they use professional-looking websites, accompanied by corporate brochures and deceptive sales tactics, which make the company appear legitimate.

Action Fraud estimates investment fraud losses in the UK each year are in the region of £1.2 billion; however, historically it is estimated that only around 10 per cent of this type of fraud is actually reported, which means the real figure could be considerably higher.

Common examples of investment include:

- **carbon credits**: where the victim is sold credit certificates or given an opportunity to invest in green initiatives;
- **share fraud**: the victim is offered shares in a company that sound attractive but are often worthless, or even non-existent. The fraudster will often state that the shares are in a company that is just about to float on a stock exchange, or has exciting new products that are about to be released;
- **wine investment**: where a fraudster offers the victim fine wine but it turns out that the wine is either very low quality or non-existent;
- **land-banking schemes**: often these involve land that is divided into smaller plots to be sold on, with the promise of a high-value return. Planning permission to build is frequently said to have been obtained.

All of the above, and many more fake investment scams in shares, property, precious stones or rare merchandise, have similar traits. The victim is cold-called or contacted through an unsolicited email or text and is offered an investment that seems too good to be true, which it normally is. The promise of high returns, low risk, and convincing and pressured selling techniques leaves thousands of victims out of pocket.

Case study—financial investment fraud

The victim was contacted unexpectedly by suspects offering him an investment in coloured diamonds which, he was told, were going to more than double in value in the space of six months. The victim paid a substantial sum of money into a bank account and was sent certificates and pictures of his supposed diamonds which, he was told, were being held in a secure bank vault. However, he is no longer able to get in touch with the suspects and on investigation into the supposed location of the diamonds, it has been discovered that it is a residential location.

....

Once the fraudsters have stolen the money from the victim, it often becomes very difficult to get back in touch with the company, which often disappears without trace.

This may also help us to understand how repeat victimisation can occur. This is where, in a bid to recover their losses, victims become repeat victims. This is encouraged by boiler room operatives, who promise high-return commodities and investments that will cover the loss. Further still, victims are convinced to keep their investment a secret to ensure the best possible return and reduce the number of other potential investors who may know about it. This acts as a convenient deception to conceal the real nature of the scheme, and also to prevent the victim discussing it with other people who might dissuade them from the scam investment. Victims are often told that if they involve the police, they will never recover their assets.

....

Case study—financial investment fraud

The victim received a cold call from the suspect company offering investment opportunities in property bonds in London, with the promise of incredible returns within months. The victim agreed to buy some bonds and made three payments by cheque and bank transfer, which resulted in the receipt of a bond certificate. However, the victim can no longer contact the company and has become aware of various warnings about the company online. The bonds have no saleable value.

....

The Financial Conduct Authority (FCA) is an independent organisation that reports to Parliament and regulates financial firms and markets in the UK. Many of the financial activities of brokers and financial advisers are covered by the FCA. It is worth noting that just because an organisation is on the FCA register, this does not indicate that the organisation is regulated in all the activities it undertakes.

Checklist—fraud prevention advice for victims of financial investment fraud

- Advise potential victims to be very careful when receiving an unexpected call. If in doubt, reject the cold call and hang up the telephone.

- In a typical cold call, fraudsters will try and pressure the victim into a deal (often one that is time-limited), offering bonuses if you invest straight away. If it sounds too good to be true, it normally is.

- When potential investors are considering investments, it is strongly advised that they check the credentials of the firm or person offering the investment, particularly by reference to the FCA register.

- Advise that before making any investment, it is best practice to:

  - take independent legal or financial advice before reaching a decision;

  - check whether the company has the appropriate authorisation and is based in the UK;

  - check the credentials of the financial company using the FCA register;

  - check the FCA warning list;

  - look for additional advice on the Action Fraud website.

- As fraudsters share information about victims, caution that it is more than likely that victims may be contacted again, albeit by a different fraudster and fake company.

Further reading

- FCA companies register: https://register.fca.org.uk/
- FCA warning list: www.fca.org.uk/news/warnings

3.3.2 **Ponzi schemes**

The term 'Ponzi scheme' is derived from Charles Ponzi, who was responsible for the first scheme of this kind, involving the purchase of 'international reply coupons'. A Ponzi scheme is typically an investment scam promising quick high-yield financial returns to those who choose to invest. A Ponzi fraudster will only ask the investor to do one thing: invest. The scheme promises high returns to investors. Participants in a Ponzi scheme are under the impression that they are earning returns from their investment; however, in reality there is no viable investment scheme and the fraudster will harvest all funding from the new investors and then often shuffle funds between accounts, distributing some of the monies to the first or existing members.

In reality:

- there is often no viable investment scheme;
- any returns that are paid are simply funded from the new investors who join the scheme;
- the scheme will eventually fail, with investors losing the money that they invested.

To give this some context, in 2008 Bernard Madoff was discovered to have masterminded the most prolific Ponzi scheme to date, having conned about $65 billion from investors.

Case study—Ponzi scheme

The victim was encouraged by a friend to invest in a company apparently specialising in foreign exchange. They invested £75,000 over three transactions of £25,000 into two different bank accounts. The suspect told the victim to tell their friends and family to invest in the company. In the early days, the victim managed to withdraw £10,000 in returns from the investment. However, they later tried to withdraw a larger amount of money but were unable to. The suspect told the victim that this was due to open trades, which tied up the funds. The victim subsequently heard of other people who had also been affected by this and was advised that it was a Ponzi scheme. The victim was unable to contact the suspect.

Further reading

- US Securities and Exchange Commission: www.sec.gov/answers/ponzi.htm

---

3.3.3 Application fraud

Application fraud involves a fraudster opening an account and using someone else's credentials without their knowledge. This type of fraud can often follow identity theft, where the fraudster has gained access to a victim's details, such as their name, address and other identifying data. The applications fraudulently taken out can be for credit cards, mobile phone contracts and mortgages.

Another variation of application fraud involves the fraudster using their own name but altering certain details within their application to gain more favourable terms. For instance, fraudsters may exaggerate their earnings so as to gain more credit on a credit card.

Case study—application fraud

A victim received an email from a bank informing him that his 'application for a credit card was being processed'. Unbeknown to the victim, a fraudster had got hold of his name, address, date of birth and other information and had used this to open an account. As the victim hadn't applied for a credit card, he contacted the bank to cancel the application.

Subsequently, the victim received a number of other alerts informing him of other accounts that had been applied for in his name, all of which had to be cancelled.

3.3.4 **Business directory fraud**

Business directory fraud involves fraudsters falsely persuading businesses into purchasing advertising space and listings. Often, the fraudster may pose as a well-known business directory service. A number of methods can be used to deceive the business into agreeing to purchase a listing:

- The business may be sent an offer of a free listing that asks them to return the form even if they do not wish to take up the offer. However, the small print will state that by returning the form they are agreeing to an order and the business will be billed accordingly.
- The business may be contacted by telephone; the fraudster will ask the business to verify their details. These verification details will then be used to state that the victim agreed to pay for the listings. Again, the business will subsequently receive invoices for the unwanted listings.
- The fraudster may contact the business, charging them for the renewal of an existing listing on a business directory.

....

Case study—business directory fraud

The fraudster employed telemarketers who telephoned businesses under the pretence that they were from a legitimate business that published business directories. The fraudsters used a variety of methods to convince the victims to agree to contracts. This included duping businesses into thinking that they were renewing supposedly pre-existing listings, or simply confirming their address.

....

3.3.5 **Government agency scams**

Government agency scams involve fraudsters contacting victim businesses via letter, email or telephone. Purporting to be a government department, the fraudster may request personal information or money from the victim. Businesses have been targeted by this type of fraud using a number of methods. Small businesses have received emails, supposedly from HMRC, asking for their bank details, claiming they are due a tax rebate. Other businesses have received fines, supposedly from government departments, claiming they have breached certain regulations.

....

Case study—government agency scam

The victim received a text claiming to be from HMRC. The text redirected the victim to a fake HMRC website that stated that the victim was eligible to receive a tax refund valued at £265.81. The website requested that the victim input their personal and bank account details to receive the refund. The reality was that, as the website was a fake, the victim would receive no money and their details would be stolen by the fraudster operating the website.

3.3.6 **Long firm fraud**

Long firm fraud involves fraudsters setting up a good relationship and credit rating with a supplier by placing several small orders and paying for them in a timely fashion. Once this good relationship is established, the fraudsters will place one or several large orders, requesting to pay by credit. Once the fraudster receives the goods, they disappear without paying.

Case study—long firm fraud

Two fraudsters cloned the details of a legitimate food company and used the details to defraud a sheep farmer in Wales. The fraudsters initially ordered sheep to the value of £4,300, paying the farmer for the livestock. They then ordered three further consignments, each worth £30,000. The fraudsters never paid for these orders but received the livestock.

3.3.7 **Short firm fraud**

KEY POINTS—SHORT FIRM FRAUD

- The fraudster will often set up their business with the sole intention of carrying out the fraud.
- The third-party address they use for the business will often be a multi-occupancy residence and the occupants will have no knowledge of the fraud.
- As in long firm fraud, the preferred goods are those that can be sold quickly and are not traceable.
- Unlike long-term fraud, this type of fraud takes place over a short timescale.

Further reading

- National Association of Business Crime Partnerships: www.businesscrime.org.uk/
- Gov.uk: www.gov.uk/guidance/crime-and-fraud-prevention-for-businesses-in-international-trade
- Get Safe Online, 'Small businesses: What you need to know about cyber security': www.getsafeonline.org/media/pdf/bis-13-780-small-business-cyber-security-guidance.pdf
- Action Fraud: www.actionfraud.police.uk/

Checklist—fraud prevention advice to reduce corporate fraud

- Advise those who are vulnerable to shred any important documentation once it is no longer needed. This includes but is not limited to letter-headed paper, financial correspondence, invoices and receipts.

- Ensure that financial details are not disclosed unless the recipient is verified as genuine.

- For small businesses, it is recommended to separate personal banking and credit cards from business accounts.

- Organisations should secure their IT infrastructures; this should involve investing in a firewall and anti-virus, malware and spyware detection software.

- Organisations should check the identities of all the companies dealt with. This can be done via credit reference agencies and Companies House.

- Organisations should ensure that all deliveries are made to genuine identifiable addresses.

- Different passwords should be used for different accounts, changing them regularly.

3.3.8 Mortgage fraud

Mortgage fraud is committed in order to obtain mortgages and larger mortgage advances than could legitimately be obtained if the correct information had been provided. Typically, the misleading information used in mortgage fraud includes:

- a fake identity (i.e. taking out mortgages in the name of someone else, who is often deceased);
- overstating income to obtain a higher mortgage/loan (this was common practice in the US sub-prime markets before the financial crash);
- providing false information about employment status;
- providing false information about other financial commitments, such as debt or hire-purchase arrangements;
- omitting information on a mortgage loan application;
- knowingly providing an overvalued price;
- failing to make any mortgage repayments;
- distorting the genuine conveyancing processes to gain an unfair financial advantage;
- manipulating Land Registry data to obtain a number of mortgages with different lenders from the same address;
- changing title deeds without an owner's knowledge.

Mortgage fraud can also occur where an individual or OCG and at least one corrupt associate (often a solicitor, as they are involved in a large proportion of property transactions) conspire to defraud a bank, a financial lending institution or individual by misrepresenting a buyer's financial position in the mortgage process.

Case study—mortgage fraud

The victim bank has provided an additional mortgage loan but, during audit checks a short time later, it has been discovered that the applicant exaggerated the value of the property in question (seemingly with the help of a chartered surveyor known to him) and overstated their income (providing falsified wage slips), meaning they obtained more funds than they would ordinarily have been eligible for.

3.3.9 Procurement fraud

Procurement fraud can take many forms, but all relate to the procurement or tender process. This kind of fraud is common when an official tender process has not been followed or procurement rules and controls are broken or circumvented. Examples of this fraud would include bids being rigged, collusion occurring between suppliers, and services or goods not being delivered or not meeting the specification of the order/contract.

Case study—procurement fraud

A former head of communications admitted to recycling old company mobile phones and keeping the proceeds. He further admitted that this escalated into purchasing new phones and tablets and selling these on almost immediately. This activity took place over a period of four to five years. The activity was discovered when the telephone provider told the victim company that several phones purchased by them in December 2014 had made their way onto the recycling market within days. Reports suggested that the phones were sold for somewhere in the region of £40,000, raised from around 385 units. This was admitted in full by the former employee.

3.3.10 Travel and subsistence fraud

This entails the exaggeration or fabrication of entries on a travel or subsistence claim that were not incurred by an employee of company. Fundamentally, the employee is stealing money from the organisation.

This type of fraud could be committed by temporary and/or permanent staff at all levels within an organisation. This type of fraud often has the additional risk of damaging the organisation's reputation, but also diminishes all the trust that the employer has in their employees.

This list is not exhaustive, but this type of fraud could include any of the following:

- claims for journeys that were not made;
- exaggerating and overstating claims (e.g. inflated mileage rates, distances travelled or claiming first-class travel when they actually travelled in economy class);
- misuse of corporate payment cards for items not related to work but claiming they are;
- claims for subsistence allowances to entertain clients, but these being false or overstated;
- forging signatures authorising payments for false travel and subsistence claims or amending claims once they have been signed off;
- misrepresenting or manipulating receipts.

Checklist—fraud prevention advice for travel and subsistence fraud

It is often impracticable to check every expense claim form in detail, but there is some fraud prevention advice for reducing the opportunities available to staff:

- Carry out regular random spot checks on travel and subsistence claims and let it be known that these are being done.

- Ensure that the organisation has and enforces a comprehensive set of controls for travel and subsidence claims, including formal processes where line managers are required to approve and review the paperwork submitted, checking claims against approved work diaries, mileage for regular destinations, and hotel bills and travel tickets.

- Insist that claimants supply substantiating documents. Follow a 'no receipt, no reimbursement' policy.

- Provide budget holders with sufficient information to monitor costs against budgets. Ideally, authorisation should be by a member of staff with first-hand knowledge of the expenses actually incurred. Thus, it would be beneficial if the organisation could ensure that travel and subsistence claims are submitted in a timely manner.

Case study—travel and subsistence fraud

A member of staff had been working for the company for a short amount of time. As part of his normal duties, he was expected to travel to different locations regularly. Procedures and policies for claiming within the company were lax, not rigorously enforced and not promoted to the workforce. The employee took advantage of this and started to submit fraudulent mileage claims that included claiming vehicle mileage rates for journeys undertaken on a pedal cycle. His manager didn't check these claims properly; he hadn't read the organisational guidance where petrol receipts were not checked. As it was 'just too easy', the member of staff then started to submit exaggerated claims, indicating that he had moved house to increase the distance he was reportedly travelling.

3.3.11 Telecommunications fraud

Mobile phone fraud

These scams can occur in an array of ways. Some of the most common are described in Figure 3.7, but this type of fraud often involves victims:

- making calls or sending texts to premium-rate services unintentionally;
- mistakenly signing up to expensive subscription services.

Figure 3.7 Types of mobile phone fraud

Missed call scams

The victim's phone registers a missed call. The number is not recognisable to the victim, who calls back and is redirected to a premium-rate service.

Phone insurance scams

After the victim buys a new mobile phone, a fraudster contacts them purporting to be from the shop and trying to sell insurance. The victim provides personal and bank details but the insurance doesn't exist and they have been scammed.

Text message scams

The victim is sent a text from an unrecognisable number suggesting they are a friend. The victim rings back thinking they are helping the person by telling them they have a wrong number, only to be charged a premium rate for the call.

Recorded message scam

The victim is informed on a recorded message that they have won a prize and is given a number to call to claim it. The number they are directed to is a premium-rate service.

Ringtone scams

The victim is contacted by a fraudster offering free or low-cost ringtones. The victim accepts the offer and the fraudster sends them ringtones charged at a premium-rate.

Telephone service fraud

This is a fraud against telephone companies and can target both landline and mobile providers. These scams can occur in an array of ways. Some of the most common are described in Figure 3.8.

Checklist—advice for victims of mobile phone fraud

- Advise potential victims not to respond to unsolicited messages, text messages or emails on their phone. The fraudster could be charging extremely high rates for the calls.
- Inform the phone provider as soon as possible if you think you have been caught up in a phone scam.
- Legitimate phone companies do not ask for sensitive personal information.
- If a phone is stolen, inform the provider—they can deactivate it remotely.
- Change any passwords for online accounts accessed via a device.

Figure 3.8 Types of phone fraud

Call selling fraud The fraudster takes out a phone service and sells people the ability to make calls using it, but the fraudster has no intention of ever settling the bill.	**Premium-rate service fraud** The fraudster directs the victims to increase their usage of a premium-rate number and thus generate revenue.
Dial Through Draft (DFT) or Direct Inward System Access fraud (DISA) The fraudster gains access to a company switchboard without the company's knowledge and sells others calls through the switchboard.	**Fraudulent application** The fraudster takes out a contract in a false name with no intention of ever settling the bill.

Further reading

- Phone-paid Services Authority (http://psauthority.org.uk) regulate UK premium-rate services and have powers to take measures against fee-charging service providers.

3.3.12 Charity fraud

Fake charities play on victims' empathy, asking them to make a contribution to a worthy—and often newsworthy—event or cause. Donations from the victim never make it to the intended charity, as money is pocketed by the fraudster. The victim's bank details are often compromised in the process if paying through a spoof website/phone line, and are then used to make further unauthorised purchases without the victim's knowledge. Phone calls are often on premium-rate numbers.

Checklist—charity donation fraud prevention advice

Genuine charities and fraudsters often use the same methods to ask for donations. Here are some crime prevention tips.

- Genuine charities are registered with the Charity Commission and print their registration details on all documentation, collection bags, envelopes, etc.

- Charity collectors are required to carry identity documents and documents from the charity confirming they are collecting legitimately. Ask to see these documents and check the details.

- Contact your local authority or police station to check whether the collector has been given a licence to collect.

- If in doubt, send your donation to the charity directly.

Further reading

- The Charity Commission will confirm that collectors are authentic. Just visit http://apps.charitycommission.gov.uk/showcharity/registerofcharities/registerhomepage.aspx, where they have an online charity register.
- Charity Commission first contact: 03000 66 9197.

3.3.13 Abuse of position of trust

This fraud occurs when the fraudster abuses the position of financial trust placed on them by the victim/organisation. Typically, the types of offences that come under 'abuse of position of trust' include:

- employees carrying out fraud against their corporate employer, sometimes called insider fraud;
- carers/support workers defrauding vulnerable people that they are meant to be caring for and supporting in their daily routine and life;
- abuse of trust fraud in the financial sector occurs because the fraudster has access to money and personal data. It is worth remembering that this type of fraud can include individuals acting independently or being drawn into working for serious OCGs.

....

Case study—abuse of position of trust

The victim's support worker took money from the victim's account without his knowledge and the bank asked the victim to report this. The victim's other support worker called to report this on his behalf. The suspect was looking after the victim on the dates concerned and the 26 transactions corresponded to the dates for the withdrawals.

In a period of eight months, 12 building society customers, who all lived or had previously lived, in similar locations had suffered various degrees of account takeover fraud. Following reimbursements to the customers affected, the building society lost a significant amount of money. Internal investigations identified that a branch manager had accessed society system records of all 12 of those customers from between one day to three months prior to the beginning of the fraudulent attacks on each customer. He was the only employee to have accessed the records of all 12 customers in the six months prior to the beginning of the fraudulent attacks. He was suspended while investigations continued and denied any involvement with the frauds, stating that he had never disclosed customer information to an unauthorised person and that he had never been approached to supply customer information. He stated that he had accessed these customer records as part of his responsibility to identify and source potential business leads for the branch. This would be a legitimate business reason for him to access customer records; however, the society suspects that he disclosed customer information to an unauthorised person and that this information was used for the subsequent fraudulent attacks on the customers.

3.3.14 Courier fraud

Courier fraud by and large relies on the victim naively trusting someone who implies that they are from a trustworthy organisation, for example the police or a bank. The fraudster will normally make contact with the victim, reassuring them and maybe even suggesting that they ring them straight back to confirm that they are trustworthy. When the victim rings back, thinking they are dialling a new phone number, the fraudster has held the phone line open so that the call is maintained and the victim unknowingly ends up speaking to the same fraudster again. The fraudster will then continue with the deception, suggesting that the organisation they are calling from has detected a fraud on their bank account (they will say that the cards relating to the accounts need to be collected in order to track down the fraudsters). They will then trick them into either visiting their financial institution and making a large cash withdrawal, to be collected in order to catch the fraudsters, or persuade them into transferring the funds into another account which is controlled by the fraudster.

3.3.15 Romance fraud

The fraudster targets those who are seeking companionship and can have devastating consequences. The offender will often post a fake online profile using a fictional name and details and wait for potential victims to initiate the first contact with them. The fraudster goes to great lengths to develop the victim's interest and trust. During this 'grooming period', the fraudster will be assessing whether the potential victim is a good financial prospect. Once the victim is drawn into the fraud, the fraudster will tell them an elaborate story and ask for money, gifts or financial details, for a variety of emotive reasons. Some examples of trends in this fraud type include the following:

- The fraudster requests monies from the victim by playing on emotional triggers, saying (for example) that they are trapped in a foreign country, need money to book a flight or hotel room, have a large medical bill to pay or have encountered financial hardship due to a run of bad luck.

- The fraudsters will sometimes ask the victim to agree to monies being transferred into their bank account and then transfer the said monies on to someone else (money laundering is a criminal offence).
- Sometimes the fraudster will ask for money to cover the administration costs or taxes in relation to a large claim they will receive, promising that they will share the money with the target in return for help now.
- Fraudsters blackmail their victims using compromising material that the victims have sent them during their communications.

Once a victim has bought into the scam, the fraudster will often re-target them, giving them further reasons for needing money.

KEY POINTS—ROMANCE FRAUD

- The victims in these types of fraud can often be reluctant to report it. They may feel like they have suffered a long-lasting emotional betrayal by someone they believed they were in a serious relationship with.
- This offence is not gender-specific; all sexes can be targeted and be the manipulators pretending to love.
- The fraudster will often be developing online relationships with multiple potential victims at the same time.

Checklist—fraud prevention advice for romance fraud

- Advise potential victims to trust their intuition and remove the emotion from their decision making, no matter how flattering or persistent the potential partner is.

- Safeguard privacy. Don't be tempted to move communications outside official sites; this is because sites will have safety procedures in place to protect and block suspicious profiles and verify new members.

- Be cautious about handing out specific information like mobile numbers, email addresses or financial information. If financial details are given, contact the relevant financial institution immediately for further specific crime prevention advice.

- Fraudsters often claim to live in the same country as the victim, but say they are currently travelling or working overseas. They may pretend to book flights to visit, but never actually come. Ask to meet—if they cannot, this should raise alarm bells.

- If the potential victim intends to meet, tell family and friends where they are going and how they will be contactable. Always meet in a busy public place, where they will feel safe and secure.

- The fraudster often overwhelms the victim with gifts and conveys strong emotional feelings very early on in the relationship. By doing this, the fraudster is often trying to deceive the victim to lower their guard.

- Watch out for cut-and-paste profiles. Use internet search engines to search for different elements of the profile to establish the date it was created. Pictures can be sourced from anywhere—so, again, use a reverse image search to check. Look closely at the emails they send you, searching for inconsistencies in what they write and what they are telling you. Do the details in the online profile match the photo?

- Avoid profiles that aren't specific enough about what they are looking for in a partner. The fraudster may be keeping all options open, allowing them to reach the widest possible target audience. Look for the following descriptions in their profiles: self-employed/professional working overseas, widow/widower with a child, claim to live near you but is currently away (though will be returning soon).

- Check discrepancies in their stories; for example, they say they have been away, yet their profile shows them not to have been. Investigate and do checks to confirm the identity of the person you are communicating with.

3.4 Identity-related frauds

Identity theft happens when fraudsters access enough information about someone's identity (e.g. their name, gender, date of birth, current or previous addresses) to commit identity fraud. Identity theft can take place regardless of whether the fraud victim is alive or deceased.

Victims of identity theft can experience fraud that has a direct impact on their personal finances and makes it difficult for them to obtain loans, credit cards or a mortgage until the matter is resolved.

Identity fraud can be described as the use of that stolen identity in criminal activity to obtain goods or services by fraud.

KEY POINTS—IDENTITY FRAUD

Fraudsters can use identity details to:

- open bank accounts;
- obtain credit cards, loans and state benefits;
- order goods;
- take over existing accounts;
- take out mobile phone contracts;
- obtain genuine documents such as passports and driving licences.

3.4.1 How identities are stolen

Criminals commit identity theft by stealing personal information. This is often done by taking documents from the rubbish or by making contact with the victim and pretending to be from a legitimate organisation. Other identity thefts occur when insiders steal personal information or penetrate databases holding private information.

The first victims may know of it may be when they receive bills or invoices for things they have not ordered, or when they receive letters from debt collectors for debts that aren't theirs.

3.4.2 Fraudulently obtained genuine (FOG) document

A FOG is a genuine government-issued document, such as a driving licence or a passport, where the criminal has used the identity of another person (fictitious or real) with a criminal's image. The document will not have been altered in any way after its issue. Possession of a FOG document is in itself a crime under section 6(1) of the Identity Documents Act (IDA) 2010, but it can also be used to obtain a credit card, loan, mortgage or other similar financial service. Where the document is used with an improper intention, this is the aggravated form and should be prosecuted under section 4(1) of the IDA 2010.

Two identities are required to apply for a FOG: an applicant and a counter-signatory. If it can be proven that these persons were complicit in the facilitation of the FOG(s), then the counter-signatory can also be charged. If the genuine holder of the identity is complicit, they too can be charged with making a false representation and allowing others to use their details (section 2(1) of the Fraud Act 2006).

KEY POINTS—FOG DOCUMENT

A UK passport, driving licence or biometric residence permit (BRP, also known as a biometric immigration document in legislation) may be seized during the course of an investigation or prosecution using search powers provided under section 19 of the Police and Criminal Evidence Act 1984 and section 44 of the UK Borders Act 2007. When seized, the case officer should notify the relevant department (e.g. Her Majesty's Passport Office (HMPO), the Driver & Vehicle Licensing Agency (DVLA) or UK Visas and Immigration) immediately to prevent the suspect declaring the document lost and obtaining a replacement.

Useful agencies:

- An inquiry can be made with the issuing organisation for copies of the application for the document, including the image. Reviewing the image will confirm whether the record is for the genuine person.
- Metropolitan Police Service, Amberhill: receives and disseminates data on false identity data.
- The National Document Fraud Unit (NDFU) deals with forged and counterfeit travel and identity documents and driving licences from around the world, and

---

can provide legal statements on the authenticity of documents and, in some cases, on their issuance processes.

- The General Register Office is for checks on the birth record for a given identity and can determine whether the person has been reported deceased. Tel: 0300 123 1837.

3.4.3 **Protecting the identity of deceased family members**

Criminals sometimes use the identities of deceased persons to commit fraud, which can be very distressing for those close to the deceased. The following websites offer deceased person mail preference services and provide further information on this issue:

- The Bereavement Register—www.thebereavementregister.org.uk
- Deceased Preference Service—www.deceasedpreferenceservice.co.uk
- Mailing Preference Service—www.mpsonline.org.uk

Checklist—fraud prevention advice for preventing identity fraud

The following advice can be given to potential victims to prevent identity fraud:

- Do not throw out anything containing your name, address or financial details without shredding it first.

- If they receive an unsolicited email or a phone call from what appears to be their bank or building society asking for security details, never reveal their full password, login details or account numbers. Be aware that a bank will never ask for a PIN or for a whole security number or password.

- If they are concerned about the source of a call, wait five minutes and call their bank from a different telephone, making sure there is a dialling tone.

- Check statements carefully and report anything suspicious to the bank or financial service provider concerned.

- Do not leave documents, such as bills, lying around for others to look at.

- If they are expecting a bank or credit card statement and it does not arrive, tell their bank or credit card company.

- If they move house, ask the mail provider to redirect their post for at least a year.

- Credit reference agencies offer a credit report checking service to alert them to any changes on their credit file that could indicate potential fraudulent activity.

- It is particularly helpful to check a personal credit file two to three months after moving house.

Payment cards

- If payment cards are lost or stolen, cancel them immediately. Keep a note of the emergency numbers to call.

- When giving card details or personal information over the phone, on the internet or in a shop, make sure other people cannot hear or see the personal information.

Documents

- Keep personal documents in a safe place, preferably in a lockable drawer or cabinet at home. Consider storing valuable financial documents (e.g. share certificates) with the bank.

- Don't throw away entire bills, receipts, credit- or debit-card slips, bank statements or even unwanted post. Destroy unwanted documents, preferably by using a shredder.

Passwords and PINs

- Never give personal or account details to anyone who makes contact unexpectedly. Be suspicious, even if they claim to be from a bank or the police.

- Do not use the same password for more than one account and never use banking passwords for any other websites. Using different passwords increases security and makes it less likely that someone could access any other accounts.

- If the victim believes they are the victim of identity fraud involving payment cards (e.g. credit and debit cards), online banking or cheques, they must report this to their bank as soon as possible. The bank will then be responsible for investigating the issue and they will report any case of criminal activity to the police. The police will then record the case and decide whether to carry out follow-up investigations.

- If the victim is not sure which organisation to call, contact Action Fraud for advice.

- The victim should contact the Royal Mail customer inquiry line if they suspect their mail is being stolen or that a mail redirection has been fraudulently set up on their address. The Royal Mail has an investigation unit that will be able to help them.

- Advise the victim to get a copy of their credit report. A credit report will show them any searches done by a lender, what date the search took place, what name and address it was done against and for what type of application. It will also show what credit accounts are set up in their name. They can contact any one of the three credit reference agencies and receive support in resolving credit report problems caused by identity fraud.

4

Digitally enabled (cyber) crime

4.1 **Introduction**

This chapter will assist investigators who want to know more about how fraud is digitally enabled and crimes that can only be committed by use of computers and the internet (so-called cyber-dependent offences). The chapter focuses on:

- offence types and basic terminology;
- case studies, which are included to aid comprehension;
- how investigations and victims can be approached;
- the 'golden hour' principles for fraud enabled by cyber offending;
- how cyber criminality can be prevented and victims protected.

In this context, the term 'cyber' is used to describe activities occurring via a network, be that the internet itself, or some other form of network.

KEY POINTS—DEFINITIONS OF CYBER-ENABLED CRIME

Cyber-enabled crime is defined by the National Computer Crime Unit as crime where a computer is used to assist or aid an offence such as fraud, harassment or grooming.

Criminal motives may range from financial gain to revenge. What remains constant is the role of the network and the systems connected to it as either conduits for criminal activity or targets in their own right.

The face of crime in the UK has changed dramatically over recent years. There has been a significant reduction in the incidence of many 'traditional' crime types, while those digitally enabled by the increasing use of computers and the internet have grown in terms of volume, threat and harm.

In 2015, it was estimated that 2.5 million cyber incidents impacted on victims in the UK annually, as well as over 5 million fraud incidents—the vast majority of which were digitally enabled. Offences of this type truly represent the high volume and priority crimes of the twenty-first century; therefore, an understanding of how these offences take place and what investigative techniques can be applied is essential.

Further reading

- Office for National Statistics, 'Improving crime statistics in England and Wales', Crime Statistics, Year Ending June 2015 Release, October 2015: http://webarchive.nationalarchives.gov.uk/20160105160709/http://www.ons.gov.uk/ons/rel/crime-stats/crime-statistics/year-ending-june-2015/sty-fraud.html.

4.1.1 **Cyber-enabled or cyber-dependent?**

A variety of definitions of 'cyber crime' have historically been used within law enforcement.

Cyber-enabled crimes

Many frauds are enabled by the prior deployment of a cyber-dependent technique. An example is the deployment of a computer virus onto a personal computer, resulting in the loss of money from the victim's bank account or the hacking of an email account in order to defraud friends or colleagues of the user of that account.

Cyber-dependent crimes

These are typically categorised as offences contrary to the Computer Misuse Act (CMA) 1990; they relate to offending that can only take place with the use of a computer. Examples include denial-of-service (DoS) attacks on corporate websites or the hacking of databases to extract data.

Some cyber-dependent crimes are not 'economic' by motivation or result; for example, the defacement of corporate websites by terrorist sympathisers or the hacking of databases by activists.

Further reading

- Fraud Act 2006: www.legislation.gov.uk/ukpga/2006/35/contents
- Computer Misuse Act 1990: www.legislation.gov.uk/ukpga/1990/18/contents

---

4.1.2 The 'cyber' criminals

Cyber crime offences reported by victims in the UK are often carried out by a group of people, either working together or operating in less defined groups. In general, these people are:

- criminals (organised or individuals);
- disgruntled insiders;
- nation-state actors (i.e. those involved in espionage), nicknamed 'hacktivists'.

Cyber criminals have a range of skills and often collaborate on a purely transactional basis, buying and selling technology and expertise as necessary. It is important that investigators understand the respective roles of such people in order to know how best to direct their investigation and what support to request.

The 'disgruntled insiders' category includes those who are seeking revenge by working to expose the internal dealings and/or data held by an organisation; for example, as in the case of WikiLeaks, a website that publishes and comments on leaked documents alleging government and corporate misconduct.

Hacktivists generally commit crimes in order to further a specific cause or to damage the reputation of a company or individual. For instance, many terrorist sympathisers commit cyber crimes in order to spread messages of hate, while other groups promote a myriad of different causes. Recent examples of loosely organised criminal groups involved in non-financially-motivated cyber crime include the so-called Syrian Electronic Army and the Anonymous group.

4.2 Cyber terminology—jargon buster

To describe the cyber world, new words and terminology have been introduced into our vocabulary. This section identifies key words and their definitions.

Botnet: A network of compromised computers that is controlled centrally by a cyber criminal. Botnets allow the criminal to undertake any number of tasks, but are most commonly used for the following:

- passing commands and configurations to launch spam campaigns;
- launching distributed denial-of-service (DDoS) attacks.

See Figure 4.1.

Figure 4.1 A diagram representing a botnet attack

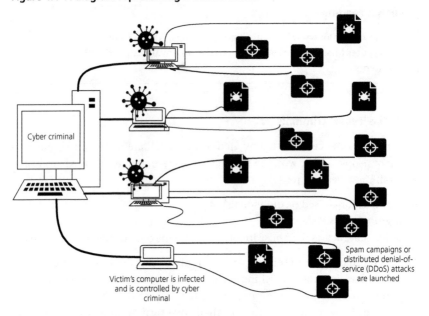

Cyber criminal

Victim's computer is infected and is controlled by cyber criminal

Spam campaigns or distributed denial-of-service (DDoS) attacks are launched

Bot: A software application that runs automated tasks over the internet, normally these tasks are simple, repetitive and done at a high speed.

Brute-force attack: Consists of quickly and systematically testing many combinations to guess passwords in order to break a security system.

Click fraud: A type of fraud where online advertisers generate income based on how many visitors click on their advertisement. The fraud occurs where automated script or computer programs are used to replicate consumers.

Cloud computing: Enables users to store and access data and programs over the internet instead of via a computer's hard drive.

Command and control server: A server that controls a botnet by issuing instructions and taking on information.

Denial-of-service (DoS) attack: A network layer attack. This is usually an attack on a website. It works by overloading the target with networked traffic.

Distributed denial-of-service (DDoS) attack: A DoS attack that distributes its traffic over a large number of infected computers. This makes it more difficult for the victim to distinguish between ordinary traffic and DDoS traffic.

Exploit kit: Used to exploit some vulnerability in a system. It is commonly used for a malicious purpose such as installing malware. Exploit kits are routinely sold by criminals to enable others to exploit a vulnerability.

Keylogger (also known as keystroke logging): A type of tool that has the capability to record information directly from the keyboard interface and send it directly to an attacker.

Malware: Short for 'malicious software'. Malware is a program designed to disrupt and infiltrate a computer and its operation.

Man-in-the-middle (MiTM) attack: When an attacker secretly intercepts and alters the communication between two systems that believe they are directly communicating with each other.

Patch: Software that fixes or improves a computer program or supporting software.

Phishing emails: Phishing emails purport to come from a legitimate organisation (e.g. a bank) in an attempt to obtain sensitive information.

Proxy server: A proxy server will act as an intermediary between an internet user and web-based services or connected resources that the user is seeking to access. It makes it difficult to trace a user's internet activity by providing a level of anonymity.

Ransomware: A type of malware that extorts money from the victim, either by locking up their important files and demanding a ransom or by using a social-engineering attack.

Root access: When a user attains administrative-level permissions.

Social engineering: An offender building an understanding of the victim and using this to control or interact with the victim to the offender's advantage.

Spam email: These can be sent to many recipients at the same time and recipients are often not personally targeted. This is a type of email that can include scripts containing malware or altered website links for seemingly genuine sites, which are actually phishing sites.

Spear phishing: A targeted and focused phishing attack aimed at a specific person. This attack usually uses data about that person to launch the attack. An email typically arrives from an apparently genuine source requesting the recipient to visit a realistic-looking website, where the recipient is asked to input personal information.

Spoofing: When a person or a program is disguised as another system or user on a network in order to launch attacks, steal data or bypass access controls. Email spoofing is when a message is forged so that it appears to come from somewhere other than the actual source.

Trojan (Trojan horse): A piece of malicious software designed to gain root access to a computer. It is usually used to bring other malware into the computer.

Virtual private network (VPN): A VPN connects remote computers or offices on a private network across a public network like the internet. A VPN uses an encrypted connection offering security over a less secure network. A VPN can also be used to circumnavigate geographical restrictions and censorship on the internet. Additionally, VPNs can be used to connect to proxy servers to conceal identity and location.

Virus: A malicious software program that infects computers by interfering with their operation. Unlike a Trojan horse, a virus replicates itself once it has been executed.

Vishing: Describes the use of social engineering to access the private and financial information of the victim over the telephone for the purposes of fraud.

Voice over internet protocol (VoIP): Enables the user to use the internet to make telephone calls. It is sometimes referred to as Internet Telephony and can be at no charge or very low cost.

Vulnerability: A design flaw that can be exploited to make a program do what it is not designed to do, such as escalating user privileges or installing programs.

Worms: A stand-alone malware computer program that is self-replicating and does not need to attach itself to an existing program in a computer.

4.3 Types of cyber-dependent crimes

The variety of specific types of cyber attack is very wide, and is expanding all the time. However, many of the basic elements of a variety of attack types are similar, as is the prevention advice that should be given to victims or members of the public. Therefore, this section describes some of the most prevalent and important threats by means of case studies—each of which demonstrates the importance of specific enablers to the criminal. By reading the following case studies, the investigator and fraud prevention officer will be able to understand many of the most common crimes and the most common vulnerabilities displayed by victims.

4.3.1 Crypto-ransomware extortion via drive-by download

This type of cyber attack can be very harmful to individuals and organisations if successful, as it results in the encryption of files accompanied by a ransom demand. The initial infection technique (which is often malware, e.g. viruses, Trojans or worms) used by the criminal in the case below, could be similar to the means by which important data (e.g. online banking credentials) are stolen in other common crimes.

....

Case study—L, the business owner

Overview

The attack described below is typical of the type of ransomware infections commonly reported to Action Fraud. While the specific details of each part of this process may differ between different attacks of this type, the basic process of target selection, delivery, infection and remittance does not alter significantly.

Background

The victim, L, is a self-employed accountant who runs a business from her home office. L has a laptop which she uses to work on her clients' accounts, storing their tax and receipt information on spreadsheet files in folders on her hard drive. She also has an external hard drive, on which she stores old account information along with her personal files, such as pictures and music.

L also uses her computer to keep up with friends on social media sites, to read the news and to access her emails. Her computer runs a popular operating system and she usually installs the security updates eventually; however, she finds the sheer number of them difficult to keep up with. She uses a free anti-virus subscription, which came pre-installed on her PC when it was bought.

Delivery

As L scrolls through her newsfeed on a social media site one day, she sees an article posted by one of her friends that catches her attention. The article is a hyperlink accompanied by a small preview of the story to which it links. She trusts this link because it was posted by a close friend on a legitimate social networking platform, and even though she has never heard of the news outlet where the story is hosted, she assumes they wouldn't post it if it were a scam.

Clicking the link opens a new tab in her browser, which takes her to the article. As the page loads she notices a pop-up window briefly appear and then disappear from her screen before she has a chance to close it herself. After this, a new tab opens in her browser window, hiding behind the tab containing the story she is reading. Although L notices this, she doesn't close the new tab immediately, waiting until she has finished reading the article.

The tab running in the background is connecting to a type of website known as a 'malware URL'. This is a web-facing server loaded with an exploit kit, which is a program written to detect vulnerable programs and operating systems and use those vulnerabilities to install malware. While L is reading the article, her computer is being infected with a Trojan horse—a type of malware that establishes root access to its victim's computer, giving an attacker the ability to install or delete programs and make changes to the victim's computer.

Installation

While L is working on her computer, the malware goes to work, disabling the free anti-virus software she has installed and allowing the attacker to download and run malicious files. The Trojan horse has been configured to install a type of malware called crypto-ransomware, which makes encrypted copies of files stored on the computer or any related drives, and destroys the originals.

She may have noticed that her computer was running slightly slower than usual while the malware was doing its work, or that windows with a black background and white writing were running behind the open windows. She may have also noticed her computer not responding when she tried shutting it down or putting it into sleep mode. This is because crypto-ransomware takes time and processing power to encrypt files, and in most cases it does not make many attempts to hide itself.

The next morning, when L opens her computer to begin work, she receives a ransom demand when she attempts to access her client information files. Opening the files triggers a pop-up window informing her that the files have been scrambled with strong encryption and that they will be permanently deleted if she does not pay a ransom demand within one week. The ransom demand also contains a unique customer reference number, instructions on how to pay using bitcoins and a sample key to unlock any two of the deleted files in order to prove that the victim will receive their files once the ransom demand has been met. L uses the sample key to unlock two files and in doing so triggers a countdown to the deletion of the files.

Recovery

Other than paying the ransom, L has three options to secure her files, she can:

- search the internet in case the criminals have reused decryption keys, and previous victims have posted those keys online;
- recover her files from a backup cloud account or her external hard drive;
- seek law enforcement assistance.

L must also be careful in this case as her computer is still infected with malware and connecting it to external drives may encrypt the files on those drives. The attackers also have the ability to install more malware onto her computer to steal information, commit DDoS attacks and click fraud, and spy on her.

Prevention opportunities

From the outset of this scenario, L has made a number of avoidable errors that led to the predicament she found herself in. To take them in order:

1 She stores important files on a live computer system that she also uses to browse the internet. This leaves her important information at risk of being compromised, corrupted or destroyed by her browsing habits. Important files, especially commercially sensitive files, should be secured and backed up regularly to a removable drive, a cloud account or a read-only medium such as a digital video disc (DVD).

2 She logs into her computer as an admin user, and does her personal internet browsing as well as her work on the same user account. An admin, or root user, is a specially privileged user of the operating system who is allowed to make changes to the computer. Tasks such as opening emails, reading files and browsing the internet are exceptionally dangerous when they are being carried out by a user who is able to make changes to the operating system. L should use the control panel to issue separate accounts for her personal and professional activities on the computer, and she should only log in as an admin user in order to make changes to the computer system, such as system updates and installing software.

3 She often puts off applying security updates and has not put a great deal of effort into finding the right anti-virus software. These are two extremely important aspects of maintaining a secure and safe computer.

4 She navigates via links posted on social media sites without paying attention to where the link will take her, or trying to verify the legitimacy of websites. Verifying the legitimacy of a link can be as simple as hovering over the link to determine whether the URL is correct.

5 L also missed a number of other opportunities to spot that something wasn't right, including a pop-up tab hidden behind the page she was viewing, unfamiliar windows running processes she had not initiated herself and slower operating speeds due to malicious applications running.

4.3.2 Private branch exchange (PBX) hacking

A PBX is hardware designed to allow circuit switching within an organisation's telephone system, namely it is the means by which calls can be routed to the correct extension or external exchange for incoming or outgoing calls. It works with both voice over internet protocol (VoIP) and the traditional public switched telephone network.

The hacking of a PBX-based telephone system can occur either through the voicemail system or vulnerable networks. The hacker diverts the outward lines to international or premium-rate numbers, which are then dialled repeatedly over a number of hours or days, causing a financial loss to the victim and an equivalent gain to the offender. Typically, small- and medium-sized enterprises or local government/public sector organisations (including education and health facilities) are most at risk from this type of crime.

....

Case study—primary school

Background

The victim, a primary school, operated an internal switchboard that meant that individuals had to call the main number and would then be rerouted to internal extensions. The switchboard was generally staffed between 08.45–15.45 Monday to Friday. They used default passwords and PINs for their voicemail facilities.

Target identification

The criminal knew that the school was likely to be closed outside school times, with no one monitoring the switchboard overnight or during the weekend. The criminal also knew that schools and other small organisations have vulnerable online security and are likely not to have altered their security settings since purchasing the PBX facility.

Delivery

The criminal dialled a range of numbers to identify those that were unused but had the voicemail facility. For more organised criminals, they may use a range of programs to identify vulnerabilities within the PBX.

Installation

Once the hacker has identified the vulnerability, they use default passwords or brute-force access to the PBX. They then reroute calls from the school to either premium-rate numbers or international destinations, where other criminals make money from receiving such calls. The school is unaware that they have been attacked until they receive a phone bill that is substantially higher than they expected, featuring premium-rate/international calls.

Recovery

The school has little option but to pay the bill; they need to follow the basic prevention advice below in order to prevent further victimisation.

PBX hacking against a school—prevention advice

From the outset of this scenario, the primary school has made a number of avoidable errors that could have prevented them being left with such a high bill:

1 The school is known to be closed before and after school hours and at weekends. This means that the criminal is aware that the switchboard will be regularly

unattended, thus providing them with time to carry out the crime. The school should consider restricting access to its telephone system outside core hours, especially at weekends and public holidays.

2 PBX passwords have been left on default settings. It should be noted that PBX hacking is often successful when weak passwords are used, as hackers use a common weak password list to test the line. Therefore, everyone should be encouraged to make all of their passwords/PIN numbers as strong as possible.

3 The school have not advised their PBX providers to remove access to premium-rate/ international numbers, which leaves them open to abuse should they be hacked.

....

4.3.3 DDoS attack

A DDoS attack generally involves flooding a network with far more traffic than it is designed to deal with—in essence, multiple computers (often remotely operated 'bots') attempt to access a website or request information from it at the same time, causing it to 'crash' or run slowly. A DDoS attack can be intended to cause the victim a financial or reputational loss, but can also be a mechanism to mask other cyber attacks (e.g. malware infections).

....

Case study—DDoS attack

Background

The victim is an online family planning forum dedicated to supporting all family planning choices as well as sharing thoughts and ideas. As a forum, it appoints a number of volunteer moderators to monitor posts and remove any felt to be offensive, inappropriate or discriminatory. However, it has significantly more posts each day than moderators.

Target identification

The hacktivists have their own protest agenda. They have undertaken a few high-profile web defacements of businesses that were contrary to their cause. They used compromised blogs to post messages stating their cause and their intention to target those they are opposed to.

The hacktivists undertook reconnaissance of a number of sites, but chose this one because it was both very popular and deemed a soft target, as it was a self-hosting site. The week before the test, the hacktivists posted a number of offensive messages on various pages of the forum detailing their agenda.

The people running the forum were aware that these groups take both physical and digital action, but did not make any assessment as they did not think they would target them ('It wouldn't happen to us'). The moderators removed the offending posts, but the site owners did not take note of the contents and were not cognisant of the threat to them.

Weaponisation

The hacktivists monitored the site for several days, testing how the forum worked to identify weaknesses and vulnerabilities. One of their observations was that each of the moderators included a document at the bottom of their post, which outlined the rules for participating in the forum. The document was approximately 3MB. They also allowed contributors to post pictures onto the site with a size limit of 5MB.

The hacktivists were not very technically skilled; however, they had access to the dark web and arranged to rent space on a botnet to carry out their activities. (The dark web is part of the World Wide Web; however, it requires specific software, configurations or authorisation to access sites. It is a platform for a significant amount of criminality, including the exchange of criminal commodities.)

Delivery

On the day of the attack, the hacktivist in control of the botnet commanded all of the computers under their control to request the rules document at the same time, repeatedly. The huge number of requests caused the servers hosting the forum to crash.

The forum owners suddenly saw a huge spike in traffic to their site before it crashed. They were unable to access the servers and at first did not realise what was happening. Their phone lines used VoIP and were based on the same servers, so they were also unable to make any phone calls. One of the workers used their mobile phone to call the police.

At first, they didn't realise what was happening and then IT informed them that they were under attack; however, they were advised to wait to see if it stopped. After nearly an hour, the attack was over.

The forum's contributors were unable to access the site.

Impact of the attack

The hacktivists used compromised social media and blog accounts to publicise their acts. They also demanded that the forum shut itself down or they would continue to attack it.

The users of the site have used Twitter accounts to raise concerns about the security of their information and their personal security. Some users have left the site, citing security concerns as their reason for leaving. The forum has also seen a marked drop in new contributors. They have spent a considerable amount of time answering media inquiries and trying to repair their reputation.

Prevention advice

There were a number of opportunities for the forum to identify that it was a possible target and put some prevention measures in place.

1 Know your threat picture: as a family planning forum, you should be aware that you may be a target for protestors.

114

2 Monitor both volumes and type of traffic to your site, as this might indicate pre-attack testing.
3 Make sure that your server setup is appropriate to your business.
4 Consider hiring a DDoS mitigation service aimed at the right level for your needs. It can undertake an assessment of your vulnerabilities and provide support.
5 Consider having a mobile phone pre-loaded with important contact details, should you become a victim again.
6 When a 'fix' is identified that will prevent the attack happening using the same methodology, make sure that you consider other vulnerabilities.
7 Reassess the situation regularly, particularly if there are public statements of intent against what your forum stands for or you receive threats directly; the risk has increased.

4.4 The initial investigation of fraud-related cyber crime

Responding to a report of a 'cyber-dependent' or 'cyber-enabled' fraud crime poses new challenges for today's investigator. A digital crime scene may appear complex, potentially consisting of compromised networked devices, servers and data centres spread over different sites and even internationally. As the amount of data passing over the internet increases at a rapid rate, year on year investigators are being faced with increasingly large 'off-site' and 'cloud-based' servers. Simply powering down and imaging (making a forensic copy of) a device is rarely going to be sufficient to provide all the evidence required, and may impede a victim's ability to continue their business functions. Like any 'traditional' crime scene, the primary objectives remain the same: to gather sufficient evidence to understand the attack vector used, to determine its scope and reach, and to identify offenders. In doing so, it is important to identify and evidence the impact and damage caused to the victim. A victim will want to understand the vulnerabilities exploited within their environment in order to remediate and protect themselves in the future.

It is helpful at the investigative stage to distinguish between a 'cyber crime' and a 'cyber attack'.

KEY POINTS—DEFINITIONS OF 'CYBER CRIME' AND 'CYBER ATTACK'

- A **cyber crime** is one that usually involves the use of a computer and/or a digital network.
- A **cyber attack** can be thought of as a collection of criminal activities undertaken mostly via computers and computer networks in order to steal money, steal information or cause damage.

Quite often, it is only at the point when damage is caused that the victim becomes aware of the cyber attack. Not all the criminal's activity will be cyber-related: equipment and infrastructure will need to be purchased; and accommodation, specialist knowledge and criminal connections will have to be acquired. More conventional investigative techniques can be applied to this non-cyber-related activity. Most financial crime, including cyber-enabled offences, will be followed by a money laundering process.

KEY POINTS—CYBER ROLES IN FORCES

A number of organisations have trained staff to assist in digital/cyber-related incidents.

Digital media investigators (DMIs)

The person undertaking the role of DMI will have broad knowledge of media technology and will have completed a relevant training course. They will be required to undertake the forensic recovery of evidential data from computer systems and provide evidentially sound technical support to officers who are investigating.

Digital media coordinators (DMCs)

The main function of the DMC is to advise on the development of an effective technology and data strategy for any investigation.

Rarely is there only one cyber criminal behind an attack and an investigator will need to give consideration to this. Viruses and exploits used to hack servers can be purchased online with relative ease. Organised crime groups offer professional money laundering services, and individuals with specific knowledge of a system and its vulnerabilities may develop code to exploit those weaknesses. While this poses challenges, it also offers investigative opportunities. This means it is increasingly important for local, national and international law enforcement agencies to cooperate and share information.

Investigators must also be conscious of the fact that a cyber attack against a victim can often consist of blended attack types; for example, as previously explained, DDoS attacks can be used as a distraction from a malware infection. Investigators must be open-minded when it comes to their evidence-gathering approach. Victims need to remain alert and ensure that the best evidence-capturing opportunities are in place.

4.4.1 'Golden hour' principles regarding cyber offences

The 'golden hour' principles hold that effective early action can result in securing significant material (including digital data) that would otherwise be lost to the investigation through attrition. Following up obvious lines of inquiry provides significant benefits, to both the investigative team and the victim (who needs to identify vulnerabilities and protect themselves against future attacks). 'Fast-track actions' are any investigative actions that, if pursued immediately, are likely to establish important facts, preserve evidence or lead to the early resolution of the investigation. This material should be recovered in a forensically approved manner and in an appropriate environment.

Further reading

- ACPO, *Good Practice Guide for Digital Evidence*, 2012: http://library.college. police.uk/docs/acpo/digital-evidence-2012.pdf
- College of Policing, 'Authorised Professional Practice—Investigation', 2016: www.app.college.police.uk/app-content/investigations/

When considering cyber offences specifically, the 'golden hour' principle is most important when identifying and securing volatile data that may evidence the interaction between the victim and the offender's attack infrastructure. This data usually exists in a volatile state and can cease to exist when power is removed from a system or hardware, such as a server. Volatile data may only be recorded for a specified period of time, and may be 'dumped' or overwritten. Volatile data can provide information regarding network connections and system processes and is often recorded in the form of event logs; this is known as 'logging'. These logs may only be retained for a brief or specified period of time. It is within these logs (and registry files) that suspicious activity can be detected. These logs can also be deleted if the device is online, so consideration needs to be given to this, as the offender could delete logs remotely.

Requesting and preserving event logs and registry files (router, application, mail server, web server, proxy server) at an early stage, before they are lost, will provide the investigator with key network information. It is also in the interests of the victim to keep accurate logs, as this will provide the incident team with the ability to deal with such incidents quickly and effectively by identifying and isolating infected machines from the network, allowing business to continue as normal. These logs may be used to ascertain what information has been lost, where that information has gone, where the attack traffic is originating from, the type of internet attack traffic that is flooding a victim and the scale and success of the attack. These logs may ultimately provide the investigative team with the information required to pursue, and successfully prosecute, the attackers.

Checklist—basic cyber strategy considerations (a DEER checklist)

- **Access points**: consider modems/routers.
- **Device**: identify and secure affected devices.
- **Examinations**: digital forensic analysis by hi-tech/digital crime unit/dept.

117

- **Email/phone**: identify email addresses and message headers, as well as phone numbers that the suspect may have used or left for contact.

- **Regulation of Investigatory Powers Act**: applications.

Evidentially securing logs may mean securing a large amount of data; the investigator must consider this as part of their incident response. Appropriate hardware storage capable of securing this data will be required, along with consideration of the need to produce the material in an evidential format. The data needs to be in a searchable format for future analysis and working copies will be required. If the data is not thought to contain direct evidence, then consideration can be given to the victim and it can be preserved as third-party material. This may have cost benefits for the investigator, but risks defence attacks on the continuity of evidence and allegations of 'tampering' if not retained by a victim or secured in the evidential chain. The victim may wish to consider securing this data in their own secure repository for analysis, in order to understand how best to protect themselves in the future.

Where any communication from the attacker is identified, including spoofed emails purporting to be from someone legitimate, then the email and email header (also known as the source code) must also be evidentially secured.

KEY POINTS—EMAIL HEADERS

- Email headers: the email header only relates to the last journey and should not, therefore, be forwarded on.
- If the victim forwards the email, the originating IP address will no longer be listed.

Email headers effectively sit 'behind' an email; they are best thought of as a digital 'envelope' containing the address and postal frank mark that the email was sent in and with. It contains valuable information about the origin of the email, the transmission route it took and the intended recipient—including the internet protocol (IP) addresses of both sender and receiver. IP addresses are the postal addresses of the internet, and, along with the time, date and time zone, may identify your suspect. Email headers can be retrieved with no specialist knowledge and any mailbox user can view their own email headers. They can appear confusing to the untrained eye—appearing in a simple text format, they will contain several IP addresses and the text content of the email, along with dates/times and other useful information. Getting to them is slightly different for each type of email. Tips on how to view email headers are readily available online with a simple internet browser search. They need to be viewed and seized from the receiving ('victim') mailbox.

Like the postal addresses used in a fraud, IP addresses can be 'spoofed' (i.e. made to appear different from what they really are). They may identify a proxy service that internet traffic is being routed through. A proxy can be thought of as similar to a postal drop box, which a suspect may use to place or pick up post or have post routed through. In these cases, you may feel that you are at a dead end; however, to a specialist cyber crime or hi-tech crime officer, it could be the starting point. Seek advice!

As touched on earlier, responding to a DDoS attack in action is like responding to an act of criminal damage in action, except that it is committed from a distance, via a computer. Defending against a DDoS attack will be the priority of the victim. There are services that can be paid for on the market that will identify and filter out internet attack traffic. Defending without these services will require the assistance of the victim's IT or network specialists. The victim will need to try and increase the amount of internet data they can receive in order to mitigate the effect of the DDoS attack (because this will enable customers to continue to use the service even as the attack is ongoing). Attack traffic is likely to have come from a large number of infected servers or computers in a botnet. If a victim is able to provide searchable logs, the most common IP addresses used in the attack can be identified and blocked (and made subject to further investigation by specialists). These IP addresses will relate to compromised devices that are simply relaying the attack traffic, and are unlikely to be the 'source' or command and control centre of the attacker.

Checklist—practical guide to investigative considerations

When taking a statement, explore the victim's digital security measures. Ask:

- What devices do they have that connect to the internet?

- Do they have any protection (e.g. anti-virus/malware/spyware/firewall) on all these devices?

- Have they opened links from unsolicited emails?

- Have they opened unusual links from friends?

- Have they noticed unusual requests for information when using websites such as online banking?

- Have they added any new friends/contacts to their social network recently? Have they verified these accounts with an actual individual?

- If money is obtained from the crime, try to establish the beneficiary account.

- Consider financial inquiries, the Proceeds of Crime Act (POCA) 2002 or the Police and Criminal Evidence (PACE) Act 1984 production orders, depending on the focus of the investigation.

119

4.4.2 **Incident response**

The initial response to a cyber incident, especially one that is affecting the day-to-day dealings of a business, should primarily be one of prevention rather than investigation (albeit with an awareness of 'golden hour' principles). The National Cyber Security Centre (NCSC) (see 4.5) is best placed to give initial advice on significant cyber incidents, especially those directed against large companies or public sector organisations. However, a variety of private firms also offer 24/7 cyber incident response facilities—and police responders can consider advising companies to consider using those services in serious ongoing cases where the need arises. See Figure 4.2.

Figure 4.2 Initial responses to a cyber incident

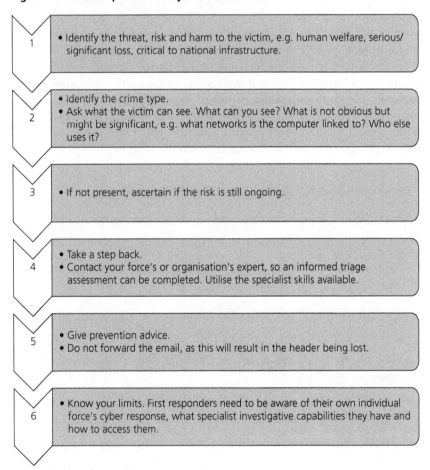

1 • Identify the threat, risk and harm to the victim, e.g. human welfare, serious/ significant loss, critical to national infrastructure.

2 • Identify the crime type.
• Ask what the victim can see. What can you see? What is not obvious but might be significant, e.g. what networks is the computer linked to? Who else uses it?

3 • If not present, ascertain if the risk is still ongoing.

4 • Take a step back.
• Contact your force's or organisation's expert, so an informed triage assessment can be completed. Utilise the specialist skills available.

5 • Give prevention advice.
• Do not forward the email, as this will result in the header being lost.

6 • Know your limits. First responders need to be aware of their own individual force's cyber response, what specialist investigative capabilities they have and how to access them.

4.5 **Roles of different agencies**

The importance of seeking specialist advice at the earliest stage of an investigation cannot be overstated, particularly to maximise and benefit from 'golden hour' opportunities. At a local level, most police forces now have either one or two of the following: a hi-tech crime unit or a digital investigation/cyber crime unit, where specialist knowledge and advice can be sought.

Checklist—roles of different agencies

- **Regional organised crime units (ROCUs)** with investigative cyber crime capabilities exist. Their role is to tackle the more serious and complex kinds of cyber criminality affecting more than one force in their area. Local police forces are connected into these units and are best placed to provide initial advice.

- **Action Fraud** is the UK's national reporting centre for all incidents of cyber crime and fraud. Reports of cyber crime and fraud can be made online or via telephone. Alongside Action Fraud sits the National Fraud Intelligence Bureau (NFIB), within the City of London Police, which is the national lead force for fraud.

- **The National Cyber Crime Unit (NCCU)** (part of the National Crime Agency) leads the UK's response to cyber crime, supports partners with specialist capabilities and coordinates the national response to the most serious cyber crime threats. By working closely with ROCUs, the Metropolitan Police Cyber Crime Unit (MPCCU), Action Fraud, the NFIB, partners within industry, government and international law enforcement, the NCCU has the capability to respond rapidly to changing threats.

- **The European Cybercrime Centre (EC3)** is the EU's facility for protecting European citizens from serious organised cyber criminality. EC3 brings together specialist knowledge and assets from member states across the EU to tackle international threats. EC3 also provides useful advice and training to European law enforcement agencies.

Further reading

- Action Fraud: www.actionfraud.police.uk/
- National Cyber Crime Unit: www.nationalcrimeagency.gov.uk/about-us/what-we-do/national-cyber-crime-unit
- European Cybercrime Centre: www.europol.europa.eu/ec3

The UK NCSC works closely with key partners to enhance the UK's ability to prepare for and manage national cyber security incidents.

KEY POINTS—RESPONSIBILITIES OF THE NCSC

The NCSC has four main responsibilities that flow from the UK's Cyber Security Strategy.

1 National cyber security incident management.
2 Support critical national infrastructure companies to handle cyber security incidents.
3 Promote cyber security situational awareness across industry, academia and the public sector.
4 Provide the single international point of contact for coordination and collaboration between national CERTs.

The Cyber-security Information Sharing Partnership (CiSP), accessed via the NCSC, is a joint industry/government initiative to share cyber threat and vulnerability information in order to increase overall awareness of the cyber threat and therefore reduce the impact on UK business. CiSP allows members from across sectors and organisations to exchange cyber threat information in real time, in a secure and dynamic environment, while operating within a framework that protects the confidentiality of shared information. CiSP membership is open to all businesses and organisations within the UK.

Further reading

• National Cyber Security Centre: www.ncsc.gov.uk
• Centre for the Protection of National Infrastructure: www.cpni.gov.uk/about/cni

---

4.6 Cyber crime prevention and protection

One of the Peelian principles upon which policing is based dictates that 'the test of police efficiency is the absence of crime and disorder'; this is a saying that remains true in situations where the crime in question has a strong cyber element.

KEY POINTS—BASIC PREVENTION MESSAGES

1 **Use reputable anti-virus software**: anti-virus products are designed to search for evidence of a wide range of cyber threats, including malware. A reputable product is a good first line of defence for the user, but it is not a panacea and will not protect against all attacks.
2 **Patch (update) software regularly**: most widely used operating systems and programs offer regular free updates to the user. As well as providing improvements in design or operation, these generally fix potential or real security vulnerabilities that have been identified.
3 **Use a firewall**: firewalls restrict the communication between computers and networks based on a set of pre-determined rules. In this way, a firewall can protect

---

the user from malicious communications from other parties. Reputable firewalls are available to purchase in a variety of places.

4 **Improve password security**: as far as possible, different passwords should be used for different services or websites—this is so that the consumer will only suffer a 'limited' compromise if a company is hacked and customers' passwords are stolen. In addition, passwords should be hard to guess and should contain a mix of letters, numbers and special characters. Ideally, passwords should be unique and should not comprise dictionary words, because these are easy for criminals to 'crack' with the right software. A variety of advice on how to safely store and construct a good password is available online.

5 **Back systems up regularly**: many cyber threats result in the victim losing the ability to access or use information held on their machine. Members of the public should therefore back up important information—either to a reputable cloud-based service, or to an external hard drive.

6 **Operate computers as a user rather than as an administrator**: PCs give owners the option to log on as a user for normal day-to-day use. This means that if they are unfortunate enough to become infected with malware, the virus will have a limited ability to spread across the system and make changes to it. For instance, some Trojan viruses make changes that enable more malware to be downloaded or allow anti-virus software to be uninstalled or avoided. These issues are less likely to occur if the victim is logged in as a user.

7 **Public wi-fi**: care should be taken when using public/non-secure wi-fi sites, as data can be intercepted by criminals.

4.6.1 **Where victims and potential victims can obtain advice**

A variety of resources are available, especially online. The details of a few are listed below. In addition to these, a number of news and intelligence services and online blogs provide current information in an easy-to-understand way. Additionally, courses are available to improve understanding (e.g. at the time of writing the Open University runs a free online 'Introduction to cyber security' course—www.futurelearn.com).

- **Action Fraud**: this is the central UK reporting mechanism for all allegations of fraud and cyber crime. In addition, the Action Fraud website (www.actionfraud.police.uk) provides advice and information to individuals and businesses on emerging and established threats.
- **Action Fraud alert**: the City of London Police, which operates Action Fraud, has a direct link to the UK Neighbourhood Watch network, which enables quick sharing of information on new threats to all members of the network. Individuals and small businesses should be encouraged to sign up to receive these email alerts (and others relating to different crime types in their local area) by visiting www.actionfraudalert.co.uk

- **Cyber-security Information Sharing Partnership (CiSP) (including regional CiSP nodes)**: the CiSP is a national initiative developed by the NCSC to share information on cyber threats with members of the business community. Interested parties can become members of the national CiSP, or of a regional 'node'—in essence, these are akin to social media portals and allow businesses to read about trends and threats that may affect them. The partnerships have strong involvement from central and local government, law enforcement and industry, and strong links to similar entities overseas. This ensures that the messages are shared in a relevant and timely manner.
- **Cyber Aware**: this is a cross-government campaign that aims to improve cyber security behaviour by individuals and businesses. Information and resources are available at www.cyberaware.gov.uk. The site also provides a link to **Cyber Essentials**, which allows businesses to identify their awareness and resilience to cyber threats.
- **Get Safe Online**: a resource offering expert advice on cyber security to both businesses and individuals in the UK. The resource is available at www.getsafeonline.org

---

KEY POINTS—CRIME PREVENTION ADVICE FOR A VICTIM WHO HAS HAD THEIR PASSWORD OR EMAIL COMPROMISED

- Don't panic!
- Install the latest software patches, and enable automatic updating to ensure the protection remains current.
- Change your password. Make sure you use a unique password for each account, especially those that hold financial information. Make passwords complex with numbers, letters and special characters. The two most commonly sought bits of information fraudsters want are your password and email address. Only use a 'remember' password facility on a machine that you are the sole user of, and don't share your passwords with any other people or leave your password in a place where it is accessible to others.
- Take care when disposing of devices holding email information and passwords, for example games consoles and smart televisions.
- If possible, change the default password on devices such as your internet router.
- Notify your family and friends. Email everyone in your contacts list so they can take steps to protect themselves.
- Monitor your bank accounts. Notify the relevant organisations or people if you notice anything suspicious.
- Scan your computer for malware.

Further reading

- Cyber Essentials Scheme: www.gov.uk/government/publications/cyber-essentials-scheme-overview

Prevention and disruption

5.1 **Introduction**

The first obligation of the police is to prevent crime and this has significant relevance for fraud. The 4Ps strategy for fraud has four elements, three of which are encompassed in traditional prevention activities: namely prevent, protect and prepare, being defined by the National Crime Agency as:

- prevent people becoming involved in serious, organised economic crime or reoffending by bringing together stakeholders—including government regulators, professional bodies and trade associations—to put in place a range of effective barriers and deterrents;
- protect UK society and economy from serious, organised economic crime by reducing the vulnerability of individuals, businesses, economic infrastructure and systems. This will also involve harnessing the collective capability of the public and private sectors to create an environment across the UK which is inimical to the presence of economic crime;
- prepare the UK for serious, organised economic crime, raising awareness about its corrosive nature and reducing tolerance of its impact on individuals, businesses and communities.

Additionally, within the Fraud Investigation Model (FIM), both prevention and disruption are key considerations in ensuring an effective response to fraud. The four questions referenced in the FIM should be considered at the earliest opportunity to prevent further offending, namely:

- What were the principle enablers that allowed this fraud to be perpetrated?
- Who else could be at risk from this or a similar fraud?
- What could have been done to remove or reduce the risk from this fraud?
- How can the lessons learned be used to prevent others from becoming a victim of a similar fraud?

The first part of this chapter describes the options available to prevent fraud and how, with knowledge of fraud typologies, use of existing crime prevention techniques and engagement, fraud prevention can be highly effective. The second part examines the opportunities for disrupting the activities of the fraudster by denying them access to the key enablers of fraud. For fraud prevention advice for specific fraud types refer to Chapter 3.

KEY POINTS—ROBERT PEEL'S PRINCIPLES RELEVANT TO FRAUD PREVENTION

Principle 1: to prevent crime and disorder, as an alternative to their repression by military force and severity of legal punishment.

Principle 3: to recognise always that to secure and maintain the respect and approval of the public means also the securing of the willing cooperation of the public in the task of securing observance of laws.

Principle 4: to recognise always that the extent to which the cooperation of the public can be secured diminishes proportionately to the necessity of the use of physical force and compulsion for achieving police objectives.

Those tasked with preventing fraud should seek to inform potential victims of the threat that fraudsters present by working with partners:

- to give relevant prevention information;
- to those at risk;
- in a timely manner; and
- in an effective and consistent way.

Designing out vulnerabilities should be a focus, as it can help individuals and organisations to avoid becoming future victims of fraud.

Many crime prevention activities have historically been shaped by focusing on the three areas referred to in the problem analysis triangle (PAT) as detailed in the College of Policing Authorised Professional Practice. This works particularly well in traditional crime and can be used as a foundation for initiating areas of prevention work in fraud-related threats. See Figure 5.1.

Figure 5.1 Crime prevention problem analysis triangle

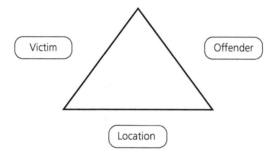

By using the PAT it is possible to look at each element and consider how it relates to fraud to determine which prevention activities would be most effective; the questions the investigator should ask include:

Victim
- Who is the victim and what is the victim group?
- Has the victim been specifically targeted or randomly selected?
- If specifically targeted, why and how?
- What can be done to prevent further frauds?
- Who is best placed to support the victim and offer prevention advice?

Location
- What is the location of the victim(s)?
- What is the location of the offender(s): digital, physical or both?

127

- What method has been used to perpetrate the fraud?
- What can be done to prevent further frauds?

Offender
- Who is the offender(s)?
- Why did they target the victim(s)?
- What is their motivation for committing fraud?
- What can be done to prevent further fraud offending?

Many fraudsters prey on victims who can be manipulated into passing over or giving access to money. Prevention activities should be focused on raising awareness of the fraudster's activities to make potential victims aware of the numerous fraud typologies. This will in turn 'target harden' individuals and organisations.

KEY POINTS—AIM OF PROTECT/PREVENT ACTIVITIES

The aim of protect/prevent activities is to minimise the impact of fraud by reducing the volume of crime, the value of the losses incurred and the impact on the quality of life for individual and organisational victims. This can be achieved through:

- an enhanced understanding of the threat, risk and harm landscape;
- empowering individuals and organisations to protect themselves;
- designed-in fraud protection.

5.2 Elements of fraud prevention

There is a strong link between providing fraud prevention advice and care for victims. This is particularly true for fraud, where repeat victimisation and the exchange of victims' details between criminals are prevalent.

Fraud prevention activities are based around three fundamental elements:

- intelligence-led and evidence-based;
- national coordination with local delivery;
- multi-agency participation.

5.2.1 Intelligence-led and evidence-based

Intelligence-led prevention will assist responders to understand who is most vulnerable to different types of fraud and why. Once this is understood, responders can direct prevention activities at the most exposed victim group and be able to identify the key enablers of that type of fraud so it can be disrupted or designed out; alternatively, additional controls can be implemented.

Evidence-based prevention, achieved through research and crime-pattern analysis, enables the responders to understand what prevention methods are effective. Developing an understanding of the fraud threat will ensure the message reaches the potential victim group in a way that will change people's behaviours and keep them protected from fraud.

Further reading

- Current fraud threats and prevention advice are available from the National Fraud Intelligence Bureau (NFIB) outputs team; contact the Action Fraud single point of contact (SPOC) for their contact details.
- Metropolitan Police Service, *The Little Book of Big Scams*, 2016: www.met. police.uk/docs/little_book_scam.pdf

---

5.2.2 **Policing national coordination with local delivery**

The responsibility for protecting communities from fraud rests with the local police force and their partners. This local responsibility is not diminished by virtue of fraud being reported centrally through Action Fraud, the National Fraud and Cyber Crime Reporting Centre.

Local priorities for prevention activities will be set by Police and Crime Commissioners (PCCs) with their chief constables. To assist their decision making, the City of London Police (CoLP) is one of the organisations that provides local threat assessments articulating the type and volume of fraud occurring in each force area, as well as an assessment of victimology within their area.

Alongside these local threat assessments, the development of national awareness-raising campaigns are directed at the:

- most harmful frauds occurring in the country;
- frauds affecting the most vulnerable members of society.

These campaigns are designed in collaboration with police forces throughout England and Wales, and are best delivered in a coordinated fashion. This allows the police to deliver targeted and consistent messages to those most at risk of becoming victims of fraud.

5.2.3 **Multi-agency participation**

Fraud prevention activities are most effective if they are delivered in partnership with non-police agencies and organisations from across multiple sectors. These have extended their reach to a wide range of victims and potential victims, and can influence their behaviours. See Figure 5.2 and Table 5.1.

Figure 5.2 Multi-agency participation contributing to reach and influence

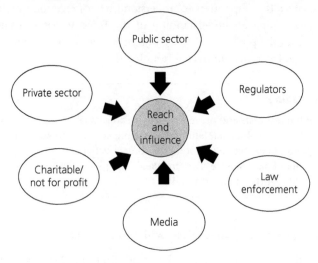

Table 5.1 Table of useful organisations

Organisation	Website	Overview
Get Safe Online (GSO)	www.getsafeonline.org	GSO is the UK's leading source of unbiased, factual and easy-to-understand information on online safety.
Neighbourhood Watch	www.ourwatch.org.uk/	Neighbourhood Watch is a voluntary organisation meant to make communities safer and provide a nationwide network.
Trading Standards	www.tradingstandardsecrime.org.uk/alerts/	Trading Standards officers are employees of the local council and investigate consumer law-related offences.
Metropolitan Police Service (MPS)	http://content.met.police.uk/Site/fraudalert	The MPS is dedicated to fraud-related matters.
Financial Fraud Action UK (FFA UK)	www.financialfraudaction.org.uk	FFA UK is responsible for leading the collective fight against financial fraud on behalf of the UK payments industry. Membership includes banks, credit, debit and charge card issuers, and card payment acquirers in the UK.

5.3 **Methods and types of prevention available**

There are a number of strategies that can be used when delivering fraud prevention. Examples include:

- **education and awareness** (aimed at enabling individuals and organisations to follow advice and protect themselves from fraudsters);
- **designing out vulnerabilities** (identifying vulnerabilities that fraudsters exploit);
- **disruptions** (aimed at disrupting identified enablers of fraud and intervening in crimes in action—see 5.7, 5.8 and 5.9).

5.3.1 **Education and awareness**

Pivotal to prevention activities is the need to empower individuals and organisations to protect themselves. Unlike other traditional crimes, a high-profile visible police presence cannot reassure the public or deter criminals from committing cyber-enabled fraud. The onus must, therefore, be on individuals and organisations to protect themselves, whilst modifying those behaviours that put them at risk of fraud.

Policing can empower the community by providing them with consistent, pragmatic and timely advice on how to prevent fraud, as well as making them aware of threats.

KEY POINTS—IMPLEMENTING AWARENESS PROGRAMMES

Considerations for implementing an awareness programme should include:

- engaging with relevant stakeholders;
- instigating a national awareness-raising campaign to influence general behaviours, which enable individuals and organisations protect themselves from fraud;
- developing a coordinated local campaign to address specific threats, developed in line with intelligence assessments;
- providing a central resource and signposting fraud prevention resources;
- ensuring that timely prevention advice is given to victims.

5.3.2 **Designing out vulnerabilities**

The production of threat assessments and working with partner organisations enable investigators to identify vulnerabilities that fraudsters target; for example, in business processes or social media. Identifying these vulnerabilities and assessing their impact allows the investigator to develop an understanding of how criminals exploit the vulnerabilities, and to establish which vulnerabilities are causing the most harm and should be prioritised for action.

Figure 5.3 Stages of the SARA crime prevention model used to design out vulnerabilities

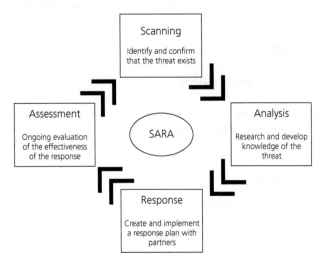

Investigators should encourage the designing in of measures to reduce the risk of fraud. The scanning, analysis, response, assessment (SARA) crime prevention model's elements form an effective framework that can be used to assist in designing out fraud-related vulnerabilities. See Figure 5.3.

However, there is often a balance to be struck between security and user convenience. Exploring how customers might be helped to make informed choices based on their individual risk appetite is a core component of this work.

....

Case study—designing out a vulnerability (courier fraud)

Courier fraud is when fraudsters phone and attempt to trick a potential victim into handing their cards and PIN numbers to a courier on their doorstep. There are many variations of the fraud, but it usually follows the method shown below.

- A fraudster will cold call on a landline, claiming to be from a bank or the police. They state that their systems have spotted a fraudulent transaction on the card.
- In order to reassure the potential victim, they suggest that they hang up and ring the bank/police back straight away. However, they do not disconnect the call from the landline. When the victim dials the real phone number, they are actually still speaking to the fraudster.
- The fraudster then asks for the PIN to be read out or typed on the phone keypad. They may ask for details of other accounts the victim holds with the bank or financial service provider.
- Finally, they send a courier to collect the bank card. The fraudster will have then obtained all the details needed to further a fraudulent transaction.

The ability of the fraudster to remain on the line is an essential part of them being able to commit this crime. This was possible due to a legacy issue with telephone systems that allowed a phone line to be left open after the recipient hung up.

Identification of this problem allowed policing (primarily the MPS) to engage with telecoms providers to highlight the issue. The issue was remedied and phone lines are now generally only allowed to remain open for two seconds. This change has helped to prevent further frauds.

5.4 **Measuring the impact of prevention**

Measuring impact is an important element of all prevention activities, regardless of whether the activity is awareness raising, designing out vulnerabilities or carrying out disruption.

Several factors should be considered when measuring impact, be it short, medium or long term. These include:

- level of reduction in harm and risk;
- whether crime or incident levels have decreased;
- cost–benefit analysis.

Measuring impact, through the production of a results analysis following any prevention activity, also enables organisational learning through:

- identifying effective practices and highlighting areas for improvement;
- preventing continued use of ineffective strategies;
- ensuring investment in what works;
- facilitating knowledge management;
- providing valuable input to knowledge products and organisational memory;
- supporting resource decisions;
- monitoring the progress of plans;
- assessing the effectiveness of pilot projects.

For results analysis to be successful, the prevention activity must have specific objectives and a process to measure them, which ought to be agreed at the outset. Any results analysis, and impact measurement, must be an honest assessment of the activities and should identify problems that occurred and any areas for improvement.

The output of a results analysis should be made available to the person in charge of the prevention activities and shared with partners to identify lessons that can be learned. They should, where possible, also be stored and made accessible in a searchable format for future reference when planning similar activities.

KEY POINTS—ASSESSMENT METHODS FOR FRAUD PREVENTION ACTIVITIES

Means of assessing the effectiveness of prevention activities can include:

- changes in behaviour;
- reductions in fraud;
- return on investment (ROI);
- counting generated website 'traffic';
- counting 'call to action' returns;
- assessing survey questionnaires based on behaviours.

5.5 Centres of best practice

Throughout this part of the chapter, a number of principles have been articulated regarding effective delivery of fraud prevention activities. There are a number of centres of best practice that can be of practical assistance to the investigator.

Checklist—centres of best practice for fraud prevention advice.

Get Safe Online (GSO) (www.getsafeonline.org/)

GSO is a joint public–private sector partnership supported by Her Majesty's Government and other organisations in banking, retail and law enforcement. They provide messaging and advice on all types of fraud and cyber threats to a range of target audiences. GSO is not just a website tool; it also provides support across all sectors in relation to fraud awareness, online safety and outreach work. It works alongside policing to deliver professional awareness-raising campaigns.

Metropolitan Police Fraud Alert (http://content.met.police.uk/Site/fraudalert)

The MPS provides a comprehensive resource centre to assist in the combating of fraud and other economic crime, it provides an excellent source of prevention material including a series titled the *Little Book of Scams* for both individuals and businesses as well as regular fraud alerts.

National Crime Agency Economic Crime Command (NCA ECC) (www.national-crimeagency.gov.uk/about-us/what-we-do/economic-crime)

The NCA ECC provides a number of useful resources including fraud alerts to inform those involved in fraud prevention.

Fraud Advisory Panel (FAP) (www.fraudadvisorypanel.org/?s=&post_type=resources& res=guidance)

FAP produce a number of resources to raise awareness of fraud and information on common fraud types and how to protect against them.

Action Fraud (www.actionfraud.police.uk/)

Action Fraud provides a very comprehensive resource centre for fraud and cyber-related offending including prevention advice and detailing the support available for victims.

Economic and Cyber Crime Prevention Centre (ECPC)

On behalf of policing, and working with the counter-fraud community, the ECPC:

- works with the NFIB, using their national and local profiles to identify those threats and potential victims most likely to benefit from prevention interventions;

- in partnership with GSO develops national prevention campaigns, working alongside the police and other partners;

- produces prevention material when it is appropriate to do so;

- works with forces to agree local priorities and helps design and support the delivery of local crime prevention activities;

- identifies, collates and shares best practice and advice.

The ECPC also coordinates the Multi-Agency Campaigns Group.

Multi-Agency Campaigns Group

The core function of the Multi-Agency Campaigns Group is to identify key economic and cyber crime threats affecting and predicted to affect UK communities that require a public prevention campaign. It is also meant to maximise efficiency by making the best use of finite resources to deliver campaigns. The role of the group is to develop and deliver an effective approach to:

- protect UK communities (organisations and individuals);

- overcome challenges in delivering campaigns/activities;

- build improved relationships, processes and policies between relevant organisations;

- lobby for new practices/policies where appropriate;

- review the effectiveness of campaigns and activities;

- enhance the national response.

Fraud Prevention Network

The Fraud Prevention Network harnesses police, local authority and other crime pre-vention resources, and equips them—as members of this network—for the delivery of economic and cyber-related crime prevention. The network is coordinated by the ECPC. In this way, the network engages with organisations at both the national level and the local level, for example the national and local chambers of commerce.

5.6 Organisational fraud health checks

The fraud health check process is a proactive counter-fraud measure that tests and examines the robustness of an organisation's ability to identify and appropriately respond to a potential threat, and is a useful tool for those engaged in fraud reduction activities. As part of building an effective counter-fraud culture, organisations and agencies should be encouraged to examine and review their own internal policies and procedures in relation to fraud prevention and awareness. The basic principles of a fraud health check model can be adapted to meet the specific needs of an organisation and provide an opportunity to identify how well prepared they are (to both make themselves a harder target for the fraudster and to promote an effective anti-fraud culture). See Figure 5.4.

Figure 5.4 Fraud health check topic areas

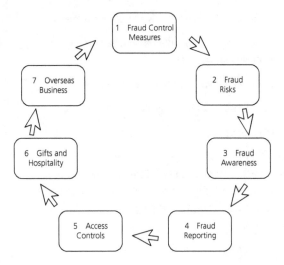

5.6.1 The process

It is important to identify and engage with the right person within the organisation who can facilitate access to both the documentation and people required during the health check. The issue of the confidentiality of the matters disclosed should be discussed and agreed before the health check takes place. Personnel with the appropriate knowledge should be identified to undertake the process, which should begin with an initial consultation at the management level to set the extent/scope of the review. Table 5.2 shows areas suggested to form the basis of the review and be considered within the scope of the check; however, each process should be targeted and relevant to the nature of the business and organisational risk.

This is not an exhaustive list and the areas examined should be tailored to meet the needs of the organisation and the nature of its business and function.

Table 5.2 Undertaking a fraud health check

Activity	Actions
Review the fraud control strategy	Review all control documents and examine them to determine if the following are detailed: • responsibility structures; • fraud risk assessment; • regulatory requirements (if any); • employee awareness; • hospitality procedures; • conduct and disciplinary standards.
Identify the fraud control measures within the organisation	Determine the actual lines of authority and coordination mechanisms for fraud control established within the organisation. Are delegated authorities and definitions sufficiently clear?
Evaluate the actions taken by the organisation to identify fraud risk areas	Establish whether a fraud risk assessment has been carried out: • What form of assessment was used? • What were the timing, date and scope of the assessment? • Were the methodology and conduct of the review sound? • Did the assessment include assessing the vulnerability to cyber-related attacks?
Identify actions taken to raise fraud awareness across the organisation	Has the organisation implemented any form of fraud training and awareness? Has the organisation developed systems and assigned responsibility for researching and/or monitoring best practice for particular areas of activity, e.g. industry-specific environmental scanning, which would assist in protecting systems and operations against fraud?
Determine the effectiveness of systems within the organisation for the reporting of suspected or known fraud/financial irregularity	Does the organisation have an active fraud reporting system in place? In particular: • Have procedures for reporting fraud and irregularity been documented and distributed in an appropriate manner to all employees? • Are all regulatory requirements relevant to the organisation being met in this area?
Examine access control arrangements to areas containing sensitive commercial/financial information	View access control arrangements and pass systems: • Do they restrict access to areas holding sensitive commercial/financial information? • Are all visitor details recorded? What are the retention periods, if any?
Establish levels of understanding with regard to the organisational policy on hospitality	Does the organisation record occasions where hospitality is offered or received? In particular: • What policies are in place to explain and regulate this process? • Is there a system of regular updating and reminding of hospitality procedures?
Establish levels of understanding with regard to organisational policy in relation to overseas business (if relevant)	Is business conducted outside the UK? If so: • Are there specific policies, procedures and ethical guidelines in place? • Is there a system of inspection to ensure that overseas business is transacted strictly in accordance with relevant legislation and policy?

Table 5.3 Traffic-light reporting system for undertaking a fraud health check

Balanced Score Card Colour	DEFINITION OF TARGET ACHIEVEMENT
Green	On target for standard set
Yellow	Minor deviation from standard set
Orange	Major deviation from standard set
Red	Seriousness weakness in performance against standard set
	No data available to inform on standard set

In order to conduct the health check, the relevant documents and policies should be gathered for review by the team. Interviews should be conducted with key members of staff across the organisation, from senior management to 'shop floor' personnel. It is important to speak with a wide variety of staff in order to gain a picture of the culture within the organisation. A final report should then be produced identifying areas of best practice and areas for development that require action.

The traffic-light reporting system can be used to show how well a particular area is performing within the review. It consists of four colours that cover performance levels and one colour that means there is no information currently available to inform on performance. The colours used and their suggested definitions are detailed in Table 5.3.

5.7 **Disruption**

Disruption activity has developed considerably over recent years as an additional way of combating fraud. This is a benefit for both the investigators and potential victims, as it provides an alternative tactic for those frauds that do not meet the threshold for investigation and prosecution. Due to the volumes of reported fraud and the current investigative capacity, activity such as requesting the suspension of websites and other cyber-enabled crime is an efficient and effective alternative means of disrupting criminality and/or preventing the organised crime group (OCG) from committing fraud.

A disruption is intended as a proportionate response used to prevent further fraud. The following sections will look at opportunities for disrupting the enablers that fraudsters exploit. These enablers, which are key to a fraudster's ability to perpetrate their fraud, include:

- websites;
- telecommunications:
- bank accounts.

5.7.1 **Enabler identification**

In order to disrupt the enablers being exploited by fraudsters, they first have to be identified. There are four main methods that policing can use to identify enablers of fraud.

- **Action Fraud reporting**: this provides the first route for identifying the enablers of fraud. From the data provided, information is extracted identifying the websites, telephone numbers and bank accounts that are linked to criminal activity.
- **Intelligence development**: while conducting offender-based investigations, investigators may identify enablers that are being used to facilitate the offending. This information should be captured and a policy decision made by the investigator on whether to allow the fraudster to continue to use the enabler to commit further crime, or to request that the appropriate private sector partner disrupt the use of the enabler.
- **Horizon scanning**: this enables the police and others to have the ability to proactively disrupt future criminality at the very early stages. With regard to websites, this is achieved through collaboration with the domain registrars.
- **External referrals**: partner organisations may identify enablers that they refer to policing via routes other than crime reporting. For example, where a legitimate company identifies a mirrored/spoofed website.

Case study—domain registrar

A domain registrar working with the CoLP proactively sought to identify websites that had been set up for a criminal purpose. For example, where a website was created in the name of a genuine company but used different digits to make it appear genuine, for example Tesc0 instead of Tesco.

5.7.2 **Stages of disruption**

Regardless of which enabler is being disrupted, there are four stages to the disruption process as shown in Figure 5.5.

5.7.3 **Due diligence**

There is a need to conduct due diligence checks on the identified enabler (see the specific guidance in 5.8 and 5.9 on due diligence for websites and telephones).

5.7.4 **Requesting disruption activity**

A number of law enforcement organisations have the ability to disrupt enablers. One of these is through the NFIB, which provides the disruption

Figure 5.5 Stages of the disruption process

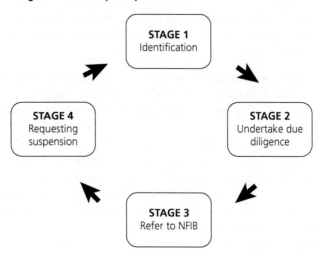

service for policing. Following identification of enablers, and the completion of appropriate due diligence regarding the enabler, the NFIB then shares data with relevant counter-fraud partners on behalf of the police, who disrupt the enabler to prevent future fraud and/or intervene in crimes in action. In order for this disruption process to be effective, it is essential that each assessing officer or staff member (i.e. the person identifying the enabler) accepts responsibility for conducting relevant due diligence before any disruption action is taken or the information is shared with the disruptions team. This involves the adoption of a transparent process that ensures all exploration of a fraudulent entity is recorded and made available for examination or audit purposes.

5.7.5 Gateways and authorities required

A suspension request of an enabler is shared between counter-fraud partners using intelligence-sharing protocols; for example, through intelligence report templates, the Data Protection Act 1998 and memorandums of understanding.

5.8 Website take down

The types of websites that may be used for criminality are:

- **genuine websites**: these are created with criminal intent to offer commodities that will not be supplied;
- **mirrored/spoofed websites**: these essentially involve viewing a real website through a different domain name system (DNS) (website address), as a

mirror image. The mirrored method involves impersonating the legitimate website perfectly, because the legitimate website is viewed through the window of the fake domain name. Criminals have been known to use this method to facilitate crime by purporting to be the genuine company/business.

Case study—the university

Information was received from an external partner, Higher Education Degree Datacheck (HEDD), regarding a website claiming to offer students huge scholarships and enticing them to sign up by giving them limited time to apply. It was established that they were not an authorised provider of degree qualifications.

The institution claimed to be on a specific road in a town in England. This was actually the address of another university, a recognised degree-awarding body. Breaches, as applied in the registrant terms and conditions, were identified. In addition, it is also an offence in England and Wales (under the Further and Higher Education Act 1992 and the Companies Act 2006) to use the 'university' title or the protected word 'university' without permission. As a result of law enforcement action, the website was terminated.

5.8.1 Stages to website take down

Checklist—website disruption

Stage 1. Identification
The identification stage is covered in 5.7.1.

Stage 2. Due diligence
Ultimately, each person assessing the website(s) is responsible for the initial outbound request(s) and must remember that if there is any doubt about suspension of a website then they should not take action/suspend it. The areas to be covered through due diligence are detailed below:

I Assess the referred website for compliance with the domain registrar's terms and conditions

- Each registrar will have their own terms and conditions and in most instances they abide by the top-level domain (TLD) rules. By consulting the registrar's terms and conditions, the identifying officer is able to evidence how these are being breached.

- Using a standalone terminal, ensuring no footprint is left (refer to force policy re the procedure for this), the identifying officer can look at each page of the website, paying particular attention to the 'Contact us' page. There are occasions when a website provides false information (e.g. a telephone number, address or other data) that can be checked relatively easily by calling (using a non-attributable phone in accordance with organisational policies), visiting the address or undertaking open-source inquiries.

- If the details on the 'Contact us' page are incorrect, then it's possible that the 'WHOIS' information is also incorrect. Therefore, a potential breach of the terms and conditions may have occurred.

II Assess the referred website against Know Fraud reports (obtainable from the NFIB)

- Reviewing Know Fraud reports allows the identifying officer to determine if there have been reports about the website, and can help to establish:
  - if the reports relate to fraudulent activity (i.e. there is criminal intent);
  - if the complaints have been generated because of bad business practice (no criminal intent).

- If there is no criminal intent, the reports are generally forwarded to organisations such as Trading Standards or the Insolvency Service, which will determine what action can be taken.

- A key function of the NFIB is to disseminate crime reports to police forces or other law enforcement agencies for investigation. When these disseminations contain details of a website that is believed to be involved in facilitating fraud, forces are advised that they have 14 days from the date of dissemination before a suspension request is instigated. This allows the investigating force to make an operational decision regarding the continued use of the website. If no response is provided by the investigating force, the NFIB will instigate the suspension process.

III Assess the referred website to ascertain who is operating it

- Suspending a website via the registrar is the preferred method of web disruption. Establishing the domain registrar can be done by checking the DNS name on the following free search tool websites: http://who.is/ and http://centralops.net/co/

- Conducting this form of due diligence also provides intelligence opportunities for the investigating officer, as additional knowledge can be obtained (including the registrant's name and address, and the internet protocol (IP) number and date with which the website was registered), which can be useful for assessing against fraud reports.

- If policing is dealing with a .co.uk domain, the Nominet database is an extremely useful tool that can be used to find other fraudulent websites that may be associated with the website and are being assessed for suspension.

Stage 3. Referring to the NFIB

The disruptions team accepts website suspension requests from law enforcement agencies and non-law enforcement organisations. All referrals should be made by completing a pre-prepared template. This template ensures that a full summary of the facts is provided, along with the full contact details of the identifying officer/member of staff and agreement to the indemnity contained on the form.

Stage 4. Requesting suspension

There are two methods for the disruptions team to request suspension of a website by a registrar:

- an email containing all the pertinent points of why a website is suspected of being fraudulent;

- a formal request for a suspension document.

The relevant method will be chosen by the disruptions team.

A registrar may choose not to suspend a website if they deem that inadequate information has been provided for them to make an informed decision. A registrar will sometimes demand a court order.

Alternatively, the registrar may simply refuse to comply with the request. In this instance, and when dealing with a .co.uk domain, the registrar will adjudicate on the matter as to whether they will support the request to suspend the domain.

Domains sometimes fall into the category of a top-level domain (TLD), i.e. in the domain name www.example.com, the top-level domain is .com and thus outside UK jurisdiction. In these circumstances, the only option is to continue communication with the organisation's registrar in order to persuade them to take action and discuss the matter with their compliance/legal department. This requires policing to communicate concerns in a clear and proportionate way, using the information that has been gathered. All reasonable methods of engagement should be considered, including liaising with a registrar via a live link on their website.

Checklist—additional due diligence

Other checks to consider will include:

- the Companies House database (http://direct.companieshouse.gov.uk/), which provides details of company addresses, directorships, secretaries, how often accounts have been filed and other useful information;

- the Financial Services Register provides comprehensive information on firms, individuals and other bodies: https://register.fca.org.uk

Liability for any request for suspension is the responsibility of the person and organisation making the request and they should ensure that all the appropriate due diligence has been undertaken.

Case study—OK Loans

The following website was identified/reported to the NFIB disruptions team as being involved in criminal activity, namely fraud (section 2(1) of the Fraud Act 2006).

Approximately 11 complaints (resulting in about £2,000 of losses) were received regarding the domain www.ok-loans.co.uk. Initial inquiries confirmed this activity to be an advance fee fraud, which is a criminal offence in the UK (fraud by false representation, section 2 of the Fraud Act). This domain was being used to request upfront payment/fees from individuals who believed they were applying for some kind of loan facility. This constitutes an advanced fee fraud, as the facility is not received.

The so-called www.ok-loans.co.uk provided registration information on the 'WHOIS' database, in particular a registrant address. NFIB disruptions contacted the owners of this address, who clarified that they took over the building two years previously when it was derelict. The building's owners confirmed that www.ok-loans.co.uk had not been at the address during that period of time.

Based on the inaccurate information being provided by www.ok-loans.co.uk and the fraud element, a full summary was provided to one of the counter-fraud community partner agencies. The website was disrupted and removed from the internet.

5.9 Telephone disruption

Disruption of the use of telephones by the disruption team is undertaken in respect of landline and voice over internet protocols (VoIPs). Fraudsters tend to use VoIPs as opposed to fixed-line numbers. This method allows the fraudster to trick victims into believing that they are phoning from certain locations in the UK; for example, the number will display a 0207 prefix, indicating that the caller is phoning from London. This provides the fraudster with a level of authenticity that helps to trick the victim, even though the offender may be based anywhere in the world.

When considering the suspension of a telephone number, the identifying officer must consider whether the request is justified, proportionate and necessary. The final decision rests with the person requesting suspension and, if in doubt, they should defer a request for suspension until more evidence is available.

Checklist—telephone disruption

Stage 1. Identification

The identification stage is covered in 5.7.1.

Stage 2. Due diligence

It is important to establish that the identified telephone numbers are being used by a fraudster and do not belong to an innocent party. Disconnecting numbers that are in use for legitimate purposes causes a reputational risk for policing and creates potential for litigation.

When establishing whether the number is used by fraudsters, the investigator should check to see if the victim has dialled it and spoken to a potential fraudster. If not, the officer should carefully consider whether it will be beneficial to dial the number to establish who answers and what company name they will use in their greetings. In line with the Police and Criminal Evidence (PACE) Act 1984, and as part of establishing the ownership of the number, policing is able to engage in short conversations as long as these do not become interviews.

If the telephone number claims to be associated with a company that exists, the investigator can try to contact the company via a recognised contact (e.g. the Financial Conduct Authority (FCA) register) to confirm that the number is not associated with them.

If the telephone number is listed on a fraudulent website or in a publication, it may still be a legitimate number. There have been rare occasions when fraudsters have mixed real telephone numbers with fake ones, just in case the victim decides to compare these to the telephone numbers for the legitimate company found in a phone book or elsewhere.

The investigator can use the list on www.telecom-tariffs.co.uk/codelook.htm to find the details of the service provider.

Once all the checks have been completed, the identifying officer needs to establish the service provider. VoIP numbers are often resold, and there may be a chain of resellers involved.

Officers should exercise caution when considering suspension of numbers that feature in historical crime and intelligence reporting, as the numbers may have been resold and now be in legitimate use.

Stage 3. Referring to the NFIB

As with website referrals, the disruptions team will accept referrals for telephony suspension requests from law enforcement agencies and non-law enforcement organisations. All referrals should be made by completing a pre-prepared template. This template ensures that a full summary of facts is provided, along with full contact details for the identifying officer/member of staff and agreement to the indemnity contained on the form.

Stage 4. Requesting suspension

The routes to requesting telephone suspensions are:

- **bulk extractions** forwarded to the Telephone UK Fraud Forum (TUFF). TUFF is requested to work with their members and assist with those telephone numbers considered most risky;
- **direct liaison** with the telephony provider.

In the instance of telephony disruptions, policing is asking industry to help prevent fraud. Suspensions are undertaken on the basis of a breach of their terms and conditions and intelligence provided by policing. As such, policing needs to ensure that it has conducted all due diligence, has articulated its findings effectively and is able to evidence that the suspension is necessary, justified and proportionate.

KEY POINTS—NFIB DISRUPTION TEAM CONTACT

The NFIB disruption team is available to provide advice and guidance to any policing resource wishing to disrupt a cyber enabler, contact the Action Fraud SPOC in your force for the disruptions team contact details.

Investigation and case management

6.1 **Introduction**

This chapter describes key elements of the Fraud Investigation Model (FIM), including gathering evidence and supporting victims. It details how reports of fraud are assessed by the National Fraud Intelligence Bureau (NFIB), how to develop a case acceptance criteria and the considerations when undertaking an investigation. It describes how to develop strategies commonly required in fraud investigations, including:

- suspect management;
- digital forensics;
- victim(s);
- covert;
- media.

The investigation of fraud requires a logical route map, as shown in Figure 6.1, and the chapter follows this journey.

Those leading fraud investigations, whether the officer in the case (OIC) in volume cases, or a senior investigating officer (SIO) in more complex cases, have a number of key responsibilities. These can be summarised under the mnemonic SHERLOCK.

Figure 6.1 Route map for undertaking a fraud investigation

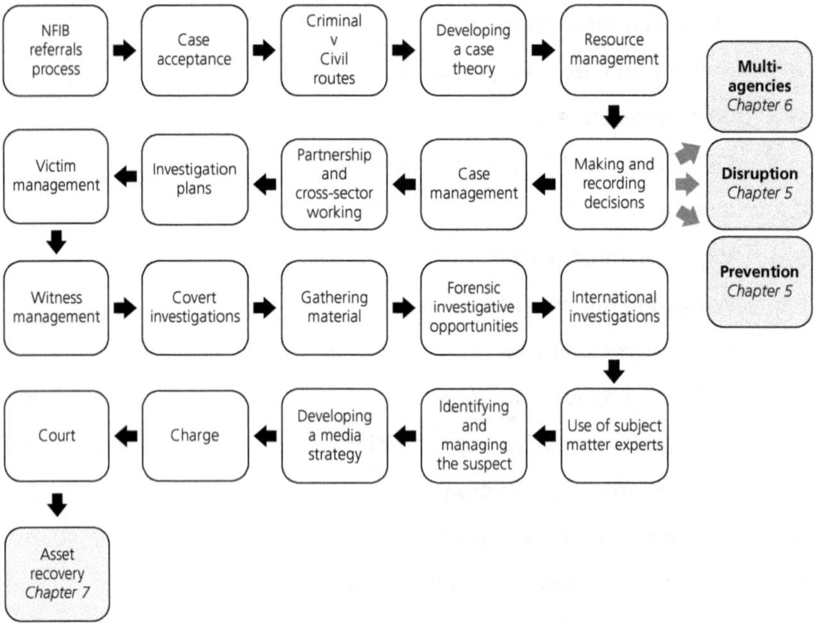

KEY POINTS—RESPONSIBILITIES FOR THOSE UNDERTAKING FRAUD INVESTIGATIONS

- Strategy: to develop both overarching and individual strategies.
- Hypothesis: to create a case theory to maximise investigative opportunities.
- Experience: to identify and engage with subject matter experts (SMEs).
- Risk management: to manage the risk to the investigation, victim and offender.
- Leadership: to demonstrate effective leadership to the investigation team.
- Offences: to identify if an offence has been committed.
- Critical incidents: to recognise and identify if a critical incident has occurred.
- Key decisions: to make and record effective decisions and supporting rationales.

Those leading an investigation have to set the investigative strategy and/or write an investigation plan, which comprises a number of key decisions across a range of areas. These can, in turn, be supported by a detailed strategy document. Investigative strategies should link directly with the case theory, referred to as the *hypothesis*. The key decisions may detail what is to be done and why, and the supporting strategy documents detail how it is to be done. These decisions and strategies should be recorded on the case management system and in the key decision log (KDL) or equivalent.

The investigation of fraud and similar offences can present a number of unique challenges to the investigator. The number of victims, the scale of loss and jurisdictional complexities can often present difficulties in the management of any investigation and the setting of parameters. It is, therefore, essential in complex cases to develop a set of comprehensive strategies focusing on key areas to enhance investigative opportunities, manage victims and set clear objectives to reduce public harm and bring offenders to justice.

KEY POINTS—ROLE OF THE SIO AND THE OIC

Complex fraud investigations should be led by an SIO, who is the lead investigator in major, complex or highly sensitive investigations. Investigations of this type are normally directed by an officer of the rank of inspector or above, who performs the role of SIO, and deputies, who fill the role of deputy senior investigation officer (D/SIO).

In addition to performing the role of OIC of an investigation, as described by the Codes of Practice under Part II of the Criminal Procedure and Investigations Act (CPIA) 1996, the SIO will also be responsible for developing and implementing investigative strategies, as well as information management and decision-making systems. Additional responsibilities include managing resources and being accountable to chief officers for the conduct of the investigation.

If the inquiry is not led by an SIO, the term OIC should be used by the investigator. The OIC is responsible for directing the criminal investigation; other responsibilities

---

include ensuring proper procedures are in place for recording and retaining records of information and other material throughout the investigation.

Appointment of the SIO/OIC

When an inquiry is allocated through the tasking process, the SIO/OIC will be clearly nominated and the details recorded.

Where the Home Office Large Major Enquiry System (HOLMES) is being used to manage the inquiry, the Major Incident Room Standardised Administrative Procedures (MIRSAP) will be followed regarding the recording of strategic decisions.

Reviews

SIOs/OICs should consider seeking reviews of their investigations; these can be a peer review or a more formal review with agreed terms of reference. Complex investigations should be presented to the tasking meeting for a 'peer' review to take place at regular intervals in accordance with organisational policy; the OIC should detail the initial information, lines of inquiry and progress to date. See Chapter 10 for further information.

6.2 National Fraud Intelligence Bureau referrals process

Action Fraud is the UK's Fraud and Cyber Crime Reporting Centre. The NFIB works proactively with Action Fraud and its cross-sector partners to protect victims and build the UK's resilience against fraud and financial crime locally, regionally and nationally.

There are three main methods of reporting fraud crime:

- via telephone to the Action Fraud Call Centre (tel: 0300 1232040);
- via the Action Fraud online reporting tool (www.actionfraud.police.uk);
- directly to the police ('call for service').

All reports of fraud are transferred from Action Fraud to the NFIB and ingested into a data warehouse called Know Fraud. The Know Fraud system processes and analyses this data against a number of 'confirmed fraud' data sets held within the system that are provided by public and private sector partners.

The Know Fraud database has an intelligence analytical tool that assesses reports and links them together via common entities to form networks. Crimes reported to the NFIB are subject to a two-stage assessment process: stage 1 is automated and stage 2 involves a manual review by a crime reviewer.

A score is given to each network through the use of a matrix, the content of which is biased towards the identification of networks that contain viable lines of inquiry. The scoring matrix is subject to revision and is periodically updated to reflect changes in NFIB priorities and/or in response to an evolving threat.

The NFIB crime review function makes use of the score attributed by this process to focus its efforts on those networks that appear to present an investigative opportunity for a police force or a non-police investigative agency (e.g. Trading Standards), or those that may present a threat to individuals, small- and medium-sized enterprises/corporate bodies or the economy as a whole.

In addition to the automated scoring process, in order to mitigate risk, a number of fraud codes are reviewed in their entirety. Additionally, crimes reported with a loss of a specific value are manually reviewed. This threshold will alter according to demand and resources.

Networks that meet the scoring threshold or those crimes subject to the mandatory review process will be subject to manual analysis by a crime reviewer. The crime reviewer will scope the network to establish its extent and the nature of any previous review undertaken and will, based on the information available, determine whether the allegation(s) amount to an offence contrary to statute. If appropriate, the network will be further assessed for viable lines of inquiry.

All networks identified as having viable lines of inquiry are enhanced through research, with a view to establishing whether the network presents an investigative opportunity for a police force or another non-police investigative body.

Checklist—NFIB referral development

The crime reviewer will identify and collate information from a variety of sources, including but not limited to:

- Police National Computer (PNC);
- Police National Database (PND);
- suspicious activity reports (SARs);
- Credit Industry Fraud Avoidance System (CIFAS);
- local crime recording systems (e.g. UNIFI);
- credit reference agencies;
- virtual office providers;
- Companies House;
- regulatory bodies;
- inquiries with financial institutions;
- telecoms operators;
- open source.

The extent of the inquiries undertaken by the crime reviewer will be determined by the quality and viability of the information contained in the network. Inquiries will be undertaken until such point that a decision can be made, with a verifiable rationale, as to whether the network is viable for further investigation.

KEY POINT—HOME OFFICE COUNTING RULES (HOCR) FOR FRAUD

The crime reviewer will determine the police force area that is to record the case for investigation in accordance with the five principles detailed in the HOCR:

1st The police force area covering the location of the fraudulent operation/suspect's address. For business-related fraud, the office address of the employee. If there is no office address, the head office of the company.

2nd The police force area with the greatest number of individual usages or offences.

3rd The police force area where the first offence was committed.

4th The police force area where the victim resides or works.

5th NFIB-determined force area.

If the victim is identified as vulnerable by Action Fraud, it will then forward the details to the NFIB, which will ensure that each report is reviewed. If there are viable lines of inquiry, the report will be sent for enforcement; if not, it will still send the report but for victim care.

If the crime reviewer identifies an enabler used in the preparation or commission of the offence, consideration will be given to submitting a referral to the NFIB Cyber Prevention and Disruption Team (see Chapter 5).

Following the completion of the automated and manual review of reported crimes, a completed Action Fraud crime package will be disseminated to the relevant law enforcement agency for further investigation.

A call for service is intended to provide the same policing response as with other crime types. For example, if a suspect can be apprehended following an assault, police could respond to that policing demand. It should be the same for fraud offences.

KEY POINTS—CALL FOR SERVICE

The criteria for 'call for service', where a police service will record fraud offences as though they were reported to the police by the NFIB, is as follows:

- offences where offenders are arrested by the police;
- where there is a call for service to the police and the offender 'is committing' or has recently committed (at the time of the call for service) all fraud types;
- where there is a local suspect.

A 'local suspect' is defined as where, through viable investigative leads:

- police can or could locate the suspect with the details provided;
- have sufficient details to apprehend an offender.

'Local' has its everyday meaning and has been used to ensure that, as with any other type of crime, where there are local viable investigative leads, police should consider the crime for investigation.

Where this is not the case and the crime needs to be transferred, the crime should be passed to the NFIB or referred to Action Fraud if appropriate. The NFIB will then deal with it in the same way as with any other reported fraud.

6.2.1 **NFIB referral quality control**

While supervisors carry out a quality control and review process, due to the high volume of crimes being reported and assessed, crime reviewers are required to exercise a certain amount of discretion. As such, they are permitted to file crimes that don't contain viable lines of inquiry. In order to ensure that risk is mitigated, all crime reviewers are required to seek authorisation from a supervisor prior to filing any crimes with a loss value of £5,000 or more.

Any force seeking to transfer disseminated crimes under the fraud section of the HOCR must do so via the NFIB crime incident registrar.

The NFIB crime incident registrar will make the decision as to whether a force seeking to transfer a crime should keep the crime or to which force it should be transferred. In the event of the transfer being authorised, the crime reviewers will be informed and will then disseminate the crime to the new force and update their records accordingly. If the crime transfer request is refused, then the crime registrar making the decision will inform the force and provide a rationale for the refusal.

6.3 **Case acceptance criteria**

Within policing the expectation is that referrals received from the NFIB should be considered for investigation. However, other investigative agencies and some police forces have their own case acceptance criteria to meet their own organisational requirements. In these cases, the investigative agency can receive both referrals and complaints of fraud from a variety of sources, for example the NFIB, direct from members of the public, corporate entities and regulators.

When this is the case, a structured decision-making process for case acceptance should be developed to record the management of new referrals. This may be recorded via a database as appropriate to the organisation's needs and internal processes. It is good practice for organisations to receive referrals and reports of fraud at a central point. This will enable defined criteria to be applied to the report that are consistent and documented, plus there will be a central record of the decision-making exercise.

The receiving organisation should consider having a screening and allocation matrix to assist in the prioritisation of referrals and be scored according to the organisational priorities.

153

KEY POINTS—ELEMENTS OF CASE ACCEPTANCE CRITERIA

Strategic assessment:

- new investigations assessed against current control strategies and threat assessments. The use of resources can thereby be aligned to the current and emerging threats of fraud.

Victim assessment:

- victim type;
- vulnerability;
- harm caused.

Offender assessment:

- position in society;
- connection to criminality (principal or minor facilitator);
- organised crime group (OCG)—establish if there are operational or intelligence development opportunities and priorities;
- professional enabler.

Evidence assessment:

- known;
- not known;
- in jurisdiction;
- outside jurisdiction.

Locality of criminality:

- local;
- national;
- international.

Scale of criminality:

- number of victims;
- number of witnesses;
- number of offenders.

Current organisational capacity:

- resource capacity for a new investigation is balanced against current workloads. It ensures resources are used effectively and known or anticipated resource implications are acknowledged and expanded on.

Community impact and proportionality:

- impact of the criminality on the community/stakeholders;
- risk of ongoing harm.

Viability of lines of inquiry:

- viable opportunities for investigation, prevention or disruption.

> **Asset recovery opportunities (Proceeds of Crime Act (POCA) 2002).**
> Other factors to consider:
>
> - current organisational capacity;
> - politically exposed person;
> - critical incident, for example likely to attract significant (not local) public or media attention.

Where the referral meets the criteria for investigation, a 'record' of the investigation should be opened at the earliest opportunity. This provides an audit trail for the assessment stage and details the decision-making process for case acceptance.

KEY POINTS—CASE ACCEPTANCE OPTIONS

- **Accepted for investigation**: the case is accepted for an investigation and the decision maker will allocate as per organisational guidelines.
- **Accepted for scoping**: the case is to be further developed before a decision is made.
- **Referral to another organisation**: the case is not accepted and is considered for referral to another organisation. The decision maker may specify the organisation This could include a referral for consideration of disruption or prevention activity.
- **Case not accepted for investigation**: the case is not accepted for further investigation and there is no opportunity to develop further or allocate to another organisation.

6.3.1 Appeals procedure

A nominated person senior to the initial decision maker should act as the appeals manager. The victim or person reporting the matter may be dissatisfied with a decision not to proceed with an investigation. A route of appeal needs to be formalised for reasons of transparency and organisational integrity. Any written representations can be considered and a written decision can be issued on the appeal verdict. Nothing within the appeals procedure affects a person's statutory right or entitlement to make a complaint to an appropriate regulator, or Member of Parliament (MP).

6.4 Criminal v Civil routes

On occasion, it may be necessary for law enforcement to engage with the private sector, with regard to expediting and taking responsibility for civil recovery, while law enforcement focuses upon prosecution. Private prosecutors and civil litigators have developed the necessary skills to trace assets worldwide, with the ability to navigate between jurisdictions and restrain funds. A joint approach between law enforcement and the private sector may be advantageous in providing the maximum prospect of compensation, and enabling law enforcement to focus on prosecution.

Provisions within the Serious Crime Act 2007 allow for the sharing of information with a specified anti-fraud organisation. Referrals should also be considered in the event that a criminal prosecution is unlikely to be achievable. Engaging with private sector asset recovery (PSAR) firms will require the exchange of information, and therefore a memorandum of understanding (MoU) and a data-sharing agreement (DSA) should be put in place.

KEY POINTS—CONSIDERATIONS WHEN ENGAGING WITH PSAR FIRMS

Key areas to be considered are:
- capacity;
- capability;
- severity;
- complexity of the offence;
- cost of using a PSAR firm.

PSAR firms are likely to utilise their own case acceptance criteria, and will also evaluate each referral on a case-by-case basis.

The cost implications of PSAR firms taking civil recovery forward will potentially erode the victim's compensation. The victim's authority is therefore required, prior to tasking PSAR firms. It is suggested that an independent scrutiny panel monitors referrals to PSAR firms, providing the public with reassurance that referrals are fair, open and transparent.

Upon each referral for investigation, consideration should be given to working jointly with PSAR firms, to expedite asset recovery and ensure that the proceeds of crime are not dissipated. Doing this enables law enforcement to focus on criminal prosecution.

6.5 **Developing a case theory**

The case theory should be developed at the earliest opportunity, as it will form the basis for a logical investigative strategy to maximise evidential opportunities. Initially, the investigator will use the process in inductive reasoning where all the material available will be gathered and analysed to develop the case theory, which in turn leads to deductive reasoning where lines of inquiry are set to gather more material to test the case theory and develop it further.

A case theory may include a variety of possible explanations for the case in question. It is important to include these in the lines of inquiry until the truth is established. Care should be taken not to fall victim to verification bias, which is where the investigator tries to prove their personal belief of what they consider has happened and limits investigations to their view at the cost of a more inclusive investigation strategy.

It is important to remember that the fraudster is often moving between the fraudulent schemes without pause and at times it is only the last scheme that initially comes to notice.

Checklist—considerations for initial case theory development in fraud cases

- The purpose is to develop the best picture of the offending with the known material.
- Ensure all sources of information instigating the investigation have been obtained, reviewed and evaluated.
- Consult those with expert knowledge to assist in formulating the case theory.
- Ensure all initial checks have been undertaken to identify further links and offending, including (where applicable):
  - NFIB;
  - SARs database;
  - PND.
- Review material from partner agencies, including:
  - National Crime Agency (NCA);
  - Serious Fraud Office (SFO);
  - Financial Conduct Authority (FCA);
  - Competition and Markets Authority.
- Consider why the fraud has been reported and by whom.
- Remember that some victims and witnesses may not be responsive and may still believe the misrepresentations being put forward by the fraudster.

The case theory in fraud cases should ultimately instigate four key investigative actions:

1 Identify and secure the relevant material.
2 Identify and support the victims, and evidence their loss and the impact they have suffered.
3 Identify the offender and recover their criminal assets.
4 Ensure preventative actions are instigated to prevent repeat offending.

6.6 **Resource management**

The cost of resourcing investigations in a modern policing/regulatory environment is an important consideration of senior leadership teams (SLTs). The management of a fraud inquiry can be costly in terms of the investment of staffing hours and budgets. Serious consideration has to be given as to the most cost-effective way that an investigation can be conducted in order to ensure that best-value principles are adhered to.

Best-value considerations start at the outset and begin with the initial evaluation or assessment of a referral. These considerations should then continue through to the tactical investigation plan and will be reviewed at the evidential evaluation stage. This consistent approach will ensure that, when the end game has been achieved, the most efficient use of resources can be evidenced at the debrief.

The responsibility for such budgets does not always lie with heads of departments, who, on evaluating a new referral, may have to make a spending review bid or look at alternative funding streams, such as an MoU, with a partner agency or victim organisation, in accordance with the FIM.

6.6.1 **Resource management considerations**

In reality, a new case is often allocated to the team that has the capacity to undertake a new investigation; however, this may not always be the most effective and efficient way of investigating a fraud. Consideration should be given to an individual investigator's experience and knowledge of a crime type, with this being offset against the opportunity to mentor a less experienced investigator; this process can also be repeated to determine the suitability of a potential first-line manager in the case.

The effectiveness of a first-line manager cannot be understated, as they will hold the day-to-day responsibility for the investigation and should be able to flag up any cost or delay issues that may occur. In cases of a large and complex nature, it may be preferable to mix staff in order to compile the most efficient and effective team.

> ### Checklist—developing a resource management strategy
>
> It is incumbent upon an SIO to have the ability to foresee resourcing and budgetary issues and be able to put in place strategies that support the department; these include the following:
>
> - Highlighting—at the initial assessment stage—aspects of the investigation that may incur increased investment in staff and cost, such as search phases and IT/forensic examination. These issues should be shared with senior management at the outset, so that they are conscious of the potential cost implications.

- Using efficient and effective policies that may dispense with or streamline unnecessary tasks or, if necessary, taking action to expedite these, thus saving time later.

- Setting tight investigative parameters for the investigation in relation to time and cost.

- Early liaison with heads of departments to look at skill sharing and obtaining advice on matters such as prioritising tasks and cost.

- Early liaison with the Crown Prosecution Service's (CPS's) Special Casework Division, which can give advice on offences, charges and points to prove, thus identifying when there is sufficient evidence to charge.

Due consideration of the above, and implementation of other best-value strategies, will ensure that the most suitable investigations are accepted and the best available procedures are followed using the right amount of staff with the most suitable skills.

6.7 Making and recording a decision

Effective decision making is a critical skill for the investigator. When failings in a crime investigation are investigated, they have often been found to be due to poor decision making. Those making decisions should counter the following factors when making decisions.

- **Confirmation bias**: directing inquires to establish an unconfirmed case theory with a tendency to ignore other lines of inquiry.
- **Fundamental attribution error**: giving a higher value to material that is in itself powerful or provided from an authoritative source, rather than material from other sources, without good reason.
- **Cultural bias**: judging material based on one's own frame of reference and personal biases, subconsciously assigning value to material without thinking.
- **Limited personal experience**: making choices without having sufficient experience to make informed decisions.
- **Working rules**: the adoption of procedures that are the 'norm' in that working environment without challenging their relevance, legality or applicability to the task at hand.

The recording of decision making in the investigation of fraud is essential and will help to protect investigators from legal challenge, whether this be prior to charge through a judicial review or at a subsequent trial of suspects.

6.7.1 **Recording decisions**

All investigations should have a record of the key decisions that form the investigative strategy and set the direction of the inquiry. This is particularly important in fraud cases due to the complexity and subsequent challenges to the methods used to gather the material during the investigation.

Where the investigation is being led by a nominated SIO, the key strategic decisions should be recorded in a KDL (or equivalent). This should not be mistaken for an action book where tactical issues are recorded.

These records will serve as a critical record of the management of the investigation and should include the rationale associated with each decision made. These records should be available (unless sensitive) for all investigators to view. In areas where a case management system is available, investigations may be managed without the need for a paper-based KDL, as they are replicated within the system.

Where the investigation is being led by an OIC, the key decisions may be recorded on the crime reporting system or equivalent. The OIC's supervisor should consider reviewing the investigative strategy on a regular basis. Where the HOLMES is being used to manage the inquiry, the MIRSAP should be followed regarding the recording of strategic decisions.

KEY POINTS—METHODS FOR RECORDING KEY DECISIONS

- SIO—key decision book (or equivalent) and case management system;
- OIC—day book and force crime system;
- local process for recording an investigation strategy/plan:
  - strategy document;
  - investigation plan;
- local method for recording investigative actions and results.

The investigation of large and complex fraud cases can often cover more than one force area with an international dimension and many can be interpreted as investigations into OCGs. Investigative methods will often incorporate both overt conventional policing methods and covert tactics. The recording of the SIO's rationale into decision making captures why policies were instigated at points in time when in possession of knowledge, evidence and information. This provides clarification later when evidence is viewed with hindsight.

The same applies to cases identified as critical incidents where investigative bodies put in place strategic gold groups to oversee case progression and manage organisational risk.

The records of decisions that are dated and signed provide a valuable record of thoughts and reasoning when making significant decisions. The rationale should consider the legality of decisions, as well as the proportionality of a tactic or decision. Due regard should be given to the Human Rights Act (HRA) 1998, which should underpin all investigative actions. These records will demonstrate that decision making was well thought out and make reference to the material considered at the time the decision was made.

An example would be considering the necessity to arrest suspects as described under the Police and Criminal Evidence (PACE) Act 1984 in preference to arranging the suspects' interviews by voluntary attendance.

A reason to arrest a number of key suspects in a coordinated raid may be that to arrest and interview suspects while all are in custody would remove the opportunity for suspects to confer and would assist the investigation in conducting coordinated interviews to obtain initial accounts from all suspects. This decision can be expanded to consider the evidence against each suspect, breaking down the roles each person plays and why arrest would be necessary to advance the investigation. The same process would then be applied to decisions and conditions around bail.

KDLs should be expanded upon to show why and what you've thought may form part of the disclosure process. Sensitive KDLs should be used for any issues that would not be automatically disclosed to the defence prior to a trial and may be subject to an application to a judge for public interest immunity (PII).

Further reading

- College of Policing, 'Authorised Professional Practice', 2016.
- ACPO, 'Practice Advice on Core Investigative Doctrine', 2005.
- ACPO, *Guidance on Major Incident Room Standardised Administrative Procedures (MIRSAP)*, 2005.
- ACPO, *Revised Guidelines for the Use of Policy Files*, 1999.
- National Centre for Policing Excellence, *Murder Investigation Manual*, 2006.
- T Cook, *Blackstone's Senior Investigating Officers' Handbook*, 2016.

6.8 Case management

Fraud investigations have the potential to generate large volumes of evidential and unused material. In addition, the number of victims, witnesses and suspects can also grow to very high levels; therefore, at the start of a fraud investigation the investigator should always plan for a challenging scenario and plan ahead to manage the case with this in mind.

6.8.1 When to use the HOLMES in fraud cases

The HOLMES computer system has evolved over time and is used in many UK police forces for various types of crime, including economic crime, particularly as fraud investigations can be large and complex, frequently involving more than one UK police force area. This requires the lead of an SIO and the use of a computerised system to assist in the document management of the investigation.

Consideration should be made for resourcing a major incident room (MIR), for particularly large and complex fraud investigations. When undertaking investigations that involve a large number of nominal records across a number of forces or international elements, the use of an MIR team can assist in the identification of unidentified nominal involved following the MIRSAP processes. An investigation should be resourced according to its size and complexity.

The HOLMES can be used in fraud investigations as a 'registration only' database, as per the MIRSAP. In these cases, all the documentation generated during the course of an investigation is recorded, scanned, searched and assessed accordingly for disclosure. This process, although suggested in the MIRSAP, should be completed by a number of MIR roles and could be conducted by the single OIC for an investigation. The OIC can effectively document manage their own material from registration stage through to disclosure and court file preparation.

6.8.2 How to use the HOLMES effectively in fraud cases

Fraud investigations have been successfully managed and run using the 'registration only' process. All material generated during the course of the investigation is registered on the database, and scanning software allows free text search in the documentation. This enables the officer to keep a record of the material generated and provides effective storage space for offices, as documentation can then be stored off site and investigators can access their material electronically from their terminal. This process also assists investigators in a phased disclosure process, and enables the ability to keep a record and audit of the records disclosed and still to be assessed. Should the requirement arise where more than one investigator is required for an investigation, the HOLMES is able to record different officers making assessments for an accountable system. The disclosure function of the HOLMES also assists investigators in meeting CPIA 1996 requirements for separate case files, without the duplication of work for separate defendants. A further benefit of the use of the HOLMES for a large and complex economic crime investigation is its ability to share the accounts nationwide, as the majority of UK police forces are on the 'Government cloud' for the HOLMES. This means investigators have the ability to obtain remote access to investigations across England, Wales and Scotland, subject to consultation with an agreement from the SIO or OIC.

6.8.3 Practicalities of using the HOLMES

The use of the HOLMES to manage case material can be utilised by the investigator. Within the system there is the option of not using all of the recognised and standard features that you would expect to see in a major investigation team (MIT). In these circumstances, the HOLMES will not be used to provide direction; rather, the system will be used as a means by which the investigator can record, retain and manage the anticipated large volume of material that might be generated. This would be backed up by conventional crime recording processes and the use of spreadsheets to assist the investigator.

The investigator needs to keep a record of the lines of inquiry that they are taking or considering. This can be achieved by recording them in a spreadsheet. Each entry should be graded as low, medium or high to prioritise the inquiries and assist the investigator in the management of their workload on that case. This record can be used by the investigator with their supervisor to review the progression of the case, and generate and record other lines of inquiry as identified during the course of the weekly/monthly review.

All high-priority inquiries will be progressed as soon as possible, with the medium ones taking second place. Some low-priority inquiries may not be undertaken and become dormant or pending action against a recorded decision and rationale.

Alongside this record, the investigator must keep details of the key policy decisions that have been made in consultation with, and agreed by, their supervising officer. These records will include not just the details of the decisions made, but also the rationales behind them.

The use of the HOLMES can only be appropriate and authorised if the investigator has the required training to input information into the HOLMES by making limited use of the system.

6.8.4 When not to use the HOLMES in fraud investigations

Investigations that are not spread across a large geographical area or are not of particular complexity or volume may not require the use of the HOLMES, but many other systems can be used to effectively record, scan, search and provide document-management solutions.

6.8.5 Strengths of the HOLMES for fraud investigations

The HOLMES allows one central location for all fraud investigations to be recorded; the service is maintained and run by a third party, which takes administrative roles and functions away from the force. The system is a nationally recognised and accredited police system in every UK police force and has, therefore, been tried and tested in court for decades in the most serious of investigations.

The registration-only functions of the HOLMES mean bespoke training is required for officers, covering disclosure and registration of documents. Adopting the 'registration only' process by a single OIC allows supervisors to effectively monitor the process of the investigation, and effectively hand over material internally and externally if required. The process is nationally recognised good practice, as well as being recognised by the CPS. The system also assists officers in producing a list of witnesses (MG9) and list of exhibits

(MG12), as long as the relevant information has been created on the database. The forms can then be extracted for the required purpose.

6.8.6 Weaknesses of using the HOLMES for fraud investigations

The limitations presented to forces when using the HOLMES are the potential cost factors for licensing and training economic departments in the creation of documents and the process of disclosure within the HOLMES.

The system also then draws the OIC away from the actions on a crime investigation, and time needs to be spent on administrative duties concerning the documentation generated (unless the OIC is supported by an administration unit).

Without the relevant knowledge and experience of the HOLMES and large major fraud investigations, the use of the HOLMES by investigators can become overcomplicated by the investigator, resulting in too much time being spent on registering material and unnecessary links being added to the database.

Further reading

- MIRSAP, 2005: http://library.college.police.uk/docs/APPREF/MIRSAP.pdf
- College of Policing, 'Authorised Professional Practice—Investigation: Managing Investigations', 2016: www.app.college.police.uk/app-content/investigations/managing-investigations/

If the HOLMES is not available, a similar or otherwise suitable computer-based system should be used in line with the principles described in this section.

6.9 Partnership and cross-sector working

Considering partner agencies is a component part of the effective use of the FIM. The challenges of budgetary constraints have encouraged counter-fraud agencies to seek more regular and mutually efficient partnerships. The arrangements often bring together diverse skills, powers and capabilities for a common purpose, yielding a greater effect and a shared benefit. The partnership working may be driven by a shared resource, particularly expertise or the engagement of relevant legal powers available to only one party.

6.9.1 Memorandum of understanding (MoU)

While the opportunities are frequent and mutually beneficial, care must be taken to ensure that the aims and objectives of each party are clearly agreed, the commitment levels of everyone are properly defined and the potential risks to each party are recognised and guarded against. The safest way to achieve these undertakings is by way of a formal MoU to which each party can resort for reference. Where one party is heavily reliant on information and/or intelligence supplied by another, it is particularly important that they have a disclaimer built in to avoid subsequent liability or litigation where they have acted in good faith upon the material supplied, which has later been found to be incomplete, incorrect or misleading.

In an increasingly litigious and resource-scarce environment, it is imperative that parties to any joint investigation define their positions and their roles.

KEY POINTS—MOU SECTION HEADERS

While each MoU may differ according to each agency's perceived requirements, the basic section headers are common to many and normally include:

- identification: of the signatories/agency and representatives;
- information: a brief background of the circumstances leading to the MoU requirement;
- objectives: the main purposes that the agreement covers;
- role descriptions: indicators of what each party will undertake to provide, resource and achieve;
- information/intelligence sharing: a description of each party's undertaking to assure the integrity, provenance, continuity and correct handling of information and intelligence, as well as the portals and controls through which it will pass;
- costs: the agreed apportioning of costs for the general or specific tasks that each party fulfils;
- litigation risks: the perceived liability of cross-reliance on material supplied by the other party and who it is agreed carries the legal risk for each area;
- proceeds of crime/incentivisation: which parties take responsibility for POCA 2002 opportunities, their ongoing management, confiscation proceedings following a successful prosecution and the ultimate benefit from POCA funds;
- data management: an undertaking for all parties to conform with the provisions of the Data Protection Act (DPA) 1998;
- prosecution: agreement as to who will be responsible for prosecuting which areas, and with mutual consent on submitted case papers;
- operational management structure: identifies the operational leads for each party, supervisor, case officer, disclosure officer, etc;
- prosecuting agency: the agreed agency taking on the joint prosecution;
- security: adherence to the Government Protective Marking Scheme (GPMS) and/or Government Security Classification (GSC), plus the handling, storage and destruction of material. It will be the responsibility of each party to ensure operational security, with mutual reporting of any breaches to counterparties, and any other procedural issues as required;
- disclosure: identifies lead disclosure responsibilities and sign-off of material. The correct management of disclosure in any prosecution will be vital;
- media: identifies relevant parties to media management, and agrees mutual consent prior to any response, release or statement;

> - health and safety/risk assessment: apportions responsibility for both to each partner agency or as otherwise agreed;
> - dispute resolution: identifies senior managers mutually recognised for oversight and resolution of key decisions;
> - commencement, amendment and review dates: sets out points in time and periods for each relating to the MoU.

The MoU should be agreed and signed off by all parties at a sufficiently senior level to ensure it accurately represents the agencies' policies and position, with an agreed commencement date. The CPS MoU template can be found in Annex F of the Disclosure Manual, which is in Appendix 1.

6.9.2 Information sharing

Working on a joint investigation raises obvious issues around the legalities of data protection when sharing data between organisations. Under the DPA 1998, personal data should be protected in line with the data protection principles, namely:

1 Data must be processed fairly and legally.
2 Data must be processed for limited purposes and in an appropriate way.
3 The processing must be relevant and sufficient for the purpose.
4 The data being processed must be accurate.
5 Data must not be kept for any longer than is necessary.
6 Data must be processed in line with an individual's rights.
7 The processing must be done in a way that is secure.
8 Data must only be transferred to countries that have suitable data protection controls.

The DPA recognises that it is sometimes appropriate to disclose personal data for certain purposes to do with criminal justice or the taxation system. In these cases, individuals' rights may occasionally need to be restricted. Section 29(3) of the DPA provides a route for sharing information in these circumstances:

- the prevention or detection of crime;
- the capture or prosecution of offenders;
- the assessment or collection of tax or duty.

6.9.3 Data-sharing agreements (DSAs)

DSAs—sometimes known as 'data sharing protocols'—set out a common set of rules to be adopted by the various organisations involved in a data-sharing operation. These could well form part of a MoU/contract between organisations. It is good practice to have a DSA in place, and to review it regularly, particularly where information is to be shared on a large scale, or on a regular basis.

> **Further reading**
>
> - DPA 1998: www.legislation.gov.uk/ukpga/1998/29/contents.
> - Information Commissioners Office (ICO), 'Data sharing code of practice', Chapter 8, 'Governance', 2011: https://ico.org.uk/media/for-organisations/documents/1068/data_sharing_code_of_practice.pdf

6.10 Investigation plans

The purpose of having an investigation plan is to provide investigators with clear direction as to the investigative priorities. The lines of inquiry in any fraud investigation can change and it is vitally important that these changes are documented throughout the life span of the investigation. A detailed aide-memoire to fraud investigation planning is to be found in Appendix 2.

An investigation plan should be created at the earliest opportunity. The purpose of doing so will be to:

- provide structure and focus;
- provide direction and clarity;
- ensure careful planning and preparation;
- detail investigative resourcing;
- set targets to maintain motivation.

The investigation plan can be said to have five main stages, which include operational learning at the end of the case to identify best practice for the future and ensure lessons are learnt from any mistakes that occurred.

KEY POINTS—INVESTIGATION PLANNING FIVE STAGES

- Defining objectives;
- setting the initial plan;
- identifying milestones;
- conducting reviews;
- identifying operational learning.

6.10.1 Structure of the investigation plan

The investigation plan should be a 'living' document that is chronological and covers the management of key areas throughout the investigation.

In fraud cases, it is important to set objectives, namely what is it that you want to achieve from this investigation? It is very important to have a clear focus on these objectives, in order to avoid becoming overwhelmed by trying to absorb the mass of information that may be uncovered in the investigation, a great deal of which may be peripheral or not relevant to the key issues in the case.

Maintaining focus on the original objectives helps to distinguish between what is worth concentrating on, and what is not.

Objectives could include:

- arresting and prosecuting known suspects;
- testing whether there is evidence to support specific charges, for example simple charges requiring minimal investigation time and resources;
- recovering and confiscating identifiable assets;
- disrupting criminal activity, where a prosecution may be deemed unfeasible.

Similarly, it is crucial to keep things as simple as possible when investigating complex fraud cases. Where possible, try and identify simple, straightforward charges that could be brought readily against the suspects, rather than committing too much time and too many resources to trying to prove complex conspiracies where the evidence may be weak or vulnerable to attack by the defence.

There is always a time and place for using conspiracy charges, but ultimately the prosecution will only succeed if it can explain the offences clearly and unambiguously to the court (i.e. the jury), leaving no room for doubt in the jury's minds.

Checklist—investigation plan: key areas to incorporate

The key areas to incorporate include the following:

- details of the OIC/SIO;

- offences under investigation;

- aims and objectives of the investigation;

- suspect(s);

- case management method;

- case summary;

- main lines of inquiry;

- resources;

- intelligence;

- victim management;

- opportunities for disruption;

- opportunities for prevention;

- multi-agency working;

- assets and restrained funds;

- international letters of request;
- joint investigation teams (JITs);
- main lines of inquiry;
- disclosure management;
- actions log.

6.10.2 **Investigation plan reviews**

It is very important to have a system of review for fraud investigations. This is especially so due to the large and complex nature of such cases, which can take much longer to complete and can involve much greater levels of detail than most other types of cases. Reviews are essential to keep track of progress and assess whether the investigation is still on track. It is best practice for supervisors to review each case monthly. Progress can be assessed against the initial investigation plan and investigators are expected to be accountable for any perceived lack of progress, the reasons for which should have been fully documented on the crime investigation database.

A useful exercise is to ask the following questions when undertaking a review:

- What does the investigation now know?
- What does this indicate?
- What else does the investigation need to know?
- Where and how can we get this information?

These help to identify areas that the investigation still needs to cover, as well as helping to close off other areas that can be considered complete. (See Chapter 10.)

6.11 **Victim management**

Victims of fraud should be treated in a respectful, sensitive, tailored and professional manner. They should receive appropriate support to help them, as far as possible, to cope, recover and be protected from re-victimisation. It is important that victims know what information and support is available to them and from whom to request help if they are not receiving it.

Definition of a victim

The Victims Code 2015 defines the victim as:

- a natural person who has suffered harm, including physical, mental or emotional harm or economic loss, which was directly caused by a criminal offence;
- a close relative of a person whose death was directly caused by a criminal offence.

169

Businesses are not included within the definition of a victim, but are still entitled to services under the *Code of Practice for Victims of Crime.*

Frauds can have a significant impact on the victim. A negligible loss to a large company, for example, could be catastrophic for a private individual or small business. Distinct communities can be targeted—for example, *Hajj* fraud that affects the Muslim community, with many losing thousands of pounds on planned trips to Mecca. Family members can be deeply affected, and, in the case of a corporate victim, employees may lose their jobs as a result of the fraud.

Although others affected may not feature as an integral element of the investigation, recognising them is essential for the accurate measurement of the harm caused and can be invaluable when presenting a case to court.

With some large-scale frauds, the number of victims can reach into the hundreds, and these can be spread across the country and to jurisdictions around the world. It is for these reasons that, within fraud investigations, victims are to be managed strategically. The task of victim management can become all-encompassing and potentially overwhelming to an individual investigator unless effective procedures are put in place.

The *Code of Practice for Victims of Crime* is the statutory code that sets out the minimum level of service victims should get from the criminal justice agencies. It sets out the time frames in which the agencies must comply and allows victims to hold the system to account if they don't receive the service to which they are entitled. The Code came into force in December 2013 and was updated in October 2015.

6.11.1 Identification of victims

Checklist—victims of fraud

Victims of fraud may be identified through a number of sources, including:

- Action Fraud reports;
- direct reporting to law enforcement;
- suspicious activity reports;
- bank accounts;
- investor lists;
- media;
- other agencies, i.e. the FCA, the Insolvency Service.

6.11.2 Initial contact

Following the identification of a victim, contact must be made not only to secure and obtain evidence for the investigation, but also to conduct a needs assessment for the victim. Be mindful that if the victim was originally identified through a third party, there may have been a delay between the initial report and their being contacted by the OIC.

Establish what support is available to the victim from family or friends and whether a referral to Victim Support, Citizens Advice Bureau or other support agencies should be considered. Fraud prevention advice may need to be provided to prevent re-victimisation via further contact with offenders.

If the victim is considered to be vulnerable, they will be entitled to an enhanced service under the *Code of Practice for Victims of Crime*. Managers should be notified at the earliest opportunity of any victim issues and/or risks in order to prevent organisational harm and reputational risk.

It is important to manage the expectations of a victim from the outset, as some victims' motives for making a complaint of fraud can be focused on recovering monies owed. If there is little prospect of them being awarded compensation, it is important that they are informed of this.

A victim is entitled to receive written information on what to expect from the criminal justice system, such as the 'Information for Victims of Crime' leaflet, or the details of the website that contains this information. This must be offered to the victim on their first contact with the police. The contact details of the investigating officer should be provided, so that the victim feels part of the process and supported at all times.

All victims, regardless of whether they are a prosecution witness, should receive the same standard of management and care. The needs assessment of a victim is an ongoing process, not just something conducted in the initial stages of an investigation. See Appendix 3 for frequently asked questions regarding the reporting, assessment and investigation and see Appendix 4 for available support services.

6.11.3 **Evidence gathering**

Victims must be advised to retain all documents and communications with the offenders until they are handed over to the investigation team. For a vulnerable victim, it may be more appropriate to obtain their evidence through a video-recorded interview instead of a witness statement.

If dealing with multiple victims, it is advisable to consider sending an initial questionnaire requesting supporting documents that evidence their losses. Ideally, these will be bank statements displaying withdrawals on their account and correspondence to show where their money has been invested or to whom it has been paid.

Once questionnaires are received, they can be reviewed and assessment made as to whether a witness statement will be taken. For large-scale fraud investigations, it may not be reasonable or practical to take a statement from every victim. In this instance, a policy decision needs to be made by the relevant case manager as to what percentage of victims will be approached for statements, with consideration given to how to represent the whole case.

Checklist—considerations to evidence scale of offending

- Timescales: commencement of the offending period, as well as its middle and end.

- Harm/loss: evidence to show large-scale losses.

- Impact: demonstrate impact.

- Consultation: with the prosecuting authority may be useful, as they may have a view as to the best practice.

Some victims may not reply at first as they may not believe that they have been a victim of crime or, for instance, may have changed address. It is essential that further attempts are made to make contact and ensure that all addresses are up to date. A policy decision will need to be made as to how many attempts should be made to engage with victims. If the victim has died, the deceased's estate will be entitled to receive any compensation, so efforts should still be made to trace an executor or next of kin to confirm any losses.

As part of any prosecution process, victims should be offered the opportunity to give a personal impact statement (PIS). The purpose of the statement should be explained to them, as well as the fact that it is their choice to complete one. If the victim is a business, then a named point of contact can provide this to fully outline how a crime has affected the business.

Some victims who are either intimidated or vulnerable may require additional support from other agencies, such as Victim Support or their local authority. In these cases an achieving best evidence (ABE) interview should be considered at the earliest opportunity by appropriately trained investigators, either using mobile interviewing equipment or at a dedicated interviewing suite.

KEY POINTS—SPECIAL MEASURES

There are a range of special measures that can be used to facilitate the giving of evidence in court by both vulnerable and intimidated victims. These measures include:

- the use of screens;
- the use of a live TV link;
- giving evidence in private;
- the removal of wigs and gowns;
- the use of video-recorded interviews as evidence-in-chief.

Vulnerable witnesses are eligible for:

- communication through intermediaries;
- the use of special communication aids.

There is substantial material available in respect of suspect, victim and witness interviewing. Should further advice be necessary, contact should be made with either local or national interview advisers.

6.11.4 Victim schedule of losses

Checklist—schedule of victims

A schedule of victims needs to be prepared to show clearly the losses of all victims and should contain, as a minimum, the following information:

- name of victim (or preferred contact, if deceased);
- contact details;
- dates of investment;
- how much was invested on each occasion;
- sort code and account number to where payment was made;
- which companies were invested in;
- any payments/refunds the victim may have received from the offender/offending company;
- supporting evidence of losses (see below);
- the gross and net loss for each victim.

Important—failure to prepare a full victim schedule could create a risk to the investigating agencies if opportunities to make payments for compensation are missed.

Supporting evidence showing the losses of each victim should ideally be referred to as a document reference and/or page number, if relevant. It must be clear to both prosecution and defence where the victim's losses have originated, as this will save court time later on. Personal trace information must, where possible, be redacted before use in the case. If an accredited financial investigator is assigned to the case, early liaison will be very useful to them in taking the schedule forward following conviction for use in confiscation proceedings and compensation.

6.11.5 Communication

In providing support to victims of fraud, it is important to recognise the needs of different individuals or groups and how best to communicate with them; a form of electronic communication sent to an IT-aware individual may not be suitable for another victim who is less IT-aware. There may also be a request for confidentiality from a partner or other family members.

KEY POINTS—OPTIONS FOR CONTACTING MULTIPLE VICTIMS

The following may be of use in cases with multiple victims:

- use of blind-copy email messages for sending bulk messages, without disclosing the recipients to each other;
- website page for victims to access securely;
- web forum;
- prerecorded telephone mailbox for inward telephone calls;
- social media;
- face-to-face localised victim workshops.

The method of contact should be agreed with each victim. Under the *Code of Practice for Victims of Crime*, they are entitled to information within five days of the suspect being:

- arrested;
- interviewed under caution;
- released with no further action (NFA);
- released on police bail or if police bail conditions are changed or cancelled.

Alternatively, the victim is entitled to information within one day if they have enhanced entitlements. Enhanced entitlements are provided to victims of the most serious crimes, persistently targeted victims and vulnerable or intimidated victims.

One of the main complaints from victims in fraud cases is the lack of consistency in the provision of updates from initial reporting through to the natural conclusion of the case. Large and complex fraud cases have a tendency to take a considerable amount of time to reach court. This can cause frustration for victims, especially if they are witnesses and are then unexpectedly required to attend court several years later.

It is also essential to update a victim of any change of OIC throughout the investigation or prosecution.

6.11.6 **Court**

It is important not only to maintain good communication throughout the investigation, but right through to the trial as witnesses are a key element to a successful prosecution.

The Witness Charter raises awareness of the use of special measures by the police, the CPS and the courts to support vulnerable and intimidated witnesses. The revised charter sets out the standards of care that all witnesses should expect to receive from the point of reporting a crime to the police through to the court trial.

Investigators should be aware of the potential for crossovers with other agencies with regard to victim contact, as there may be another agency involved in the investigation. For instance, the Insolvency Service may become involved if a company goes into compulsory liquidation or a bankruptcy order or debt relief order is made. The Insolvency Service's official receivers are responsible for the administration and investigation of the case. They have a responsibility to identify creditors, which may be the same as the victims in the case under investigation, and may seek compensation on behalf of their creditors.

Care is needed if a victim has already been recorded as a creditor with the Insolvency Service, so that they are not compensated twice.

6.11.7 Developing a victim management strategy

Although it is not exhaustive, the checklist below outlines some of the factors investigators need to consider when developing a victim management strategy.

Checklist—victim management strategy

- Identify all the victims in the case.
- Assess vulnerability and identify a management process.
- Ensure a victim management strategy is documented.
- Victims should complete questionnaires and provide supporting documents to evidence their losses.
- Assess the victims' evidence to identify their suitability as prosecution witnesses.
- Maintain communication with victims, ensuring regular updates are provided.
- Comply with the *Code of Practice for Victims of Crime* and the Witness Charter.
- Make policy on any deviations from the Codes of Practice.
- Victim schedule: record all victims, not just witnesses for the prosecution.
- Identify risks and make management aware of these at the earliest opportunity.
- Consider referral to other agencies where appropriate (e.g. Victim Support).
- Manage the expectations of the victims.
- consider in appropriate cases an additional level of victim care, through a named contact or a family liaison officer (FLO).

See Appendix 5 for an example victim management strategy.

Further reading

- Ministry of Justice (MoJ), *Code of Practice for Victims of Crime*, updated October 2015: www.gov.uk/government/uploads/system/uploads/attachment_data/file/476900/code-of-practice-for-victims-of-crime.PDF
- The Witness Charter: www.cps.gov.uk/victims_witnesses/witness_charter.pdf
- Critical incident principles: www.app.college.police.uk/app-content/critical-incident-management/

6.12 Witness management

It is imperative at the outset of any inquiry that witnesses are treated in accordance with best practice. In some instances, it may be that a statement is taken from a witness who is neither vulnerable nor intimidated; in these cases, no special measures would normally be required in court.

In other cases, investigators may encounter vulnerable, intimidated, significant or hostile witnesses. Significant witnesses, sometimes referred to as key witnesses, are those who:

- have or claim to have witnessed, visually or otherwise, an indictable offence, part of such an offence or events closely connected with it (including any incriminating comments made by the suspected offender either before or after the offence);
- have a particular relationship with the victim or have a central position in the investigation.

Due to the very nature of fraud investigations, there may be many witnesses who are deemed to be significant. In these cases, the investigator should consider visually recording the interview. Visually recorded interviews with significant witnesses can also have the additional benefits of:

- safeguarding the integrity of the interviewer and the interview process;
- maximising the fine-grain detail given by the witness;
- increasing the opportunities for monitoring and for the development of interview skills.

KEY POINTS—VULNERABLE AND INTIMIDATED WITNESSES

Section 16, Youth Justice and Criminal Evidence Act 1999—vulnerable witnesses

Allows special measures for witnesses who are under 18 years of age or in circumstances where the court deems that the witness's evidence may be diminished due to their experiencing mental ill health, demonstrating a significant impairment of intelligence and social functioning, having a physical disability or suffering from a physical disorder.

Section 17, Youth Justice and Criminal Evidence Act 1999—intimidated witnesses

The witness is eligible for assistance (special measures) by virtue of this section if the court is satisfied that the quality of evidence given by the witness is likely to be diminished by reason of fear or distress on the part of the witness in connection with their testifying in the proceedings.

Source: www.app.college.police.uk/app-content/
investigations/victims-and-witnesses/

It is vital that any vulnerable or intimidated witness is identified and treated accordingly from the outset. This enables the use of potential protection measures at any future trial, with a number of different special measures available.

The National Police Chiefs' Council provides guidance in this area, stating that interviews with significant witnesses 'should be video recorded unless the witness does not consent or it is impracticable to do so'.

Should a hostile witness consent to an interview, it should be recorded on video unless they object.

Further reading

- Criminal Justice Act 2003: www.legislation.gov.uk/ukpga/2003/44/contents
- Youth Justice and Criminal Evidence Act 1999: www.legislation.gov.uk/ukpga/1999/23/contents
- Mental Capacity Act 2005: www.legislation.gov.uk/ukpga/2005/9/contents
- PACE Act 1984: www.gov.uk/guidance/police-and-criminal-evidence-act-1984-pace-codes-of-practice
- MoJ, *Code of Practice for Victims of Crime*, 2005: www.gov.uk/government/publications/the-code-of-practice-for-victims-of-crime
- Ministry of Justice, *Achieving Best Evidence in Criminal Proceedings: Guidance on interviewing victims and witnesses, and guidance on using special measures*, 2011: www.cps.gov.uk/publications/docs/best_evidence_in_criminal_proceedings.pdf
- National Policing Improvement Agency, 'National Investigative Interview Strategy', Briefing Paper, 2009: http://zakon.co.uk/admin/resources/downloads/investigative-interviewing-strategy-2009.pdf

---

6.13 **Covert investigations**

Fraud investigations are subject to the same specialised covert tactics that can be used for most criminal investigations that involve an element of organised crime. The use of covert methods can prove extremely effective in a fraud investigation, especially if you are dealing with a prolific offender or a fraudster who is trying to distance themselves from their criminal activity. Use of these tactics may attract PII considerations and, where appropriate, decisions concerning their use should be recorded in a sensitive KDL or via another recording method used by the organisation.

6.13.1 Legislation

The use of any deployment of a covert nature is governed by the Regulation of Investigatory Powers Act (RIPA) 2000 to ensure that it is legal, necessary and proportionate to utilise the above investigatory powers. There is also a requirement to show that all aspects of a subject's human rights have been considered, paying particular attention to the following Articles within the HRA 1998:

- Article 2: the right to life;
- Article 6: the right to a fair trial;
- Article 8: the right to respect for private and family life.

6.13.2 Deployment authority

Each type of covert deployment being considered requires a different level of authority but will in any case need to go through an authority office, which is usually headed by an authorising officer (AO) at the rank of detective superintendent. It is their responsibility to ensure that the application requested is legal, necessary and proportionate.

It is essential that the relevant department of a force responsible for covert methods of investigation is contacted to discuss the objectives of the investigation and the suitability of covert methods to achieve the required aims.

There are a number of covert tactics that can be utilised to provide an effective means of obtaining intelligence and evidence. The following list identifies the main covert methods available:

- **surveillance**: private premises/vehicles (intrusive) or public places (directed);
- **covert human intelligence sources** (CHISs): undercover officers (UCOs);
- **access to communication data**: subscriber details, itemised billing, cell sites, internet protocol (IP) data.

Surveillance (directed)

Directed surveillance is covert and conducted in public places. It is conducted for the purpose of a specific investigation or pre-planned operation in a manner that is likely to result in private information about a person being obtained.

The use of directed surveillance is a common covert method utilised in fraud investigations to identify a suspect's lifestyle, associates, assets and/or further premises owned or used by fraudsters to commit their criminal activities. Refer to the RIPA 2000 for authority requirements and liaise with the force's covert policing department to ascertain local procedures.

Surveillance (intrusive)

Intrusive surveillance is covert and relates to surveillance taking place in private, by means of a surveillance device in residential premises or in a private vehicle. Due to the naturally heightened expectation of retrieving private information, this covert method requires a higher authority. Consultation with your covert policing department is recommended.

Covert human intelligence sources (CHISs)

CHISs can be very useful in all fraud investigations, although it is likely that their motivations will differ from those of the CHISs found in more traditional criminal offences. A fraud CHIS is more likely to be driven by jealousy or a feeling of having been wronged on a professional level, and is less likely to be criminally involved. The CHIS will be managed by a unit that specifically and only deals with this covert resource. This is to ensure that the safety and management of the CHIS are in line with the RIPA and a level of sterility is maintained in the information passed on. The unit should register and manage the CHIS and conduct regular reviews. A CHIS can be tasked and it is essential that close liaison is maintained with the team managing the CHIS.

Undercover officers (UCOs)

Specialised UCOs have proved to be an effective tool, particularly in investigations involving the internet, whether it is cyber-enabled crime or cyber crime. Where unsuspecting members of the public are engaged with fraudsters on social media, the use of UCOs to gather evidence against the organisers of the offence is highly successful. This method targets the OCG rather than looking at the recipient account holders (mules), who often know very little of those behind the fraud. Due to the high volume of crimes belonging to this emerging fraud type, an umbrella authority under the RIPA can be run over an extended period of time, identifying specific subjects of the operation when necessary. This allows deployment against these criminals to take place over a rolling period of time with maximum effect.

With many of the deployments that involve this level of covert activity, there is often an element of risk. A specialist financial UCO may be deployed in the capacity of a money launderer and be required to move monies through accounts to gain trust from their criminal associates. The UCO will require access to many accounts across different banks, and money will be moved between them. UCOs will be run by an undercover officer, who will advise on options, required authorities, the boundaries within which their officers can operate and risk.

Access to communication data

The need for access to communication data has grown substantially. Mobile phones, computers and digital devices have become commonplace, and fraudsters use these by the very nature of their criminality. Compelling evidence is captured on these devices and has proved extremely useful to investigators in proving association, providing intelligence and yielding strong and secure evidence.

There is usually a single point of contact (SPOC) identified within law enforcement when utilising this legislation. An application requires different levels of authority depending on what information is requested.

6.13.3 Considerations before deploying covert methods

Covert deployments should be used when other methods of investigation have been considered but are not applicable or effective. An application to request a covert method should also show what has been considered and why covert activity is the preferred option.

It is imperative that, before each deployment, there are clear objectives from the outset. These objectives may change as the investigation develops, and this should also be recorded in any application/review process.

> ### Checklist—covert deployments considerations
>
> The following points should be considered to enable the setting of clear objectives:
>
> - **Resources**: the use of covert methods can be labour-intensive (surveillance) and so can often be more expensive than other investigative methods. Every force will have a tasking process to get access to a surveillance team. An authority office will advise on the protocol, which will vary from force to force.
>
> - **Defined parameters**: fraud investigations can often take place over a long period of time. For example, requesting communication data (subscriber/itemised billing) without a defined time period can be costly and time-consuming. All material will need to be examined, along with other investigative demands.
>
> - **Disclosure**: the use of covert techniques can lead to an increased amount of material produced that needs to be analysed appropriately for disclosure. Much of this will be of a sensitive nature and must be managed to ensure that it is not disclosed with other material. Often such techniques and the material they produce can lead to the need for PII in preparation for trial. You should notify your detective inspector of the sensitive material, and they will attend a PII hearing with you.
>
> - **Collateral intrusion**: with any covert technique, particularly the use of surveillance, there is a risk of collateral intrusion. This risk must be considered and any risks managed effectively.

- **Regular reviews**: it is necessary to regularly debrief and review the product of your covert technique. This may change the direction of the investigation and objectives. All reviews and intelligence should be recorded through a formal review of your authority.

Once a covert tactic has been authorised, there is a requirement for regular review and any new intelligence must be added so that the AO is confident that the deployments remain legal, necessary and proportionate.

6.13.4 Developing a covert investigation strategy

Checklist—covert investigation strategy

- Consider what evidence or intelligence is being sought?

- Is it relevant to the operation under consideration?

- What is the least intrusive means of securing the required evidence/intelligence?

- Has the least intrusive method been attempted? If not, why not?

- What is the likelihood of collateral intrusion against the privacy of persons not being investigated?

- How will collateral intrusion be minimised or prevented and how will the product be managed?

- Does the use of this tactic cause any risk to the organisation or its staff?

- Are there risks to the public or specific third parties through the deployment of such tactics?

- What are the risks to the subject of the investigation?

- Have all legal requirements been met?

- Does the proposed action comply with the HRA 1998?

- Seek advice from the director of intelligence/covert manager.

- Liaise with the relevant force's covert policing department to obtain advice and identify local procedures.

Further reading

- Office of Surveillance Commissioners, 'Procedures and Guidance', 2014: www.welhat.gov.uk/CHttpHandler.ashx?id=11156&p=0
- Surveillance Codes of Practice: www.gov.uk/government/publications/ covert-surveillance-and-covert-human-intelligence-sources-codes-of-practice

6.14 **Gathering relevant material**

Gathering relevant material is one of the most important aspects of fraud investigation and features in the FIM. The procedure adopted for gathering the material often comes under close scrutiny during the judicial process, and it frequently forms a significant area of examination for the defence.

The term 'material' is widely used throughout the legislation and procedures used by the investigator during a criminal investigation; it is referenced throughout the PACE Act and the CPIA. The material gathered during an investigation only truly becomes evidence once it is presented to the court.

Definition of the term 'material'

Material is material of any kind, including information and objects, which is obtained or inspected in the course of a criminal investigation and which may be relevant to the investigation. This includes not only material coming into the possession of the investigator (such as documents seized during the course of searching premises) but also material generated by him (such as interview records).

(Revised CPIA 1996, Code of Practice under Part II, March 2015)

In many fraud-related cases, the evidence of the offence is not rebuttable, so the defence will closely examine how that material has been gathered and how disclosure has been handled throughout the investigation. The investigator requires a comprehensive understanding of both the legislation and the procedure for gathering the various types of material encountered during an investigation. Investigators should be aware of the fraud challenge triangle, which illustrates where the challenges may be made in a typical fraud-related trial. See Figure 6.2.

Figure 6.2 The fraud challenge triangle

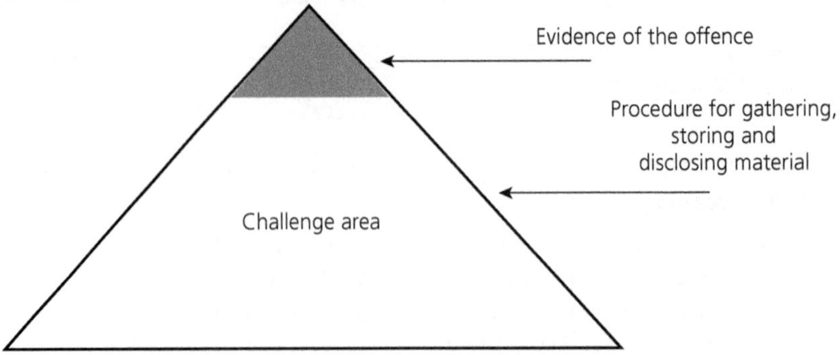

The investigator should apply a logical approach to the investigation and will benefit from prioritising the recovery of material throughout the investigation. The starting point for this process is to think about the nature of offending and identify the offence type(s). This will assist in identifying the nature of the material to be sought. For example, in a typical fraud the investigator will be looking for material relating to false representation, dishonesty and financial gain or loss.

Once the nature of the material has been identified, the next question to be answered is to identify its likely location and who is responsible for permitting access to it and whether they are likely to assist. In a fraud investigation, this will often be dictated by the type of fraud under investigation. See Figure 6.3.

Figure 6.3 Material recovery—typical locations

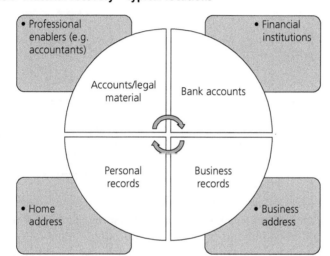

After the type and location of material have been considered, the order of recovery should be prioritised, seeking to identify what should be secured at the earliest opportunity. The method of recovery should then be decided. This can range from gaining consent through to obtaining a production order. The investigator will need to carefully consider the access conditions for each recovery method to ensure they are fully met. It is important to record the rationale for the decisions made during this process. In volume and priority cases, the investigating officer may record their decisions on the crime-recording system or progress sheet; in serious and complex cases, the SIO may use the key decision book for this purpose. See Figure 6.4.

6.14.1 'Golden hour' considerations

The golden hour principles are as important in fraud cases as they are when investigating more traditional crime types. The concept originated from medical emergencies and the response during the first hour to trauma, which, if effective,

Figure 6.4 Material recovery—process diagram

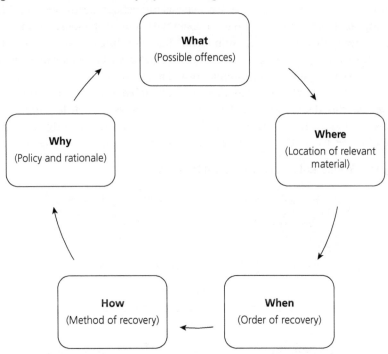

can reduce harm and save lives. In criminal investigations, the term relates to securing the maximum amount of material, minimising material attrition and maximising the opportunities to identify the offender. In fraud cases, the principles are the same as in other crime types. 'Golden hour' doesn't actually refer to a period of 60 minutes: it is a period of time that could be days, or even weeks.

These principles should drive fast-track actions to secure material subject to attrition at the earliest opportunity. From the moment the offence is reported, material attrition should be considered and responded to. Attrition is the wearing down of available material; this could be through the disposal of evidence by an offender or the diminishing memory of the victim or witness. By minimising material attrition, the investigation will gather as much relevant material as possible, enabling the fullest picture possible to be presented to the court.

KEY POINTS—FAST-TRACK ACTIONS

In fraud cases, the investigator should consider the following to reduce material attrition:

- record a statement from the victim (consider method if intimidated or vulnerable);
- secure relevant digital material and records held by the victim;

- secure material held by third parties;
- secure material held by the suspect relating to the fraud;
- consider passive data-gathering opportunities (CCTV etc).

6.14.2 **Types of material**

All material encountered by the investigator will fall into a specific category. It is crucial to correctly identify the type of material, as this will dictate the appropriate recovery method. If done correctly, this will help to negate any subsequent challenges in the judicial process. The types of material are, in the main, detailed in the PACE Act. See Table 6.1.

Further reading

- PACE Act 1984: www.legislation.gov.uk/ukpga/1984/60/contents

Table 6.1 Types of material

Section	Material type	Example(s)
PACE Act 1984, section 8	All material that does not consist of or include items subject to: • legally privileged material; • excluded material; • special procedure material.	Suspect's own financial data held at their home address.
PACE Act 1984, section 10	Legally privileged material. **Note:** items held with the intention of furthering a criminal purpose are not subject to legal privilege.	Correspondence between a professional legal adviser and his or her client in connection with or in contemplation of legal proceedings and for the purposes of such proceedings.
PACE Act 1984, section 11	Excluded material: • personal records; • journalistic material (held in confidence); • human tissue or tissue fluid.	Human tissue that has been taken for the purposes of medical treatment and held in confidence. Documentary records relating to an individual's health/mental health.
PACE Act 1984, section 14	Special procedure material: • material acquired or created in the course of any trade or business and held in confidence; • journalistic material, other than excluded material.	Banking records. Account opening records. Bank manager's notes.

6.14.3 **Methods of recovery**

Often, the appropriate method of recovery will be obvious to the investigator. The criteria to access each method are clearly detailed in a number of Acts and procedural documents, including the PACE Act 1984 and the POCA 2002. However, great care should be taken to consider each investigation on its own merits and look closely at the type of material to be recovered. The investigator should avoid adopting 'working rules', which can lead to poor practice and challenges throughout the judicial process. It is critical that the investigator fully understands what they are doing and why. The use of the powers available to the investigator is always underpinned by the HRA 1998; the investigator should ensure their actions are proportionate, legal, accountable and necessary.

Further reading

• The Human Rights Act 1998: www.legislation.gov.uk/ukpga/1998/42/contents

---

The rationale for the chosen method of recovery should be recorded in sufficient detail to ensure the investigator can recall at a later date why that decision was taken.

The choice of recovery method and its application, particularly search warrants and production orders, have been the subject of a significant number of judicial reviews, following which there has been adverse comment on both the individual investigator and their organisation. Often, the investigator has failed to understand the nature of the material being sought, has not been sufficiently transparent in their application or has taken material during the search that was not covered by the search warrant. It is in these areas that the investigator needs to be diligent and, if in doubt, seek expert advice.

KEY POINTS—METHODS OF MATERIAL RECOVERY FREQUENTLY USED IN FRAUD-RELATED INVESTIGATIONS

These include:

• consent;
• Serious Organised Crime and Police Act (SOCPA) 2005, section 62—disclosure notice;
• DPA 1998, section 29—sharing of information;
• PACE Act, section 18—entry and search after arrest;
• PACE Act, section 19—general power of seizure;
• PACE Act, section 32—search upon arrest;
• POCA 2002, section 345—production order;
• POCA 2002, section 352—search and seizure warrant;
• PACE Act, section 8—search warrant;

- PACE Act, section 9, Schedule 1—production order (first set of access);
- PACE Act, section 9, Schedule 1—production order (second set of access);
- Criminal Justice and Police Act 2001, section 52—used in conjunction with the above powers;
- PACE Act 1984, Schedule 1—production order (section 12, warrant application).

Once the investigator has identified the type of material sought, they should identify the appropriate recovery method and ensure the access criteria are fully met.

6.14.4 Consent

Gaining the consent of the holder of the material is the least intrusive measure that can be utilised by the investigator. In nearly all cases, the victim and most witnesses will hand material to the investigator with their consent. The consent given by the subject must be true consent and the investigator is under an obligation to be truthful and transparent as to the purpose of the request for the material.

6.14.5 Disclosure notices (section 62 of SOCPA 2005)

The section 62 notice is a particularly valuable tool when dealing with a reluctant witness in a serious case. The notice was introduced under the SOCPA 2005 and was intended to mirror the powers already available to the SFO to compel individuals to cooperate with investigations by producing documents and answering questions. The legislation allows investigators from the police, the NCA and Her Majesty's Revenue and Customs (HMRC) to seek a notice from a prosecutor directing a person to:

- answer questions with respect to any matter relevant to the investigation;
- provide information with respect to any such matter as is specified in the notice;
- produce such documents, or documents of such descriptions, relevant to the investigation as specified in the notice.

This can be done in relevant offences that are listed in the Act and include lifestyle offences listed in Schedule 2 to the POCA 2002: corruption, false accounting (where the gain or loss exceeds £5,000) and money laundering.

The access criteria for using the notice include demonstrating that there are reasonable grounds for suspecting that a person has committed an offence, and that the person subject to the notice has material relevant to the investigation that will be of substantial value. Section 64 details a number of restrictions on the information that can be required, including legally privileged and special procedure material. Any statement made by the person subject to the notice cannot be used against them in criminal proceedings, unless they fail to comply with a disclosure notice, give a false declaration or make a statement contrary to section 5 of the Perjury Act 1911.

Failing to comply with the notice is a summary offence of failing to comply with a disclosure notice. The maximum penalty is a level 5 fine or a term of imprisonment of 51 weeks (in Scotland, 12 months) or both. The section also creates an offence of making a false or misleading statement, which, if tried on indictment, is punishable by a fine, up to two years' imprisonment or both.

6.14.6 DPA 1998—section 29

The primary purpose of the DPA 1998 was to protect personal data held by organisations to ensure it is processed lawfully.

KEY POINTS—SCHEDULE 1—THE DATA PROTECTION PRINCIPLES

Part I The principles

1 Personal data shall be processed fairly and lawfully and, in particular, shall not be processed unless:
   (a) at least one of the conditions in Schedule 2 is met, and
   (b) in the case of sensitive personal data, at least one of the conditions in Schedule 3 is also met.
2 Personal data shall be obtained only for one or more specified and lawful purposes, and shall not be further processed in any manner incompatible with that purpose or those purposes.
3 Personal data shall be adequate, relevant and not excessive in relation to the purpose or purposes for which they are processed.
4 Personal data shall be accurate and, where necessary, kept up to date.
5 Personal data processed for any purpose or purposes shall not be kept for longer than is necessary for that purpose or those purposes.
6 Personal data shall be processed in accordance with the rights of data subjects under this Act.
7 Appropriate technical and organisational measures shall be taken against unauthorised or unlawful processing of personal data and against accidental loss or destruction of, or damage to, personal data.
8 Personal data shall not be transferred to a country or territory outside the European Economic Area unless that country or territory ensures an adequate level of protection for the rights and freedoms of data subjects in relation to the processing of personal data.

Source: https://ico.org.uk/for-organisations/guide-to-data-protection/data-protection-principles

---

The provisions detailed in section 29 of the Act give an exemption for the non-disclosure principles, permitting personal data to be shared for the prevention of crime, the apprehension of offenders and the assessment or collection of any tax or duty or imposition of a similar nature. Many organisations will accept an application under section 29; however, the onus is on the data controller to agree to hand over the material requested. An application made under section 29 does not compel the recipient to hand over the material requested, and if they refuse an alternative form of recovery will need to be considered.

6.14.7 PACE Act 1984, section 18—entry and search after arrest

The power under section 18 allows a constable to enter and search any premises occupied or controlled by a person who has been arrested, if there are reasonable grounds to suspect that, on the premises, there is evidence (not legally privileged material) that relates to the offence for which they have been arrested or for a similar indictable offence. This power requires the written authority of an inspector, either before the search or retrospectively if the person's presence was required elsewhere for the effective investigation of the offence (an inspector should be informed as soon as is practicable).

6.14.8 PACE Act 1984, section 19—power of seizure

Section 19 gives a constable who is lawfully on premises a general power to seize anything, except legally privileged material, that they have reasonable grounds to believe has been obtained as a result of an offence or is evidence of an offence that is being investigated, or any other offence. They must believe it is necessary to seize the material to stop it being concealed, altered, lost or destroyed.

6.14.9 PACE Act 1984, section 32—search upon arrest

This section gives the constable the power to search an arrested person under certain criteria for, among other things, anything that might be evidence relating to an offence. If the suspect has been arrested for an indictable offence, then a search may be conducted of any premises he was in when arrested or immediately before for evidence relating to the offence if there are reasonable grounds to believe there is evidence of the offence on the premises. Any material discovered may be seized if it is evidence of an offence or has been obtained in consequence of the commission of an offence.

KEY POINTS—CASE LAW—JUDICIAL REVIEW—RELIANCE ON SECTION 32 POWERS IN PRE-PLANNED OPERATIONS

Lord Hanningfield of Chelmsford v Chief Constable of Essex Police [2013] EWHC 243 (QB)

The case concerned an investigation into Lord Hanningfield and an investigation into claims he made whilst engaged by Essex Council. He made a number of

---

challenges to the police procedures adopted during the investigation. One of these areas was a decision made by the SIO to rely on the arrest to trigger the use of the section 32 search powers. The court ruled that, where the necessary criteria for arrest are not met, the process should not be relied on as an alternative to obtaining a search warrant if a search is considered necessary.

Mr Justice Eady, in his summing up, stated that 'the burden clearly rests on the Defendant (Essex Police) to establish that it was necessary to arrest Lord Hanningfield to effect a search of his home without obtaining a search warrant'. In this particular case, the necessary criteria were not fulfilled. Mr Justice Eady further stated that: 'It was in the light of that knowledge that the SIO decided that the s.32 route would be the most appropriate for the case in hand. One can see that it was in some ways convenient for the officers to take this course, without having to obtain a warrant, but that is clearly not a sufficient justification. I can, therefore, see no justification for by-passing all the usual statutory safeguards involved in obtaining a warrant.'

6.14.10 **POCA 2002, section 345—production order**

The POCA legislation is designed to remove the benefit of crime from the offender. It comes with a whole raft of powers, including the ability to access material through the service of a production order.

KEY POINTS—POCA 2002, SECTION 346—REQUIREMENTS FOR MAKING OF A PRODUCTION ORDER

(1) These are the requirements for the making of a production order.
(2) There must be reasonable grounds for suspecting that:
    (a) in the case of a confiscation investigation, the person the application for the order specifies as being subject to the investigation has benefited from his criminal conduct;
    (b) in the case of a civil recovery investigation, the property the application for the order specifies as being subject to the investigation is recoverable property or associated property;
    (c) in the case of a money laundering investigation, the person the application for the order specifies as being subject to the investigation has committed a money laundering offence.
(3) There must be reasonable grounds for believing that the person the application specifies as appearing to be in possession or control of the material so specified is in possession or control of it.
(4) There must be reasonable grounds for believing that the material is likely to be of substantial value (whether or not by itself) to the investigation for the purposes of which the order is sought.

---

(5) There must be reasonable grounds for believing that it is in the public interest for the material to be produced or for access to it to be given, having
regard to:

(a) the benefit likely to accrue to the investigation if the material is obtained;

(b) the circumstances under which the person whom the application specifies
as appearing to be in possession or control of the material holds it.

Source: www.legislation.gov.uk/ukpga/2002/29/section/346.

The application should be made to a judge by an appropriate officer, a term
which includes police officers. The application should state that the person
detailed in the application is subject to either a confiscation or money laundering investigation or is subject to a civil recovery investigation. The order should
confirm that the order is sought for the purposes of the investigation and that
the specified person is in control of that material.

6.14.11 **POCA 2002, section 352—search and seizure warrant**

A judge can issue a search and seizure warrant if the application relates to
either a money laundering or confiscation investigation or is subject to a
civil recovery investigation. The warrant can be issued where a production
order has not been complied with and there are reasonable grounds for
believing that the material is on the premises specified in the application
for the warrant. Additionally, a search warrant can be sought where it is not
practicable to communicate with a person against whom the production
order could be made, or with any person who would be required to comply
with an order to grant entry and where the investigation might be seriously
prejudiced unless an appropriate person is able to secure immediate access
to the material.

6.14.12 **PACE Act 1984, section 8—search warrant**

This is the material recovery method that is used extensively in fraud-related
investigations and is the main 'tool' used to search for evidence of an offence.
The access criteria are clearly articulated and should be carefully considered
when contemplating whether it is the correct material recovery method. Over
recent years, there have been a significant number of judicial reviews examining the application, execution and recovery of material relating to the service
of section 8 search warrants; in many of these cases, the procedure adopted by
the investigating officers has not been sufficient and this has led to significant
criticism of law enforcement agencies and their ability to comply with the law.
See Figure 6.5.

Figure 6.5 Simplified flow chart—PACE Act 1984, section 8—warrant applications

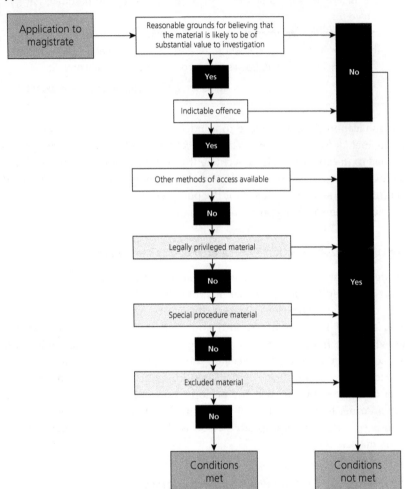

In October 2013, the Lord Chief Justice introduced a set of new search warrant application and warrant forms. The changes were made to ensure closer compliance with the requirements laid out in the PACE Act. The new template forms were introduced to ensure those completing the documents properly consider the access criteria and give sufficient detail for the magistrate or judge to make a considered decision on whether to grant the warrant or not.

There are three warrant application forms, each with a specific purpose. Care has to be taken to select the right form. See Table 6.2.

Table 6.2 Summary of warrant applications

Warrant Applications—Summary

	Application	Purpose
A	Application for search warrant—Criminal Procedure Rules, rule 6.30; PACE Act 1984, section 8.	Search warrant under section 8 of the PACE Act 1984.
B	Application for search warrant—Criminal Procedure Rules, rule 6.31; Criminal Justice Act 1987, section 2.	Search warrant under section 2 of the Criminal Justice Act 1987—for use in connection with an application by a member of the SFO for a search warrant under section 2 of the Criminal Justice Act 1987.
C	Application for search warrant—Criminal Procedure Rules, rule 6.32; PACE Act 1984, sections 15 and 16.	Search warrant under legislation (the main search power) to which sections 15 and 16 of the PACE Act 1984 apply, other than section 8 of the PACE Act.

Checklist—preparation of the application for a section 8 search warrant

- Apply in writing, giving:
  - an estimate of how long the application will take.
- Provide the applicant's details, including:
  - their address and telephone number.
- Detail the status of the applicant, ensuring it:
  - satisfies the court of their entitlement to apply;
  - includes the police, the NCA and HMRC.
- Arrange the application with the court, by:
  - adding an estimate of the time for application;
  - identifying opportunities to utilise a live link.
- Detail the offence under investigation, including:
  - the indictable offence (this also applies to a summary offence under the Immigration Act 1971 (section 28D)).
- Explain in detail the material sought, by:
  - providing details of why the material will be of substantial value;

- providing the maximum amount of detail re the material sought;
- confirming that it does not consist of legally privileged, excluded or special procedure material.
- Detail why access criteria are met, explaining:
  - why it is not possible to communicate to person entitled to grant entry;
  - why entry will not be granted by a person who could be communicated with;
  - why entry will not be given unless a warrant is produced;
  - why the purpose of the search will be seriously prejudiced unless a constable can secure immediate entry.
- Provide information that might undermine the application.
- Specify the premises to be searched by:
  - indicating if they will be searched more than once and why;
  - specifying as many sets of premises as possible.
- Detail others to be involved in the search by:
  - identifying others by function or description;
  - giving the reason why others need be involved in the search.
- Declarations:
  - by the applicant to the best of their knowledge and belief that all information relevant to the application has been presented to the court and the application is true;
  - that a senior officer has reviewed and authorised the application.
- Serve an application on an officer of the court.

The Criminal Procedure Rules were updated in October 2015 regarding the way the application for search warrants should be made to the court and the procedure that should be closely adhered to.

Checklist—applying for a search warrant (Criminal Procedure Rules, October 2015)

- The application should be made in private.
- The applicant should be present (can be by live link, if the court permits).
- Check that sufficient time is available to make the application.

- The application should be made on oath.

- The applicant should disclose all information, including issues that might undermine any grounds of the application.

- The court is responsible for making a record of any questions and answers during the application.

- Questions and answers must be on oath and the truth.

- If the applicant cannot satisfy the court, then the court may detail what further information is required and give directions to any revised application.

Further reading

- **Duty of disclosure when making an application for a warrant**: when applying for warrants, there is a duty of full disclosure on the applicant. The court should ensure they take a diligent and inquisitive approach to the application. See *R (on the application of Chatwani and others) v The National Crime Agency and another* [2015] EWHC 1284 (Admin).
- **Failing to comply with the PACE Act when making an application for a warrant (warrant quashed)**: see *R (on the application of S, F and L) v Chief Constable of the British Transport Police* [2013] EWHC 2189 (Admin).
- **A section 8 warrant should record the address to be searched (warrant quashed)**: see *R (on the application of Bhatti and others) v Croydon Magistrates' Court and others* [2010] EWHC 522 (Admin).
- **Failing to give the full information in application (material returned)**: see *R (on the application of Kouyoumjian and another) v Hammersmith Magistrates' Court* [2014] EWHC 4028 (Admin).
- **Failing to give sufficient detail what property could be seized (ordered to return property)**: see *Lee and others v Solihull Magistrates' Court and another* [2013] EWHC 3779 (Admin).

6.14.13 **PACE Act, section 9, Schedule 1—production order (first set of access)**

Section 9 of the PACE Act 1984 permits access to excluded and special procedure material, which can be sought by making an application under Schedule 1 to the PACE Act 1984.

Schedule 1 details two sets of access conditions:

- the application for special procedure material (see Figure 6.6);
- the application for excluded material (see Figure 6.7).

See also Figure 6.8.

Figure 6.6 Simplified flow chart—PACE Act 1984, section 9—production order

(Schedule 1, section 2, first set of access conditions)

Special procedure material (not excluded material)

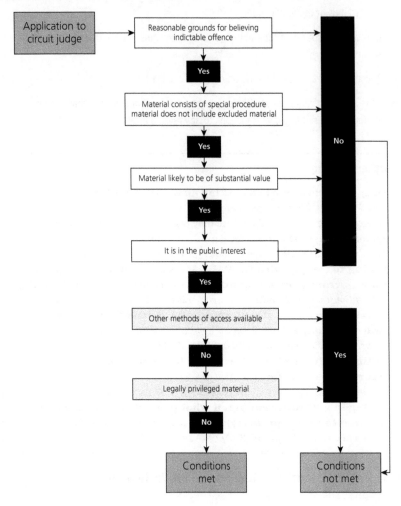

....

Case law

R (on the application of Faisaltex Ltd and others) v Preston Crown Court [2008] EWHC 2832 (Admin)

This case gives guidance on special procedure material.

The Honourable Mr Justice Eady:

Special procedure material is, by virtue of section 14, essentially material held by a person subject to an undertaking to hold it in confidence. It is particularly likely to be found at premises occupied by solicitors or accountants because of the nature of their professions, and it may then include various business documents concerning their clients' business. But there is no reason why one should expect business documents held by the clients themselves at their business or domestic premises to be held subject to an undertaking to hold them in confidence.

....

6.14.14 Criminal Justice and Police Act 2001, sections 52–62

An understanding of the use of the section 52 notice and the processes connected to its serving is essential for the investigator. The legislation was introduced to rectify a defect in law identified as a result of the case *R v Chesterfield Justices and Chief Constable of Derbyshire, ex parte Bramley* [1999] All ER (D) 1237.

This case highlighted the point that the PACE Act 1984 did not authorise the police to seize material for the purpose of examining it elsewhere to ascertain if it was relevant unless they had a specific power to do so. In the case of Bramley, a large quantity of material was taken from his business premises to sift through elsewhere; it was determined that this process could be construed as 'trespass'. As such, this could have led to claims being made and could have resulted in large amounts of compensation being paid to those whose material had been taken.

Figure 6.7 Simplified flow chart—PACE Act 1984, section 9—production order
(Schedule 1, section 3, second set of access conditions)
Special procedure material (***includes excluded material***)

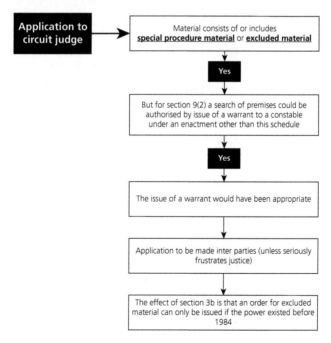

Figure 6.8 Executing a Schedule 1 warrant

Application
- Circuit judge
- Written authority
- Inter partes
- Notice served

Search warrant
- Not practicable to communicate with any relevant person
- May seriously prejudice the investigation

Search procedure
- OIC responsible for minimum disruption
- Ask for documents concerned
- If not satisfied, may search

Sections 50–62 of the Criminal Justice and Police Act 2001 provide a legal basis for material to be taken from the person/scene when it is not known if it is relevant or not (see Figure 6.9). They explain the process for such seizures and are particularly detailed in relation to the way such material is to be recorded and handled. Section 50 deals with seizures from people and section 51 details seizures from premises.

The serving of a section 52 notice is a supplementary process and has to be carried out in conjunction with an existing power of search. It enables those exercising an existing power of search to remove material from the scene to another location to determine whether something is or may contain something for which they are authorised to search. The reasons why this might be done are detailed in the 'reasonably practicable' test. The main considerations are:

1 How long will it take to carry out separation or determination of the material?
2 How many persons are required over a reasonable period?
3 What damage would be caused if the search/examination were carried out in situ?
4 What specialist equipment or apparatus would be required to undertake the examination?
5 Would separation of material at the initial point of search be likely to prejudice the subsequent use of seized material (i.e. the audit trail)?

If there are grounds to believe legally privileged material is held on a computer that is to be seized (as it may contain other material relevant to the investigation), then it is critical that a section 52 notice is served.

The section 52 notice should be served when the material is taken and a copy given to the person from whom the material was taken. The material should

Figure 6.9 Criminal Justice and Police Act 2001—relevant sections

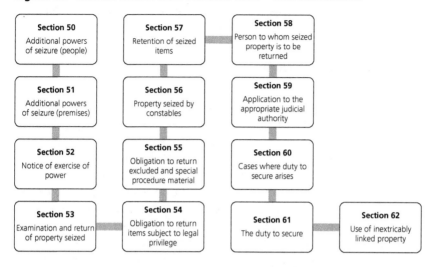

be examined as soon as is practicable and stored in a separate area of the property store. The owner of the material should be notified that they can make representations to the Crown Court to have the material returned before it is examined. In some circumstances, they are permitted to be present when the material is examined.

Further reading

- Criminal Justice and Police Act 2001: www.legislation.gov.uk/ukpga/2001/16/contents
- PACE Act Codes of Practice, Code B, paragraph 7.7: www.gov.uk/government/uploads/system/uploads/attachment_data/file/306655/2013_PACE_Code_B.pdf

---

6.15 Forensic investigative opportunities

Forensic analysis of exhibits and documents within the area of fraud investigation broadly follows normal practice for other types of crime. This section aims to outline some of the principles pertinent to fraud investigation and detail some of the options that the investigator may not have come across in other types of investigation.

Typically, fraud investigations need close management with a well-written forensic strategy. Drafted at the start of any fraud investigation, this will assist the investigator(s) in focusing on what is important and relevant to the case and controlling what reasonable inquiries should be undertaken.

Any forensic strategy should be formulated in consultation with a forensic officer or force forensic manager. Again, this will focus the aims of such a process and control the financial commitments of the investigation.

6.15.1 **Documentary evidence**

Most fraud cases collect a large amount of documentation, the content of which is normally the primary evidence. However, consideration should be given to the benefits of analysis of things such as handwriting, paper technology (type, standard, watermarking, etc), chemical fingerprint development and DNA. Expert witnesses exist in these and other documentary evidence fields, and further advice can be gained from your force forensic manager, national databases or industry. Fingerprint evidence gained from seized documents can be invaluable, but the temptation here is to seize as much paperwork as possible during searches and to test every piece of paper. Clearly, this is not practicable and early decisions will need to be made about what material is to be seized and what will then be tested. Again, the forensic strategy should be a guide to this process and will assist in demonstrating thought processes and financial constraints at any subsequent court cases.

6.15.2 **Voice analysis**

Many financial and associated businesses routinely record calls in and out of their buildings and can supply excerpts in evidential format. These calls can then be compared with suspect interviews or other recordings by an expert who will then be able to give an opinion on the similarity of the voice and ultimately link a recording to a suspect. Liaise with the force's forensic department, which will be able to assist with access to experts.

6.15.3 **Phone and computer downloads**

Complex frauds can involve many people at different levels of crime. The downloads of phones, other media devices and computers can lead to the collection of a large amount of data that will need careful and thoughtful analysis; adherence to the original strategy will assist here.

Options such as taking data forensic experts with you on premises searches need to be considered, and any non-police officers need to be specifically mentioned on warrant applications.

Powers of 'search and sift' under sections 50 and 51 of the Criminal Justice Act 2001 should be considered when seizing phones, computers and other means of electronically storing data.

Before any download work is commenced, consideration should be given to the existence of DNA or fingerprint evidence on seized items. The inside of a phone or computer case can provide good evidence of ownership prior to any data analysis.

The checklist below outlines some of the factors investigators need to consider when developing a forensic evidence strategy.

Checklist—forensic material recovery

- Consider writing a forensic recovery and examination strategy for your case.
- Set the legislative/procedural framework for the recovery, examination and retention of items seized.
- Remember to reference 'traditional' forensic opportunities:
  - DNA and fingerprinting techniques are relevant in fraud investigations.
- Consider fraud-specific forensic opportunities:
  - it may be important to attribute an individual user to a particular digital device.
- Control the size of the inquiry by being clear about what you are trying to achieve.
- Section 50/51 notices must be served and adhered to in 'bulk' seizure searches.
- Remember fraud investigation forensics rely on different expert testimony and can lead to high budget costs.
- Seek early legal advice in cases involving LPP material.

6.15.4 Digital evidence

Obtaining digital evidence requires careful consideration from the outset; otherwise numerous electronic devices will be seized, creating unnecessary and expensive work for the investigation team. Early consultation with hi-tech crime units is essential in deciding what types of devices will need seizing and what devices can be imaged at the scene. These decisions can only be made after the SIO/OIC has decided what offences are being investigated, who is being investigated and what material is being sought from the electronic devices.

Following the seizure of devices, a digital forensic strategy should be written outlining how the devices will be imaged, what material will be extracted for examination, how that material will be examined by an investigator and how this work will be recorded.

The strategy is a useful document to remind the investigation team of what is expected of them during the examination stage, and highlights relevant legislation that is associated with digital evidence.

The size of the investigation will normally dictate how many devices will be seized. If a number of different types of devices have been seized, different options can be used at the imaging stage. For instance, memory cards could be subject to 'triage' review to determine their contents. Meanwhile, computers and laptops might have to be subject to a full imaging process due to the volume of material stored on the different media.

Following the extraction process, the data needs to be examined. The examination process is the part that will take the longest time to complete and is the most resource-intensive element. As per the Attorney General's guidelines, not all material needs to be examined in voluminous cases. Using keywords will reduce the amount of data to be examined. Keywords need to be relevant, and early engagement with defence teams will reduce the risk of abuse arguments later in the judicial process.

For larger cases, there are e-discovery products available to assist with examining lots of data en masse or by a number of examiners. These products are available from private companies and can be expensive to use.

6.15.5 Passive data generators

Passive data generators are automated systems that gather and collate information for purposes unconnected with criminal investigation, but can be accessed by investigators. The most common examples for fraud investigations include:

- financial information;
- CCTV;
- computer-based electronic evidence;
- telecommunications information, including subscriber details and cell sites.

What distinguishes passive data generators from other types of record keeping, such as patient records, is that they are automated and require no judgement on the part of the person making them. They are also stored in systems that require technical expertise to access.

It is vitally important that parameters are set when obtaining passive data, as the results can be voluminous or result in further requests. The data will then need to be examined by the investigation team, while managing the other inquiries.

Consideration will first have to be given to the legal framework to obtain the data and determine how long it will take the organisation to retrieve the data. Importantly, the wider the parameters, the longer it may take for the data to become available.

6.15.6 Social media

Social media, as in other crime types, can help to provide intelligence on the associations between suspects, their background and their current whereabouts. Apart from establishing this from open-source inquiries, it is highly likely that evidence from social media will be stored on the suspect's mobile telephones and tablets.

Obtaining evidence of the account's content from the companies themselves will require a letter of request being sent to a foreign jurisdiction, as the companies are often based outside England and Wales.

In certain investigations, consideration could be given to deploying an undercover officer (UCO) within the virtual world to gain further information and/or evidence. This course of action would need to be discussed in detail with the relevant force's covert policing department and, if agreed, would require the use of RIPA applications.

Although it is not exhaustive, the checklist below outlines some of the factors investigators need to consider when developing a digital evidence strategy.

Checklist—digital forensic strategy

Developing a digital forensic strategy

- Early consultation with a hi-tech crime unit;
- clear decisions from the SIO;
- the different imaging options;
- the Attorney General's guidelines;
- the use of keywords for examination;
- early engagement with defence teams.

A *Passive data generators*

- Set realistic parameters for the date range of the data;
- identify the framework required to obtain the data;
- length of time needed for the organisation to provide the data;
- provision of adequate resources to examine the data.

B *Social media*

- Consider where evidence can be found on the suspect's property;
- letters of request will be required to obtain evidence from overseas-based organisations;
- consider the use of covert tactics to obtain evidence.

C *Digital forensic strategy headings and considerations*

1 Introduction;

2 background information;

3 priorities;

4 objectives;

5 timescales;

6 imaging;

7 preservation for fingerprint analysis;

8 broken or damaged hard drives;

9 analysis:

- graphics material;
- office-style documents;
- encryption;
- internet evidence finder;
- areas not to be examined and rationale;

10 examination:

- training;
- keywords;
- evidential product;
- disclosure;

11 sources of support;

12 welfare, health and safety;

13 review of results;

14 dealing with documents in foreign languages;

15 material subject to legal professional privilege;

16 illegal images;

17 retention of exhibits;

18 relevant legislation/guidance.

Further reading

- Passive data generators: www.app.college.police.uk/app-content/
  investigations/investigative-strategies/passive-data-generators
- RIPA 2000: www.legislation.gov.uk/ukpga/2000/23/contents
- PACE Act 1984: www.legislation.gov.uk/ukpga/1984/60/contents
- Criminal Procedure and Investigations Act 1996: www.legislation.gov.uk/
  ukpga/1996/25/contents
- Criminal Justice and Police Act 2001: www.legislation.gov.uk/ukpga/2001/
  16/contents

- Attorney General's guidelines on disclosure, 2005 and 2011: www.gov.uk/guidance/attorney-general-s-guidelines-on-disclosure-2005-and-2011
- Attorney General's guidelines on disclosure, 2013: Disclosure Manual, Annex H: www.cps.gov.uk/legal/d_to_g/disclosure_manual/annex_h_disclosure_manual/
- ACPO Good Practice Guide for Digital Evidence, 2012: http://library.college.police.uk/docs/acpo/digital-evidence-2012.pdf
- The Regulation of Investigatory Powers (Covert Human Intelligence Sources: Relevant Sources) Order 2013: www.legislation.gov.uk/uksi/2013/2788/pdfs/uksi_20132788_en.pdf

6.16 **International investigations**

International/cross-border investigations have become increasingly common as communication systems advance and the 'world shrinks'. It is important to recognise that, with just a few exceptions, the jurisdictions engaged with will have their own legislation and guidance that need to be adhered to. Any action contradicting these may well endanger the ability to use any material provided.

KEY POINTS—MATERIAL SOUGHT FOR INTERNATIONAL INVESTIGATIONS

The material sought for international investigations is best divided into two sections:

- non-evidential, i.e. information and intelligence;
- evidential, i.e. material obtained for inclusion in a prosecution.

Information and intelligence exchanged with foreign jurisdictions has to be carefully assessed, properly authorised and auditable. Some transactions are covered by agency- or case-specific international bilateral MoUs or wider national agreements. In each case, however, the content needs to be properly evaluated, appropriately marked under the Government Protective Marking Scheme (GPMS) and deemed suitable for dissemination with an appropriate level of supervision. In supplying such material to a foreign jurisdiction, it is also important to define the agreed use and level of dissemination that the recipient should observe.

Evidential material is normally supplied between jurisdictions under the auspices of formal bilateral mutual legal assistance treaties (MLATs), unless otherwise accommodated. Obtaining evidence abroad normally involves the submission of a letter of request from the competent prosecuting UK authority (e.g. CPS) via the UK Central Authority (UKCA) at the Home Office. This letter (colloquially 'LOR' or 'commission rogatoire') is normally drafted by the investigating officer for agreement and finalisation by the prosecuting agency, who then submit it via the UKCA. The UKCA will then check the letter and advise the investigating officer on any changes that are necessary before transmitting it to the appropriate central authority for the country in question and in a format agreed by the relevant MLAT. The LOR may request the most relevant corresponding agency to seek and obtain the required material independently, or may include a request for the investigating officers to travel to obtain the material, assisted by the former. It is important to remember, however, that while obtaining material abroad in this way, it is under the legislation and codes of practice of the host country and UK powers cannot normally be invoked.

If an investigation crosses international borders, then early consideration should be given to drafting an LOR, as failure to do so can cause considerable delays to the evidence-gathering process, either through a local lack of capacity or resources or due to political interference. Reaching out via the Foreign and Commonwealth Office (FCO) to UK embassies/ambassadors and local law enforcement can greatly increase the chances of success.

Additionally, if officers travel to the relevant jurisdiction to conduct inquiries, they must be aware of the legislation and codes of practice of the host country. Also, their movements, and the management of the request, will be carried out within the time frames of the assisting law enforcement officer or court officer. Therefore, it is essential that they engage early with local law enforcement or the relevant agency, so that a realistic time frame can be agreed prior to travelling.

Where joint or parallel investigations affecting both jurisdictions exist, there are a number of processes available for managing them. These are normally under national agreements or specific MoUs, as mentioned earlier.

Another way of recovering material from overseas jurisdictions is to form a joint investigation team (JIT). A JIT is an investigation team set up for a fixed period, based on an agreement between two or more EU member states and/or competent authorities, for a specific purpose. Non-EU member states may participate in a JIT with the agreement of all other parties. The advantage of entering into any JIT is that it enables the exchange of evidential material without the need for an international letter of request. JITs have been used to facilitate both the prosecution and disruption of OCGs for fraud-related offences. JITs are facilitated through Eurojust, situated in The Hague. It is imperative that, at the commencement of any JIT, the roles of each country are clearly defined to prevent any future confusion over the prosecuting jurisdiction. The objectives should be clearly defined to minimise misunderstandings. When embarking on joint investigations, communication is key to a successful outcome. Officers should ensure that relevant legislation is explored within both jurisdictions, to guarantee that the most appropriate prosecution venue is identified. Officers should ensure that any agreement to enter into a JIT is documented and reviewed accordingly.

6.17 **Use of subject matter experts (SMEs)**

The use of an SME in court proceedings is outlined in the Criminal Court Procedure Rules.

KEY POINTS—DEFINITION OF AN EXPERT

An expert is defined as 'a person who is required to give or prepare expert evidence for the purpose of criminal proceedings, including evidence required to determine fitness to plead or for the purpose of sentencing'.

Source: Criminal Procedure Rules, rule 19.1, October 2015

The SME has a duty to the court to give an opinion that is objective, unbiased and within their area of expertise. They may be required in both the investigation and the subsequent court case. This will usually occur when there is an area that requires specialist knowledge. SMEs will have gained experience in the pertinent area as a result of experience, practical knowledge and, often, qualifications. They will usually be undertaking a day-to-day role within their area of expertise, have recently undertaken such a role or supervise those undertaking the role.

The SME will understand a topic area better than the audience (in this case, the judge and jury) and should be able to explain the matter in simple terms, without the use of jargon and industry-specific terminology. An effective SME will also have experience of court procedures and will be able to differentiate between what is relevant to the case and what may be important to them but is not required for an understanding of the particular areas relevant to the court case.

Sourcing an SME with the relevant experience may be difficult, particularly when the area of expertise is unusual. Colleagues in the same or other forces may be useful sources of information. The NCA also hold details of the experts used in criminal cases. In addition, the Police OnLine Knowledge Area (POLKA) is a useful source of information.

It is important to check the track record of the SME. Confirm that their knowledge is up to date and relevant and that they are able to pass their knowledge on to an audience.

An SME will have gained considerable experience in the area and, as such, will be able to command an appropriate level of remuneration for their work. Discuss the appropriate level of work and consider whether some of the work will be undertaken by the investigation team, with the SME only being required to state conclusions or give opinions.

Those instructing SMEs must ensure that there are no conflicts of interest. The SME cannot work for both sides in a court case, unless instructed to do so by the court. A conflict check should be undertaken by SMEs to ensure they are not being instructed by both parties. This must be included within the agreement between those instructing and the SME.

KEY POINTS—THE AGREEMENT WITH AN SME

This should be a formal, binding contract that must contain details of:

- the level of work required from the SME;
- deadlines for the delivery of the product;
- how disclosure of the product will be dealt with;
- the rate charged for the work;
- the rate charged for appearing at court;
- the names of all parties in the case;
- details of the case;
- the documentation that will be provided to the SME;
- confidentiality;
- ownership of the product and whether it can be used elsewhere;
- confirmation of the experience and expertise of the SME;
- a dispute resolution process.

Advice should be sought from lawyers in drafting such an agreement if a standard agreement is not available.

If SMEs are instructed by both sides in a case, the court may order a meeting of experts to take place before or during trial in order to produce a list of agreed and non-agreed areas. This should have the effect of reducing the time spent by the experts in giving evidence. Care should be taken to ensure that the expert is not forced into agreeing areas that could be damaging to the case, though this is heavily dependent on the strength of the individual expert. Again, this demonstrates the need to source a relevant expert with the correct level of experience.

In general, it is useful to engage an SME at the earliest opportunity, but this must be balanced by the potential for the SME to charge additional fees.

Expert witnesses will generally have experience of the Civil Procedure Rules but they should be made aware of the additional requirements of the CPIA in respect of the disclosure, recording and retention of material. The additional work is not onerous and will generally be part of the expert's normal procedures.

It is also useful to ensure that the expert is aware of how criminal trials with a jury differ from civil or tribunal cases. The expert must take account of the different audience—jury and judge rather than only a judge—when preparing any report.

KEY POINTS—CONTENT OF AN SME REPORT

- Qualifications, expertise and accreditation;
- details of materials relied upon in report;
- statement setting out the substance of all the facts;

- who carried out any relevant tests/examinations;
- any 'qualifications' on the opinion given;
- summary of conclusion;
- declarations.

6.17.1 **Forensic accountants**

Forensic accountants are often instructed in criminal cases in order to convert seemingly complex financial data into a form that is easily understood by a jury. In many cases their work will overlap with that undertaken by the financial investigator, but it will tend to concentrate on the investigation and prosecution of the case rather than restraint and/or confiscation.

Forensic accountants are skilled in reading and interpreting accounting data and should be able to isolate fraudulent transactions from 'business as usual' data. They should present their findings without using jargon, and they should not be so complex that they cannot be understood by the non-expert.

It is important to differentiate between the work required to progress a criminal investigation and the work that the CPS may require in order to present the evidence to the court and provide opinion-based evidence on the facts.

Forensic accountants are employed in both areas, but it is important to establish at an early stage what is required of the accountant. When acting as an expert witness and giving an opinion on matters, it is important that the instructions given to the expert are:

- clear;
- unambiguous;
- not subject to misinterpretation.

When instructing an expert witness, the independence of the expert must be considered at an early stage. An expert witness should not be involved in the investigation of the case. The job of the expert is to provide opinion-based evidence on the facts as given. For this reason, it is important that excellent records are maintained of the instructions given to the expert, the documentation that is provided for review and any discussions that are held. In addition, it is important that the instructions constrain the work that the expert is required to do. It is not the job of the expert to investigate. If, however, the expert feels that an area requires further work, this may be undertaken provided that this is in line with any investigative strategy that is already in place.

Contrast this with the work that may be undertaken by a forensic accountant who is involved with the investigation, and who would not normally be considered to be independent and thus not act as an expert witness.

KEY POINTS—ROLE OF THE FORENSIC ACCOUNTANT IN FRAUD INVESTIGATIONS

The responsibilities of the forensic accountant include:

- review of accounting records for evidence of how transactions have been dealt with:
  - investigation of the data on an accounting package;
  - interpretation of hard-copy accounting records;
- extraction of key accounting transactions and the presentation of them in a straightforward manner;
- application of statistical techniques to identify anomalies in transactions;
- analysis of bulk data, not always accounting for data differentiation between 'business as usual' data and irregularities.

As with expert witnesses, the instructions given to an investigating forensic accountant must be clear, unambiguous and not subject to misinterpretation.

It is likely that few investigations would warrant the use of an external forensic accountant who is heavily involved in the investigation process, principally because of the fees that would be charged. Budget holders would be well advised to check whether the skills and experience exist in-house before going external.

In some cases, the CPS will require a forensic accountant to be instructed, particularly in cases where one is instructed by the defence.

Those instructing expert witnesses in criminal cases should ensure that the expert has suitable qualifications and experience. The expert's CV should be obtained and scrutinised.

6.18 Identifying and managing the suspect

The development of an effective fraud suspect management strategy is vital to any fraud investigation and is part of the FIM. Fraud is rarely opportunistic and is often an offence that can require a high level of planning and organisation. When developing a suspect management strategy, the following should be considered:

- Who is/are my suspect(s)?
- Where is/are my suspect(s)?
- What do I need to do in relation to the suspect(s)?
- When do I need to act? (Consider reducing further harm.)
- How am I going to manage the suspect(s)?

KEY POINTS—WRITING A FRAUD SUSPECT MANAGEMENT STRATEGY

Format of the strategy document:

1 Title page:
- author;
- date;
- version.
2 Purpose and scope of the strategy.
3 Introduction:
- background;
- case-specific information.
4 Suspect identification:
- known; or
- unknown.
  Consider:
  - digital footprint;
  - financial investigation;
  - linking—Action Fraud/PNC/PND, other agencies;
  - covert tactics;
  - use of false identities (identity theft).
5 Partner agencies:
- make inquiries with partner agencies.
6 International inquiries:
- make inquiries with international partners (if applicable).
7 Suspect management options:
- multiple suspects;
- voluntary attendance;
- arrest suspect(s);
- asset management—liaise with the relevant financial investigation unit (FIU) to prevent the dissipation of criminal proceeds and incorporate POCA strategy into the suspect management strategy.
8 Suspect interview:
- planning;
- selection of interviewers;
- managing the interview.
9 Post-arrest management:
- consider bail conditions;
- remand in custody;
- establish the needs of the victim(s) to inform decisions regarding bail conditions;
- review bail conditions regularly to ensure they are still necessary.

10 Charging decisions.
11 Referencing:
- note key information sources/policies/procedures/legislation referenced in the strategy.

6.18.1 Suspect identification

As with any other complex and premeditated crime, it is likely that the perpetrators will have taken measures to evade detection, adding to the challenge presented to the investigator, who will have to diligently unpick the chain of events. This often involves detailed inquiries to 'follow the money'. Inquiries to trace, identify and gather evidence against fraud suspects can be complicated by the fact that offenders frequently operate under one or more assumed identities and do not necessarily visit a physical 'scene of the crime'.

Those committing fraud can, and often do, remotely perpetrate a wide range of offences, nationally and internationally, from various digital devices. These devices are invariably mobile and use internet connections that cannot always be linked to an individual user—for example, an unregistered and disposable pre-paid SIM card or public access wi-fi. It is also a common tactic to employ others to undertake more exposed roles—for example, a 'dupe', who visits a bank branch purporting to be someone else to facilitate a transaction.

Digital footprint

In most cases, the suspect will leave their twenty-first century 'fingerprints' in both their chosen method of communication with the victim and the financial transactions between the parties involved. These offer investigative opportunities that should be robustly pursued. These records are usually held by third parties, which are often the key to unravelling the fraud and identifying the perpetrators. Computers, mobile phones and payment instruments all leave electronic traces; these offer the investigator their most significant investigative opportunities. When this type of data features in an investigation, inquiries can be made with the service provider or bank to obtain account, payment and location details and other useful evidential material.

This data can supply valuable lines of inquiry when tracing a suspect. For example, if an unregistered internet dongle used to commit an offence were topped up at a supermarket, it would be possible to identify the payment card used for that transaction or secure CCTV of the suspect at the premises. Equally, if you have a known suspect, you can cross-reference the digital history of items found either in their possession or registered in their name against the digital footprint of the offence. This could assist in attributing a telephone number to your suspect or place them at a particular location at a significant time.

Forensic analysis

DNA, fingerprint, facial recognition/mapping, voice and handwriting analysis can assist with identifying suspects or evidencing a link between an offence and an identified suspect.

Covert tactics

Static and mobile surveillance can assist in both identifying unknown suspects and capturing evidence of the criminality.

False identities

Fraud suspects often operate under assumed identities using counterfeit identity/financial instruments and false drop addresses to perpetrate their offences. Proffered identity documents should be carefully examined and caution exercised when confirming a fraud suspect's particulars.

6.18.2 Suspect management

In fraud investigations, it will be necessary to interview the suspect to obtain information about the offence, the suspect's account and possible admissions. There are many competing factors to consider when deciding whether it is necessary to request that the suspect voluntarily attend for interview or to arrest a suspect to achieve those aims and manage them over an extended period of police bail. The legal framework that determines how this decision is reached is the PACE Act 1984, Code G, Revised Code of Practice for the statutory power of arrest by police officers (also refer to the Human Rights Act and the Police Code of Ethics).

Voluntary attendance and interview

If a suspect agrees to assist with an investigation and attend the police station (or another location) for an interview voluntarily, and this is the only investigative action required, this will usually negate the necessity for their arrest.

KEY POINT—REASONS TO USE VOLUNTARY ATTENDANCE AND INTERVIEW UNDER CAUTION FOR FRAUD INVESTIGATIONS

Having suspects attend voluntarily and be interviewed under caution is often done in fraud investigations for the following reasons:

- **compliance with the provisions of Code G**: where the *only investigative action* required is to interview the suspect and they are willing to attend the interview;
- necessity criteria not met;
- **timing**: in order to make the best use of the custody detention period, it may be more appropriate to conduct a voluntary interview, especially when dealing with a protracted and complex fraud investigation, to give the suspect an opportunity to provide their initial account.

Suspect arrest

As with all other criminal investigations, the decision to arrest a suspect is an operational decision that is made at the discretion of the investigator, who must decide which of the necessity criteria apply (PACE Act 1984, Code G).

The following factors may support the need to arrest a suspect as part of a fraud management strategy.

- **Destruction or concealment of evidence**: if a search of a suspect or a search of the premises occupied by them has not taken place, this may seriously negate the effectiveness of any subsequent search. With prior warning, key evidence (e.g. a SIM card used in an account takeover fraud) could easily be disposed of or destroyed. The PACE Act 1984 (Code G, point 2.9(e)(i)) gives the example that a necessity criteria may be met in these circumstances.
- **Retrieving evidence from a suspect**: it is only possible to search and/or examine a suspect to establish their identity or to photograph marks, features or injuries that would provide evidence of identity if they are a detainee at a police station. If it is pertinent to your investigation to secure this form of evidence, then the arrest of your suspect will be considered necessary in accordance with the PACE Act 1984, Code G, point 2.9(e)(iv). An example would be a suspect who has approached bank employees to attempt to corrupt them and incite them to supply account security information to an OCG. That suspect may have a mark or feature like a tattoo that gives them a distinctive appearance described by the witnesses. It would be prudent to photograph that mark or feature as part of the prosecution case.
- **Suspect evidential comparison**: it is only possible to compel a person to provide evidential samples such as fingerprints and DNA and use force in order to achieve this within the provisions of the PACE Act 1984 if that person is under arrest. It would therefore be necessary to arrest them to ensure a prompt and effective investigation as per the PACE Act 1984, Code G, point 2.9(e)(iii). Think laterally and consider the evidence in your case and the forensic opportunities that are potentially available. This may include ATM skimming equipment or banking documents submitted for fingerprint examination. However, it should be kept in mind that an arrest cannot be necessary if it is purely to take routine fingerprints or samples. There must be a reason for the investigating officer to believe that taking such samples would prove or disprove the person's involvement in the offence, or help to confirm their identity.
- **Risk of absconding**: suspects in fraud cases often dissipate the proceeds of crime abroad, and your investigation may establish that they have connections and assets outside the UK. If there is a risk that they will abscond, you may want to consider arresting them to allow them to be remanded in custody or for bail conditions to be applied to prevent their disappearance (e.g. the forfeiture of their passport or a prohibition on them applying for travel documents). Consideration should also be given to their access to counterfeit

documents. Reporting conditions can be added where necessary (PACE Act 1984, Code G, point 2.9(f)).

- **Threats against or intimidation of witnesses**: where there are reasonable grounds to believe that this is the case, then it may be necessary to arrest the person to allow suitable bail conditions to be applied. This might include exclusion from a geographical area or a prohibition on direct or indirect contact with the witness. This necessity may be particularly relevant when investigating interpersonal fraud offences, such as romance fraud or courier fraud (PACE Act 1984, Code G, point 2.9(e)(i)).
- **Contact between co-suspects/conspirators**: where there are reasonable grounds to believe a suspect will make contact with co-suspects or conspirators, the PACE Act 1984 (Code G, point 2.9(e)(i)) states that it may be necessary to arrest that person to prevent that contact from taking place. The management of contact between multiple suspects needs to be carefully considered for each phase of the investigation: at the point of arrest, while they are in custody and post-arrest.

6.10.3 Suspect interviews

An effective suspect interview is paramount to any fraud investigation, as the information gleaned from this process can often direct the next stages of the investigation or can impact on the prosecution case at court if the correct procedures have not been adopted.

The PEACE model provides an effective framework to assist in the interviewing process, it consists of five elements.

- **P**lanning and preparation;
- **E**ngage and explain;
- **A**ccount;
- **C**losure;
- **E**valuation.

The planning and preparation phase is considered to be the most important aspect of this framework, as this is where the information held is analysed and objectives that may impact on the whole investigation are identified. See Appendix 6 for a template for developing an overarching fraud interview strategy.

Planning for the interview

The planning stage of a suspect's interview is vital, particularly with complex fraud investigations. A number of factors need to be considered, including:

- **custody officer briefing**: preparing a separate brief for both arresting and custody officers to prevent the unnecessary leakage of disclosures;
- **pre-interview disclosure**: the interview team has a number of options for pre-interview disclosure, full disclosure, staged disclosure or indeed no

disclosure. There is a significant amount of case law concerning this topic which investigators should make themselves familiar with. In fraud cases there is often a very strong rationale for making a full disclosure of the material held. Often it is the suspect's own material and it is in the interests of the investigation that they should be given the opportunity to view the material prior to interview. It is best practice that the pre-interview disclosure to the defence lawyer should be recorded.

Interviewing officers should be fully prepared in the event of a 'prepared statement/no comment' interview.

Given that fraud offences are indictable and often involve multiple offenders, careful consideration needs to be given to the many procedures and powers under the PACE Act, coupled with other tactical options as follows (this list is non-exhaustive):

Checklist—fraud interviews

- Holding suspects incommunicado;
- delaying access to legal advice;
- removal of a solicitor;
- suspects changing their minds regarding legal advice;
- urgent interviews;
- use of appropriate adults;
- briefing and debriefing police doctors;
- fitness to be interviewed;
- use of interpreters;
- significant statements/silence;
- special warnings under sections 36 and 37 of the Criminal Justice and Public Order Act 1994;
- further arrests under section 31 of the PACE Act;
- downstream monitoring under Home Office Circular 50/1995;
- extensions of detention;
- introduction of bad character, including foreign convictions;
- challenge interviews;
- adverse inferences.

Consideration can also be made under sections 71–75 of the Serious Organised Crime and Police Act 2005, offenders assisting investigation and prosecutions, should a suspect wish to make admissions and potentially give evidence against others. Advice should always be sought from appropriately trained officers. Furthermore, the undertaking of the CPS would be required.

Further reading

- College of Police, 'Authorised Professional Practice—Investigation: Investigative Interviewing', 2016: www.app.college.police.uk/app-content/investigations/investigative-interviewing/

6.18.4 **Post-arrest management—bail**

If a decision has been taken to arrest a suspect, their bail needs to be regularly reviewed to ensure that it continues to be necessary. Fraud investigations can be lengthy, and while it may have been necessary to arrest a suspect, it may not continue to be necessary to retain them on police bail if circumstances no longer warrant it.

Checklist—bail

1 **Pre-charge bail**

The following are examples of when pre-charge bail can be granted (source: CPS):

- Section 37(2) of the PACE Act is cited and the custody officer has authorised the release of the suspect, having determined that there is currently insufficient evidence to charge. He or she may be released pending the obtainment of further evidence. Where necessary, conditions of bail can be attached to prevent the suspect from failing to surrender, offending on bail, interfering with prosecution witnesses or otherwise obstructing the course of justice, or for their own protection.

- Where section 34 of the PACE Act is cited (e.g. where a detailed and lengthy investigation is required and no assessment of the evidence can be made), no conditions of bail can be imposed—see *R (on an application by Torres) v Metropolitan Police Commissioner* [2007] EWHC 3212 (Admin).

- Where the police consider that there is sufficient evidence to charge, but the matter must be referred to the CPS for a charging decision (section 37(7)(a) of the PACE Act).

- See section 37B of the PACE Act and the Director's Guidance on Charging for guidance and procedures relating to the provision of charging advice by the CPS. In order to obtain this advice, the police may release a suspect on bail to return to the police station at a future date and may impose conditions on that bail (section 47(1A) of the PACE Act). Such advice will normally be provided under the Full Code Test of the Code for Crown Prosecutors prior to the suspect's return.

2 Post-charge

Where there is sufficient evidence and the suspect is charged with an offence (section 37(7)(d) of the PACE Act), the police can keep the suspect in detention or release them on bail to appear at court at a future date and may impose conditions on that bail (section 47(1A) of the PACE Act). It should be noted that (either pre- or post-charge) the police cannot impose conditions on a suspect:

- to reside at a bail hostel;

- to attend an interview with a legal adviser;

- to make themselves available for inquiries and reports;

- that contain electronic monitoring requirements.

3 Bail conditions

Bail conditions should only be imposed in order to address any of the risks that would be inherent in granting unconditional bail. In proposing (or considering) conditions of bail, prosecutors must ensure that they are necessary, reasonable, proportionate and possible to enforce. Consideration should also be given to the extent to which they meet the objections to bail. Conditions that are unsuitable may give rise to a continuing risk of further offending, of absconding, or of harm to the victim(s) or public, and prosecutors should be prepared to challenge their imposition or seek further evidence from the police before acceding to them, should they have any concerns.

4 Types of condition

- **Reporting to a police station**: this must be necessary to avert the risk it is designed to meet. For example, care should be taken to ensure that the interval between reporting times is not so long as to be insufficient to prevent a defendant from absconding.

- **Doorstep condition**: it was held in *R (CPS) v Chorley Justices* [2002] EWHC 2162 (Admin) that a doorstep condition was not contrary to the European Convention on Human Rights. Where it is proportionate and necessary to enforce a curfew, or a residence condition has been imposed for one of the statutory purposes, then such a condition may be appropriate.

- **Murder cases**: under section 115 of the Coroners and Justice Act 2009, a Crown Court must impose conditions in accordance with section 3(6A) of the Bail Act 1976 providing for the medical examination of the defendant. The court need not impose the conditions if it is content that satisfactory reports have already been obtained.

- **Not to drive**: the court must be satisfied that such a condition is necessary and, in doing so, ought to consider whether its imposition might have unexpected and unjust results. See *R v Kwame* (1974) 60 Cr App R 65.

- **Sureties** can be expressed as being continuous throughout the court proceedings and, if they are taken on these terms, there is no requirement for the surety to attend each hearing. Prosecutors should be prepared to assist the court to explore the status and means of the potential surety, in the interests of justice and the surety. The prosecutor should be prepared to ask for time to make inquiries as to the sufficiency of the surety.

- **Securities** should be lodged with the court or, in exceptional circumstances, with the police, and not with the CPS.

- **Electronic tagging**: where the court is satisfied that there is local provision for electronic tagging, and the offender would not be granted bail but for their being tagged, it may order that this condition be imposed (section 3AB of the Bail Act 1976).

Source: CPS www.cps.gov.uk/legal/a_to_c/bail/

Consideration needs to be given to the management of contact between suspects post-arrest while they are on bail. A witness may be more vulnerable for reasons of age, mental health or cooperation with the investigation, and bail conditions might be necessary to protect that individual from intimidation and any attempt to pervert the course of justice.

Further reading

- Bail Act 1976, section 7: www.legislation.gov.uk/ukpga/1976/63/section/7
- PACE Act 1984: www.gov.uk/guidance/police-and-criminal-evidence-act-1984-pace-codes-of-practice
- College of Policing, 'Authorised Professional Practice', 2016: www.app.college.police.uk/

6.19 Developing a media strategy

Over the past few years, there has been a rise in the appetite and uptake from the media in relation to fraud cases. While the complexity of fraud cases has been a barrier, the human interest story, from the victims' and offenders' perspectives, creates opportunities that the media can utilise. This, in turn, develops an environment whereby the SIO can develop a balanced media strategy. The SIO can use the media effectively to:

- identify further victims;
- identify further lines of inquiry;
- provide awareness and education messaging;
- disrupt and prevent further offending;
- demonstrate effective enforcement activity;
- reduce potential harm to the public.

Whether the case concerns an opportunistic fraudster or an OCG found guilty of fraud at court, the media should be utilised to promote the 'good news' story of what the police and their partners have achieved, provide a clear deterrent message and maximise awareness of fraud as a growing threat to the community.

6.19.1 Media strategy considerations

A media strategy should be defined by the SIO in conjunction with your force's press office and it should describe the aims and objectives and which elements of the media will achieve maximum coverage of the target audience and therefore serve the specified key messages. While there is a sharp focus on suspect and witness identification (balanced with public reassurance) in other areas of policing, in fraud investigations the emphasis is more likely to be on victim identification and messaging to encourage reporting.

6.19.2 Critical elements to all media strategies

There are two key elements that should be woven into *all* media engagement.

1 Action Fraud: the promotion and utilisation of Action Fraud—the national fraud and cyber crime reporting centre—will reinforce the policing model for reporting fraud and cyber crime. Action Fraud is, therefore, a resource to utilise to receive and therefore absorb any increase in reporting in response to a media appeal. Promotion of web-based reporting is essential.
2 PROTECT messaging: due to the increasing scale and complexity of fraud and the absence of geographical boundaries, all media strategy should look to encompass PROTECT messaging. The current volumes of fraud in the UK are not matched by law enforcement resources and the Peelian principles of crime prevention are an important key message in all media releases. The latest PROTECT messaging for specific crime types and cases can be obtained from Action Fraud, the NFIB website or HMG-backed initiatives such as 'Get Safe Online'.

6.19.3 Timing

The timing of the media engagement must be considered so that a balance is achieved between protecting future victims (if there is an ongoing threat of fraud from offenders) versus the impact of alerting suspects and/or frustrating the investigation. The added complication in fraud investigations is where the alleged offending could be linked to a lawfully engaged entity and a decision will be required by the OIC/SIO to determine the stance and content of the messaging. A written record should be made that describes the decision and reasoning, if naming a company/individual is deemed the right course of action. The balance is between placing your suspicions on record versus failure by the police to share information and warn the public. Media releases prior to conviction must have clear and concise objectives, with consideration given to the right to a fair trial. The reasons for conducting a targeted media appeal prior to conviction must be fully considered and any decisions recorded.

6.19.4 **Victims**

To maximise media coverage, the engagement of the victim can assist in explaining the impact of the crime; however, before this takes place a full risk assessment should be undertaken. If and when the victim gives a media interview, there is a responsibility on the police to provide ongoing support and revisit a risk assessment at regular intervals.

6.19.5 **Suspect identification**

Although in fraud cases it is less likely that the media will be used to identify suspect(s), as with other guidance, where the media engagement seeks to identify an unknown offender, adherence to the latest policy and PACE Act legislation must be followed. Any media appeal for a known suspect must not prejudice any future and/or potential identification procedure, nor contravene any court-imposed media restrictions on any ongoing trial.

KEY POINTS—TACTICAL DEVELOPMENT OF MEDIA ENGAGEMENT

- All media engagement should be conducted through your force's corporate communication team with an accurate audit for sign-off and agreement.
- Investigators must ensure that material is retained in order to comply with disclosure purposes.
- Should specific expertise be required at either the SIO level or the corporate communication level, consideration should be given to seeking advice from the City of London Police, as the national lead force for fraud.
- Consider the wider implications of your messaging. Could there be data held by the NFIB that supports and corroborates the extent and scale of the fraud type you are investigating that will increase the media's appetite? This will also ensure consistent and up-to-date messaging.
- Action Fraud should be given a short briefing note and made aware of any media campaigns that are likely to result in an increase in demand on Action Fraud contact centre resources.

6.19.6 **Media channels**

The strategy should consider the best media channels it could use in order to meet its objectives. There will always be a balance to be struck between the local and national extent of the engagements. Newspapers, television and radio are traditional media outlets, but it can be a struggle to instigate instant pick-up.

Social media engagement, through both local and national channels, is an efficient and effective way of reaching a broad audience and has the potential for further pick-up from the aforementioned outlets.

Checklist—media strategy

- Engage with the force's communications team at the earliest opportunity.

- Ensure that an agreed briefing note of current facts and key information is included.

- Identify the key messages to be conveyed.

- Identify which elements of the media should be considered.

- Identify a SPOC from the investigation team (if required).

- Provide relevant contact details (where applicable).

- Provide adequate/appropriate resources to receive information (where applicable).

- Adhere to the local force's media guidelines.

- Reference Action Fraud and PROTECT messaging.

- Review the process in place to ensure the relevance of the strategy against case development.

- Assign a spokesperson in case of interview requests.

- Ensure resources are in place to respond to any upsurge in reporting by victims or other interested parties.

Fraud and financial investigations

7.1 **Introduction**

The College of Policing Authorised Professional Practice (APP) describes a financial investigation as 'any investigation into a person or person's financial matters. It could also involve the investigation into the finances of a business or private limited company. A financial investigation can determine where money comes from, how it is moved and how it is used.'

A fraud investigation is, in essence, a financial investigation and features in the Fraud Investigation Model when both gathering material and securing the offenders' assets. *Blackstone's Senior Investigating Officers' Handbook* states that financial information can reveal evidence of the offenders' motives, gains, links to others and modus operandi (methods). The early engagement of a financial investigator (FI) is essential in fraud investigations to:

- assist in obtaining financial information;
- give consideration to potential confiscation proceedings;
- recover the value of the assets that have benefited that individual, such as cash, properties or vehicles.

The primary objective of confiscation in fraud cases is to recover assets so that they can then be used to compensate victims if appropriate. This value can be recovered following a successful conviction by applying to the court for a confiscation order. There is also the power to restrain assets where this is necessary to stop a person who has benefited from their crime from being able to dissipate, spend, sell, transfer or hide their assets or property before they can be confiscated.

KEY POINTS—FINANCIAL INFORMATION

Financial information can be used to identify:

- offences (including money laundering);
- suspects, witnesses and victims;
- associations with others and/or links to places/premises;
- information around a person's location and movements;
- use of services such as phone and transport;
- motives;
- lifestyle and habits.

Further reading

- The College of Policing, 'Authorised Professional Practice—Investigation: Financial Investigation', 2016: www.app.college.police.uk/app-content/ investigations/investigative-strategies/financial-investigation-2/

7.2 **The role of the financial investigator (FI)**

FIs are trained to understand financial intelligence and have access to specific sources of intelligence that the non-accredited investigator does not. They are also trained and accredited to use the specialist powers relating to restraint and confiscation available under the Proceeds of Crime Act (POCA) 2002.

FIs can be utilised at any stage in an investigation, from the initial intelligence-gathering phase, through the evidence-gathering and presentation at court stages, and then post-conviction when confiscation and compensation are considered.

When engaging in an investigation into fraud, consideration should be given to involving financial intelligence officers (FIOs), or FIs, from the start. Their use should be reviewed throughout the investigation, including during conviction and sentencing. It should be noted that if confiscation is a possibility, then the input of an appropriately qualified FI should be included when charges are being considered and if a basis of plea is offered at any time. This is because these two events can have a significant impact on any subsequent confiscation or compensation request.

KEY POINTS—TYPES OF FINANCIAL INVESTIGATION

- **A money laundering investigation**: a criminal investigation into a person (or persons) engaged in laundering the proceeds of crime. This can be either the criminal themselves or a third party facilitating the retention of the criminal's benefit from their criminal conduct.
- **A detained cash investigation**: an investigation into the origins and intended use of cash seized under Part 5 of the POCA 2002. The ultimate aim is to forfeit the cash in civil proceedings in the magistrates' court, and this can be achieved as long as it can be shown, on the balance of probabilities, that the cash derived from, or was intended for use in, unlawful conduct.
- **A confiscation investigation**: an investigation into the extent and whereabouts of a person's benefit from their criminal conduct. Confiscation is dealt with along with other financial matters, such as compensation post-conviction, in the Crown Court as part of the sentencing process. A confiscation order is an order made by a Crown Court for the defendant to pay a sum of money, which represents their benefit from their criminal conduct, to the court. To preserve assets being considered for confiscation, a restraint order can be obtained in the Crown Court at any time from the commencement of an investigation.
- **A civil recovery investigation**: an investigation into assets that are derived from or intended for use in unlawful conduct, with the ultimate aim of forfeiting them in civil proceedings in the High Court, as long as it can be shown, on the

---

> balance of probabilities, that the cash derived from, or was intended for use in, unlawful conduct. Civil recovery cases are primarily (but not exclusively) dealt with by a specialist unit within the National Crime Agency (NCA), and most law enforcement agencies refer appropriate cases to them.

Post-conviction, the investigation of a person's benefit from their criminal conduct and their assets not only enhances the confiscation investigation—thereby ensuring that the convicted person does not retain the proceeds of their criminal activity—but can also assist with any compensation claim from the victim(s).

Section 378 of the POCA 2002 identifies who can exercise powers under the various sections of the Act. Primarily, these can be summarised as constables, NCA officers, officers of Her Majesty's Revenue and Customs (HMRC), immigration officers and FIs. FIs are regulated by the NCA Proceeds of Crime Centre (POCC), and can be employed by a variety of public bodies, all of which are listed in the Proceeds of Crime Act 2002 (References to Financial Investigators) (England and Wales) Order 2015.

The specific roles, accreditation and continued professional development (CPD) requirements needed to maintain accreditation are detailed in the NCA's 'Proceeds of Crime Centre Registration, Accreditation and Monitoring Policy', which is available from the NCA POCC or can be downloaded by anyone with access to the Financial Investigator Support System (this will include any FI). Once qualified, there is an ongoing requirement for FIs at any level to undertake CPD to ensure that their knowledge and skill levels remain sufficient and up to date.

KEY POINTS—ROLES REGULATED BY THE NCA POCC

These are:

- **Financial intelligence officers (FIOs)**: these officers are trained in identifying and accessing financial intelligence through both open sources and specialist databases and gateways. The material they generate is primarily for intelligence purposes only, but can be very useful for determining the scope of an investigation or the parameters of a financial order.
- **Financial investigators (FIs)**: these officers exercise the investigative powers under Part 8 of the POCA and the cash seizure powers under Part 5 of the same Act. They can be utilised to get the appropriate POCA court orders to obtain material that can be used evidentially or to enhance the intelligence process. They are also trained to make the appropriate applications at the magistrates' court in relation to cash seizures and forfeitures.
- **Confiscators**: they are trained to carry out confiscation investigations and any linked restraints. They work closely with the officer in the case and the prosecutor, and should be included in any discussions regarding potential charging strategies and the basis of pleas.

It should be noted that police staff investigators who hold powers under Schedule 4 to the Police Reform Act 2002 do not hold the same powers as an accredited financial investigator (AFI) unless they have been separately trained and accredited to do so by the NCA.

Checklist—financial investigation strategy

- Early engagement of an FI and/or relevant financial investigation unit (FIU) to assist in developing the strategy, ensuring it covers the following:
  - setting the objective;
  - specialist advice—what is required;
  - financial intelligence requirement;
  - use of POCA 2002 powers;
  - gathering evidence.
- Consider bank account information (pre-order inquiries) to establish evidential priorities and protection of assets.
- Ensure the investigative strategy incorporates an asset recovery strategy.
- Ensure ongoing liaison with the FI throughout the investigation.
- Establish investigative objectives and utilise POCA legislative tools accordingly (e.g. account monitoring orders, customer information orders, disclosure orders and/or cash seizures).
- Identify assets early.
- Liaise with the Crown Prosecution Service (CPS) early regarding the prospects of confiscation.
- Develop an understanding of POCA legislation.

Further reading

- The Proceeds of Crime Act 2002 (References to Financial Investigators) (England and Wales) Order 2015, giving a schedule of agencies who have AFI: www.legislation.gov.uk/uksi/2015/1853/pdfs/uksi_20151853_en.pdf

7.3 Legislation

The primary legislation used in financial investigations is the POCA 2002. This deals with the accreditation of FIs, confiscation and restraint, civil recovery and cash seizure, money laundering, investigative powers and criminal taxation.

Other useful legislation linked to this area is the Money Laundering Regulations 2007, which detail many of the obligations financial institutions are required to abide by. These regulations cover customer due diligence, record-keeping procedures, training, supervision and registration, as well as outlining the offences covering failure to comply with these regulations. When dealing with fraud investigations, it is often worth considering whether or not any of the Money Laundering Regulations have been breached alongside the more traditional criminal offences.

The Criminal Procedure Rules and the Civil Procedure Rules govern the practicalities of the legislation and processes, and the various codes of practice also assist in the practicalities and procedures involved.

7.3.1 **POCA search powers**

As well as search powers under other legislation, such as the Police and Criminal Evidence (PACE) Act 1984, the POCA 2002 provides some additional search opportunities.

Where a production order has not been complied with or would not be appropriate, then it is possible to obtain a search and seizure warrant under section 352 of the POCA 2002 for a money laundering investigation, a confiscation investigation or a detained cash investigation. The orders are obtained in the Crown Court and can be applied for by an AFI, a constable, an officer of HMRC or an immigration officer. A warrant can also be obtained in the case of a civil recovery investigation or an exploitation proceeds investigation by an NCA officer.

Where a search is specifically for cash, which is considered to be derived from or intended for use in unlawful conduct and is over the minimum threshold, currently £1000, and is to be seized under the civil cash seizure provisions of the POCA 2002, then prior authority should be obtained from a justice of the peace or, if not practicable, a senior officer (an officer of at least the rank of police inspector or equivalent). The power can be exercised by an officer of HMRC, a constable or an AFI and currently relates to premises and people.

KEY POINTS—DEFINITION OF CASH UNDER POCA

Defined by section 289(6) of the POCA as notes and coins in any currency, postal orders, cheques of any kind (including traveller's cheques), bankers' drafts, bearer bonds and bearer shares, found at any place in the UK. Cash also includes any monetary instrument which is found at any place in the UK.

If searching premises, the person carrying out the search must already be lawfully on the premises, as there is no power of entry attached to this authority and, if searching a person, this does not include an intimate or strip search but does include any article they have with them.

The other linked search provision in the Act is the confiscation seizure power, which is dealt with below.

Checklist—search and seizure powers in relation to confiscation and restraint

- If a restraint order is already in force, a constable, an AFI or a customs officer may seize any realisable property to which it applies to prevent its removal from England and Wales (section 45(1) of the POCA 2002).

- Excluding cash or exempt property, a constable, an AFI, an officer of HMRC or an immigration officer can seize property that might otherwise be unavailable for confiscation or that the value of the property may be diminished as a result of the conduct of the defendant or any other person (section 47C of the POCA 2002).

- There is a power of search attached to this requiring appropriate approval from a justice of the peace (sections 47D–G of the POCA 2002).

- If planning to use either of these powers, liaison with an appropriately qualified AFI is key, as many organisations have restrictions in their policies and procedures as to who can exercise these powers.

7.3.2 Cash seizures

Cash, as defined in section 289 of the POCA 2002, can be seized by a constable, an AFI or an officer of HMRC. The officer should be lawfully on any premises or have reasonable grounds for suspecting that a person is carrying cash (which is recoverable property or is intended by any person for use in unlawful conduct) and the amount of cash is apparently not less than the minimum amount, currently £1,000. Once seized, the cash can be detained for up to 48 hours (excluding weekends and bank holidays) before it has to be either returned or further detained by order of a magistrates' court. There is no specific power of arrest under the POCA 2002, and AFIs do not possess a power of arrest unless they are also in a role that allows them this power, such as that of a constable.

7.3.3 POCA investigative orders

There are three main investigative orders available under the POCA that can be applied for by an appropriate officer, namely:

- production orders;
- customer information orders;
- account monitoring orders.

229

Authorisations need to be by a senior appropriate officer, which for the police would be an officer of the rank of inspector or above, except for customer information orders, where it is required to be an officer of the rank of superintendent or above. A fourth type of order is also available, a disclosure order, but it tends to be used less frequently.

7.3.4 **Production orders**

These are available to support a money laundering investigation, a confiscation or a detained cash investigation, they can also be used for a civil recovery or exploitation proceeds investigation. The principles are similar under the POCA 2002 as they are when obtaining a production order under other legislation such as the PACE Act 1984 or the Drug Trafficking Act (DTA) 1994. The orders are applied for in the Crown Court and can be applied for ex parte as long as this can be justified to the judge. The main purpose for the application should determine which type of order to go for, so if the main reason for the order is to gather evidence for a fraud then the PACE Act rather than the POCA would be the appropriate legislation to apply for. To prevent future challenge, it is worth ensuring that this reasoning is documented clearly in the case file. If appropriate, an order to grant entry can also be applied for under section 347 of the POCA.

7.3.5 **Customer information orders**

These orders are only available under the POCA and are available for money laundering or confiscation investigations. They can also be used for a civil recovery or exploitation proceeds investigation; they are not available for detained cash investigations.

KEY POINTS—CUSTOMER INFORMATION ORDERS

Customer information orders require the disclosure of the following information where it is available:

- account number(s), including those for any safe deposit boxes;
- the person's full name;
- the person's date of birth;
- the person's most recent address and any previous addresses;
- the account opening and closing date(s)/safe deposit box start of use and finish of use date(s);
- any identity evidence provided as part of the anti-money laundering requirements when opening the account/safety deposit box;

- the full name, date of birth, address and previous addresses of any person who holds or has held an account jointly with the person at that financial institution;
- the account number(s) of any other account(s) to which they are a signatory at that financial institution, along with the details of the person holding the other account(s).

7.3.6 **Account monitoring orders**

These orders are only available under the POCA and are available for money laundering or confiscation investigations, they can also be used for a civil recovery or exploitation proceeds investigation. They are not available for a detained cash investigation. These are forward-facing orders, whereas a production order only provides historic material up to the date of the order. An account monitoring order requests transactional information from the date of the order to a period of up to 90 days hence. These are particularly useful tools in covert investigations, and they support a pre-arrest phase. They can be very time-intensive for the financial institution, so good liaison with them before making the application is crucial to identifying what they can do and in what timescales. For most investigations, a fax or email at the start of the business day detailing the transactions carried out the day before is more than sufficient. Real-time information is difficult for them to obtain and should only be requested in the most serious of cases.

7.3.7 **Disclosure orders**

There are two types of disclosure order under the POCA. The first is linked to restraint—the court can make any order it believes is appropriate to ensure the effectiveness of the restraint order. This may include a requirement for the person being restrained to disclose information about the nature and whereabouts of some or all of their assets. It should be noted that if such an order is made, the resulting information cannot be used for any other purpose; if it is used to assist the criminal investigation, then the resulting material gathered may be tainted as a result.

The second type of disclosure order can only be made in relation to a confiscation investigation or a civil recovery or exploitation proceeds investigation. It requires any person who is considered to have relevant information, who has received notification in writing, to either answer questions in person, provide specified information or produce specified documents or described document types that are considered to be relevant information. The application is made by a prosecutor on behalf of the appropriate officer, and there is a linked code of practice in relation to this.

> **Further reading**
>
> - Proceeds of Crime Act: codes of practice, www.gov.uk/government/
>   publications/proceeds-of-crime-act-codes-of-practice

7.4 Protocols

Most organisations have their own protocols in place for requesting the assistance of an FIO/FI. As a general rule, the more information you can supply them with, the easier their job will be and the more effective their assistance will be to your investigation. Early engagement and regular communication are key to a successful investigation.

FIOs and FIs have access to the Financial Intelligence Gateway, which is administered by the NCA. It provides a communication channel between financial institutions and law enforcement.

> **Further reading**
>
> **Codes of practice**: there are a number of codes of practice in force that relate to the POCA. These can be found using the links below:
> - Recovery of cash search powers: www.gov.uk/government/uploads/system/
>   uploads/attachment_data/file/423104/48397_Code_of_Practice_Recovery_
>   Accessible.pdf
> - Search, seizure and detention of property: www.gov.uk/government/uploads/
>   system/uploads/attachment_data/file/423100/48394_Code_of_Practice_
>   Search_Seizure_Accessible.pdf
> - Investigations: www.gov.uk/government/uploads/system/uploads/
>   attachment_data/file/423102/48396_Code_of_Practice_Investigation.pdf
> - Issued by the Attorney General for prosecutors' use of investigation powers
>   (disclosure orders): www.gov.uk/government/uploads/system/uploads/
>   attachment_data/file/424777/49416_Un-Act_Code_of_Practice_Accessible_
>   v0.1.pdf
> - APP: www.app.college.police.uk/app-content/investigations/investigative-
>   strategies/financial-investigation-2/effective-financial-investigation/

7.5 Restraint and confiscation

The purpose of a confiscation investigation is to ensure that a criminal does not retain the proceeds of their criminal activity. To do this effectively, confiscation should be considered in the early stages of the investigation and the FI will run their inquiries in tandem with the senior investigating officer (SIO)/officer in the case (OIC) for the criminal investigation.

As confiscation proceedings commence post-conviction, the defendant may attempt to dissipate their assets before that time. Particular crunch points can be around the time of arrest, the time of charge or at the start of trial. To prevent this from happening, it is possible to obtain a restraint order that prohibits the defendant (and some linked third parties, where appropriate) from dealing with their assets without the permission of the court.

This is a power that can be applied for at any time from the commencement of an investigation; given the length of time many fraud cases take to come to trial, it can remain in place for many months or even years. To ensure that the matter is dealt with expeditiously, the court must now, when granting a restraint order, ensure that regular reporting requirements are adhered to.

An important point to note in relation to restraints is that the witness statement provided by the FI to the court to support the application needs to be disclosed to the defendant when the restraint order is served on them. The court requires full and frank disclosure in any application, so it is crucial that the FI and the officer in the case liaise beforehand to ensure that the material that will need to be disclosed to the defendant will not jeopardise the investigation, particularly if at the pre-arrest stage. The need to restrain assets may need to be weighed up against the need to keep the investigation covert, and the timing of the application should be adjusted to reflect that.

Confiscation investigations require the FI to examine the defendant's finances to identify the financial value of the benefit they obtained from their criminal conduct. This will be directly influenced by the matters on the indictment, which is why there should be consideration of confiscation at the charging phase. Ideally, the FI would be included in the discussions with the CPS about charging.

While the onus is on the defence to show the court that they have insufficient assets to meet the benefit figure, the prosecution will need to ensure that any known assets that can be identified are brought to the attention of the court. Information from interviews and searches can be very helpful in this regard, and if it is possible for the FI to attend any search then this can often pay dividends.

Confiscation proceedings should commence on or before the time of sentencing and are instigated by the prosecutor or the court. At the time of writing, it is only possible to carry out confiscation in the Crown Court, so if a case in the magistrates' court is being considered for confiscation, then a request will need to be made by the prosecutor for the matter to be committed to the Crown Court for sentencing and confiscation.

If a person fails to pay their confiscation order in full within the time period specified by the court, then they are liable to have an additional sentence of imprisonment imposed on them, which is to be served at the end of any term of imprisonment handed down for the criminal offences.

KEY POINTS—JOINT ASSET RECOVERY DATABASE

- The Joint Asset Recovery Database (JARD) is managed by the NCA and is a national, inter-agency database holding details of all cash detention and forfeiture orders; all confiscation, restraint and financial reporting orders; and all civil recovery and criminal taxation cases.
- As well as being an inter-agency administrative tool (various parts of the system are used by the police, agencies such as HMRC, the NCA, the Department for Work and Pensions (DWP), the Financial Conduct Authority (FCA), the Serious Fraud Office (SFO), immigration enforcement, the Home Office, Her Majesty's Courts and Tribunals Service (HMCTS) and the CPS, as well as local authority AFIs), JARD is also a useful intelligence tool. A search on JARD for FIs should be routine.

8

Fraud and disclosure

8.1 **Introduction**

Disclosure is one of the main areas for challenge in fraud and economic crime cases. Investigators should be in no doubt that there could be intense scrutiny of both their disclosure decisions and the methods used to gather material during the course of the investigation. If the prosecution fail to discharge their disclosure obligations from the outset, then this provides the defence with reasons to challenge the basis of the prosecution. Failure to comply with the legislation, guidelines and codes of practice may jeopardise any prosecution case. This chapter describes the elements to be taken into consideration regarding disclosure in fraud cases. It is important that those dealing with disclosure are suitably trained to undertake that role.

> Disclosure is one of the most important issues in the criminal justice system and the application of proper and fair disclosure is a vital component of a fair criminal justice system. The 'golden rule' is that fairness requires full disclosure should be made of all material held by the prosecution that weakens its case or strengthens that of the defence.
>
> (Lord Goldsmith, HM Attorney General, Foreword, Attorney General's guidelines on disclosure, 2005)

Historically, the police and other investigators have not paid enough attention to the disclosure process or have not resourced it sufficiently; this has led to challenges and ultimately failed fraud prosecutions. This has led to a change in the charging stance of specialist fraud prosecutors, such that the Crown Prosecution Service (CPS) now frequently requires confirmation that disclosure is well advanced and in good order before charges are authorised. Disclosure, therefore, needs to be prioritised from the start of a fraud case.

Fraud cases, by their very nature, can be material-intensive, raising particular challenges in the disclosure process. Common issues that arise from disclosure failures are:

- abuse of process applications and possible stay of prosecution;
- increased costs;
- significant work needed to rectify problems;
- acquittals—with loss of compensation to victims and confiscation opportunities.
- failure to secure third-party material.

Further reading

- The Criminal Procedure and Investigations Act (CPIA) 1996, as amended by the Criminal Justice Act 2003: www.legislation.gov.uk/ukpga/1996/25/contents

---

- Disclosure Code of Practice under section 23(1) of the CPIA: www.gov.uk/ government/uploads/system/uploads/attachment_data/file/447967/code-of- practice-approved.pdf
- Protocol for the control and management of heavy fraud and complex criminal cases, 2005: www.cps.gov.uk/publications/docs/control_protocol. pdf
- Attorney General's guidelines on disclosure, 2013: www.gov.uk/government/ uploads/system/uploads/attachment_data/file/262994/AG_Disclosure_ Guidelines_-_December_2013.pdf
- Criminal Procedure Rules, 2014—in particular, Parts 1–3 and 22 and the Disclosure Practice Direction issued under them: www.legislation.gov.uk/ uksi/2014/1610/contents/made
- 'Disclosure: A Protocol for the Control and Management of Unused Material in the Crown Court', protocol issued by the Court of Appeal, February 2006: www.judiciary.gov.uk/wp-content/uploads/JCO/Documents/Protocols/ crown_courts_disclosure.pdf

8.2 Disclosure and the principles

8.2.1 Relevance tests

With regard to all relevant material, investigators are required to retain, record and reveal anything that appears to have some bearing on any offence under investigation or on any person being investigated, unless it is incapable of having an impact on the case. Relevance needs to be properly determined as early as possible. Failure to do so can necessitate a time-consuming exercise by prosecutors to rectify the situation.

There is a common misconception that simply everything must be scheduled and disclosed. This is incorrect; the disclosure officer must rigorously apply the relevance test to ensure that all the parties are not burdened with masses of irrelevant material. Much of the material gathered during the course of a fraud investigation that is not prosecution evidence will be unused material and will fall within the definition given. Additionally, some statements may initially form part of the evidence but subsequently become unused material.

What is relevant may change as the investigation develops and the defence case becomes known. The prosecutor's duty of disclosure is a continuing duty, and the question of relevance must be kept under review.

8.2.2 Disclosure test

The prosecutor must disclose to the accused any prosecution material that has not previously been disclosed (e.g. prior to interview), and that might reasonably be considered capable of undermining the case for the prosecution or of assisting the case for the accused. It is for a disclosure officer to identify the material that he or she believes meets the test for disclosure and work with the prosecutor to ensure that all such material is identified and disclosed.

8.3 Disclosure roles

8.3.1 The disclosure officer

The disclosure officer is responsible for examining the material retained during the investigation, revealing material to the prosecutor and certifying that this has been done, and disclosing material to the accused at the request of the prosecutor. In essence, they are responsible for the day-to-day management of unused material and complying with all legal obligations.

This is a key role and the importance of it should be recognised at the outset of the investigation. It is a requirement of the legislation that the disclosure officer must be suitably trained.

In routine investigations, it may be appropriate for the investigation and disclosure roles to be undertaken by one person. In large-scale fraud cases, it will be necessary to separate the roles in order to avoid the investigating officer (IO) becoming overwhelmed. In these cases, the work of the disclosure officer has the potential to make or break the case at trial.

Checklist—the disclosure officer must provide different certifications in the course of the disclosure process

The certifications should cover:

1 revelation of all relevant retained material;

2 whether material satisfies the disclosure test;

3 whether material satisfies the disclosure test following a defence statement.

8.3.2 The investigating officer (IO)

The IO is the person conducting or assisting in the conduct of a criminal investigation. It is not necessary to always maintain schedules of unused material from the start of all investigations, but this is usually beneficial and should be judged on a case-by-case basis. In the early stages of an investigation, it may not be possible to decide whether particular material will eventually form part of the prosecution case, or will remain unused.

8.3.3 **The senior investigating officer (SIO)**

The SIO is responsible for strategies and decision making from the beginning to the end of a case. The scale of the investigation will determine the size of the disclosure task. The SIO should have a logical and focused investigative strategy that takes full account of and is achievable given the disclosure implications of different decisions. Large-scale fraud investigations can quickly get out of hand if the SIO does not maintain rigid case parameters. Fraudsters often have multiple scams ongoing at any one time, and it is necessary to concentrate on those lines of inquiry that will yield the best evidence and chance of conviction. Once a certain threshold of fraud offending is reached, especially in terms of value, proving further offences will not attract any greater sanctions from the courts, but can tie up limited resources in onerous disclosure tasks. Should these become unmanageable, the case could be unsuccessful, whatever the quality of the evidence.

8.3.4 **Crown Prosecution Service (CPS)**

The support of an experienced prosecution lawyer is vital to the investigation team, and in major cases a consultation should be sought as soon as possible. This will enable all parties to work towards the same goal and work on key issues together (e.g. defining 'relevance')

The prosecution should discharge their disclosure obligations in relation to the retention, recording and revelation of material within a reasonable time frame.

When making a charging decision, a prosecutor must be satisfied that the disclosure process is being properly managed, and that disclosure obligations can be discharged. If not, the consideration as to whether there is a realistic prospect of conviction will be negatively affected.

8.4 **Manual guidance (MG) forms**

The preparation of properly detailed schedules saves time and resources throughout the disclosure process, and promotes confidence in their integrity.

The disclosure officer is responsible for preparing signed and dated schedules of unused material, to be submitted with a full file.

KEY POINTS—DISCLOSURE SCHEDULES

The disclosure officer will prepare two main schedules of all items of material relevant to the case, describing:

- non-sensitive unused material (MG6C);
- sensitive unused material (MG6D).

Each description of an item should contain enough detail to allow the prosecutor to make an informed decision as to whether he or she needs to inspect the material before deciding whether it should be disclosed or not.

Any comments or explanations regarding the schedule's contents should be made on the MG6 form accompanying the submission of the MG6C and MG6D. The disclosure officer should aim to submit the schedules with the file, but this may not be possible due to the volume of unused material. The prosecutor should be informed of the volume of unused material and this should be revealed to them in phases within agreed timescales. It is important to enter into a dialogue with the prosecutor and explain the nature and extent of any problem as it arises, reach an agreement and keep each other fully informed.

8.4.1 Police schedule of relevant non-sensitive material (MG6C)

This is disclosed to the defence. In the description column of every schedule, each item should be individually described clearly and accurately and be consecutively numbered. The description must be sufficient to allow an informed decision on whether it could satisfy the disclosure test. Documents should not be referred to using jargon or by numbers that are meaningless to third parties. The relevance of the material should be described, so that the information and not the documentation will form part of the descriptive schedule. This is similar to, for example, describing the contents of a book rather than just giving its cover title and nothing else.

Where there are numerous items of a repetitive nature (e.g. messages) it is permissible to describe them by quantity and generic title. Care is necessary to avoid overuse of this technique leading to the prosecutor and the defence requesting to see the items. The disclosure officer must ensure that items that might meet the disclosure test are also described individually. Examples of items that can be grouped together in the disclosure list are:

- police emails: these can be grouped according to particular themes on the schedule. For instance, 'all relevant internal emails between police officers and staff re transmission of exhibits';
- witness packs: rather than being listed separately and scattered across the schedules, it is helpful if all documents relating to one witness are either listed together in sequential order or as one item. This includes draft statements, relevant emails, correspondence and any officers' notes.

Emails and correspondence between the police and the prosecuting legal team are sensitive (privileged) and should not be disclosed on the MG6C. Special attention is to be paid to documents held by officers electronically. Large-scale cases should be managed with a central folder, and all officers should save their case material to subfolders within the central folder. Police email systems can be set up to delete emails after a set period of time, so steps should be taken to preserve all relevant emails.

Other items that must be specifically disclosed on MG6C schedules include:

- any previous convictions of prosecution witnesses;
- the names of any witnesses who may have relevant information, but who have not made witness statements.

8.4.2 **Police schedule of relevant sensitive material (MG6D)**

This schedule details unused material that the disclosure officer believes should be withheld from the defence because disclosure would give rise to a real risk of serious prejudice to an important public interest. This schedule will not be disclosed to the defence. The MG6D must contain enough detail for the prosecutor to determine whether it is necessary to make an application to the court for permission not to disclose sensitive unused material that would otherwise satisfy the disclosure test, on the grounds of public interest immunity (PII).

In cases where there is no sensitive unused material, the disclosure officer should endorse and sign an MG6D to this effect. An item may move from the MG6D to the MG6C (e.g. when an ongoing inquiry is completed)

KEY POINTS—SENSITIVE MATERIAL

Examples of sensitive material in fraud cases include the following:

- Information provided under an obligation to report suspicious financial activity (while financial institutions etc are under such obligations and therefore do not give suspicious activity reports in confidence, their protection must be considered in disclosure decisions).
- Information from the public, agencies, commercial institutions and communications service providers in circumstances where there is some legitimate expectation of confidentiality (e.g. Crimestoppers material).
- Details of measures taken to protect witnesses from intimidation and harassment. Confidential methods of detecting and fighting crime. Exposure of investigative techniques makes the criminal community more aware and therefore better able to avoid detection. The Crown should neither confirm nor deny the use of a human intelligence source.
- Issues related to national security, including economic interests.

Each item must be considered independently before it is included in the sensitive schedule and before any PII is made. Some items, by their very nature, will reveal why disclosure should be withheld.

Checklist—sensitive material that satisfies the disclosure test

The disclosure officer should provide to the prosecutor detailed information on the following:

- why the material is sensitive;

- why it is considered that disclosure will create a real risk of serious prejudice to an important public interest;

- the consequences of revealing to the defence:

  - the material itself;

  - the category of the material;

  - the fact that an application may be made;

- the significance of the material to the issues in the trial;

- the involvement of any third parties in bringing the material to the attention of the police;

- where the material is likely to be the subject of an order for disclosure, the police view on continuance of the prosecution;

- whether it is possible to disclose the material without compromising its sensitivity.

The prejudice that is anticipated from disclosure of a document must be a serious, not a minor, risk. Again, as with 'real risk', this is an assessment that must be made on an individual basis, having regard to the risk of possible cumulative damage to the public interest.

Where material is disclosed having been edited to protect the public interest, the original should not be marked in any way. The defence should be informed of the action taken, although this will normally be clear from the appearance of the document itself. An application will have to be made to the court to withhold the remainder of the material if it requires disclosure.

For disclosure purposes, the law makes no distinction between covert and non-covert material. The disclosure officer signs to certify that all relevant material has been retained and revealed to the prosecutor. To this end, covert units will usually participate in the disclosure process and the disclosure officer should have access to all the material in their possession in order to fulfil their duties. If the issue is so sensitive that the disclosure officer cannot be informed, then the covert unit will approach the CPS directly on the subject.

8.4.3 Disclosure officer's report (MG6E)

Defence requests for disclosure of material from the MG6C will only be complied with if the CPS or the police consider that the material meets the disclosure test.

The disclosure officer should review the unused material schedules for any items so listed that meet the disclosure test. All items that do will require an entry on the MG6E, cross-referenced with the original entry. The reason why an item meets the disclosure test will be recorded after each entry, and copies of any disclosable material will accompany the MG6E schedule. Any requests from the defence for material listed on the MG6C schedule must state why they say it meets the disclosure test, connecting its relevance with the defence case statement.

The disclosure officer should be objective and fair-minded, and should think from the defence's point of view. This includes all issues and not just major points; the defence may want to put small pieces of evidence together that might ultimately place doubt in the jury's minds as to whether a person is guilty or not.

Checklist—types of material that may be included on an MG6E

- Previous convictions or cautions for prosecution witnesses.

- Any material that might affect the credibility of a prosecution witness or the accuracy of any prosecution evidence. This category covers any material that is detrimental to the witness, such as any previous convictions or rewards. Other examples include a witness who gives inconsistent versions of events. There is a distinction to be made between a person who makes additional statements to clarify information and a person who changes their story.

- Any material that may have a bearing on the admissibility of any prosecution evidence.

- Any information that may cast doubt on the reliability of a confession, such as information relating to the accused's mental or physical health or their intellectual capacity.

- Information suggesting that a person other than the accused was or might have been responsible, or which points to another person, whether charged or not (including a co-accused), having involvement in the offence.

Any material that supports or is consistent with a defence put forward in interview, in the defence statement or which is otherwise apparent from the prosecution papers, should be supplied to the prosecutor. This includes anything that points away from the accused, such as information concerning a possible alibi. If the disclosure officer believes that material satisfies the disclosure test, it should be brought to the prosecutor's attention, even though it suggests a defence inconsistent with, or alternative to, any defence already put forward by the accused.

A wide interpretation should be applied when identifying material that might satisfy the disclosure test. The disclosure officer should consult with the prosecutor where necessary to help to identify material that may require disclosure, and must specifically draw material to the attention of the prosecutor where the disclosure officer has doubts as to whether it might satisfy the disclosure test.

KEY POINTS—PROSECUTOR'S RESPONSIBILITIES

The prosecutor is required to advise the disclosure officer of:

- items described on the MG6C that should be on the MG6D and vice versa;
- any apparent omissions or amendments required;
- insufficient or unclear descriptions of items.

To avoid confusion, numbering of items submitted at a later stage must be consecutive to those on the previously submitted schedules.

8.5 Disclosure officer's policy file and CPS disclosure management document

The disclosure officer should create and regularly update a disclosure policy file. The day-to-day management of material is planned and recorded in this document. It should not just be a statement of the law, but should instead form a comprehensive audit trail, capable of demonstrating that the police have control of the material. Key points must be recorded, such as an invitation to the defence team to suggest keywords to use when researching digital material (see the following section), and reviews triggered by the receipt of defence case statements. The prosecution must account for what it is doing, as well as what it will not be doing.

In larger fraud cases, the CPS, often in conjunction with counsel, will produce a separate disclosure management document (DMD). This written statement sets out the position of the prosecution regarding the management of the unused material, to assist the court and the defence. It demonstrates to the court what has been done, as well as when and how.

KEY POINTS—DISCLOSURE MANAGEMENT DOCUMENT (DMD)

- Ensure a clear and transparent approach to the management of the disclosure process by the prosecution.
- Reassure the court that the prosecution is complying with its disclosure obligations.
- Prompt the defence on disclosure issues in advance of trial, thus helping to highlight and accelerate their resolution.
- Enable the defence to see and understand what the prosecution is doing and to make any challenges by application to the court.
- Enable the defence to know the extent to which they should be making their own inquiries.

The use of DMDs is now embodied in the Better Case Management initiative, introduced across Crown Courts in 2016.

8.6 Digital disclosure strategy

Material stored on digital media is a critical area in most fraud investigations. Its correct management, in terms of disclosure obligations, is absolutely vital. There are an increasing number of fraud cases in which a huge amount of material is held on computers, smartphones, in the 'cloud' and on other digital storage systems. Investigators cannot leave analysis of seized computers to the end of an investigation. In general, any digital media the police seize has to be imaged and searched for material, which may be evidence, or which may undermine the prosecution or assist the defence. This process takes time, so an early start is always beneficial.

KEY POINTS—FRAUD OFFENCES

In July 2011, the Attorney General issued guidelines stating:

[T]he disclosure officer's obligation to inspect retained material may be fulfilled in relation to digitally stored material by using search terms or dip sampling methods, so long as the material is described on the schedules as clearly as possible and the manner and extent of the inspection is recorded along with the justification for adopting that approach. . . . The objective of these Guidelines is to set out how material satisfying the tests for disclosure can best be identified and disclosed to the defence without imposing unrealistic or disproportionate demands on the investigator and prosecutor.

The guidelines specify the way in which defence disclosure requests for material stored on computers and other digital material are to be dealt with, so that the prosecution can comply with its duties of disclosure. In particular, it is set out that where the material is extensive, dip sampling and searches using lists of search words may be used, so as to make the task manageable. The rationale and methodology for the same should be made clear in the DMD, being drawn up in collaboration with the defence team.

In December 2015, the Court of Appeal Criminal Division (CACD) issued a redacted judgment in the case of *R v R and others* [2015] EWCA Crim 1941. The prosecution had been stayed following defence submissions on disclosure of digital material, and the CACD allowed a prosecution appeal. Although the case had not yet come to trial, the CACD issued the redacted judgment as it was recognised that the guidance was urgently needed in the public domain, as there was a perceived need to avert the danger of large fraud cases becoming unprosecutable.

The background to the case involved the seizure of many computers, containing in total some seven terabytes of data. The prosecution had been unable to move forward on the resulting disclosure issues, leading to a successful defence application to stay the case as an abuse of process. In overturning this decision, the CACD specifically stated that it was beyond argument that there had been no deliberate misconduct or bad faith on the part of the prosecution. Every effort had been made to comply with its disclosure strategy. The key guidelines were as follows:

KEY POINTS—KEY DISCLOSURE GUIDELINES

- The prosecution must be in the driving seat at the stage of initial disclosure.
- This requires the prosecution to get a grip on the case and its disclosure requirements at the outset. Initial disclosure must be considered and adequately resourced, and there should be an emphasis on the front-loading of disclosure tasks. A 'thinking' approach is to be adopted that is tailored to the individual needs of the case, and a 'one size fits all' mentality is not appropriate.
- The prosecution must encourage dialogue and prompt engagement with the defence.
- The assessment of material for disclosure needs to be informed by the analysis of the cases for both the prosecution and defence, by reference to the issues in the case. Therefore, the disclosure officer may not be able to identify all disclosable material during the initial phase.
- The law is prescriptive of the result, not the method.
- It is recognised that vast amounts of data preclude the reading and scheduling of every single item. The prosecution cannot be, and is not, required to do the impossible. Sampling is allowed. The prosecution team is under a duty to properly record the analytical techniques used to search the data. As the case progresses, the exercise may need to be revisited. It is vital that realistic deadlines are set by the courts and the prosecution needs to actively manage expectations as to what can be achieved in particular timeframes.
- The disclosure process should be subject to robust case management by the judge (this includes initial disclosure). The CACD is clear that judges must take an active role in preventing cases going off track. The defence should be prevented from aiming to stall progress in a case by claiming that the initial disclosure is not complete. Progress can be made in parallel with disclosure continuing alongside the overall preparation of the case. The CACD concluded: 'A search for perfection in this area is likely to be illusory.'
- Flexibility is critical.
- Disclosure should not be seen as a box-ticking exercise and it is not part of the prosecution's duty under the CPIA to improve the material seized. Thus, there is no obligation on the part of the prosecution to give the defence a searchable database or means to navigate metadata. *R v R and others* [2015] EWCA 1941.

With the above principles in mind, the following general guidelines can be used to assist in adopting a reasoned and professional approach to the digital disclosure task.

8.6.1 Targeted search strategy

The seizing of many devices can be problematic to case management if there are insufficient resources to examine and schedule their contents for unused material. Investigators should consider their investigative strategy carefully so that only those that are believed to be likely to contain relevant evidence are seized. As with any forensic decision making, wholesale seizure of old computers and telephones, or from people at the periphery of a case, may ultimately prove to be more of a disclosure burden than an investigative benefit. If possible, consideration can be made for the imaging and/or examination of a digital device's contents at the search scene, as this can prevent the seizure of irrelevant items and also minimise disruption to businesses. In large-scale fraud cases, a separate digital media strategy document can be considered. This could be used to set parameters, and could be divided into sub-groups, with different policy decisions regarding the examination of computers and mobile telephones.

KEY POINTS—ATTORNEY GENERAL'S GUIDELINES

The Attorney General's guidelines are meant to help officers and staff:

It is important for investigators and prosecutors to remember that the duty under the CPIA Code of Practice is to 'pursue all *reasonable* lines of enquiry including those that point away from the suspect'.

It is not the duty of the prosecution to comb through all the material in its possession—e.g. every word or byte of computer material—on the look-out for anything which might conceivably or speculatively assist the defence.

(Attorney General's guidelines on disclosure, 2011: 'Supplementary Guidelines on Digitally Stored Material')

8.6.2 Keywords and other forms of sampling

Investigators need to know what is technologically possible, as this is constantly changing. As digital media files are generally too large for every file/message/ image, etc to be examined, a sensible approach to sampling has to be adopted. Traditionally, the first technique to be employed is keyword searching. This will be in the investigative phase, but the involvement of the disclosure officer, or the keyword list taking disclosure issues into account, can save the exercise having to be repeated later. Similarly, consulting the defence for keywords can also save time and resources. Any requests for additional searches proposed by the defence that are relevant to an issue in their case should be encouraged. Requests for keyword searches may be set out in the accused's defence statement, and should be supported by sufficient justification to enable the prosecution to understand what underlying material the accused is seeking and why that material satisfies the test for disclosure. Even if the defence do not respond at any stage, or reply with a list that contains too many words or too many common words, details of the consultation must be recorded in the disclosure officer's policy log. In this way, it can be demonstrated to the court that the cooperation of the defence was actively sought, especially if they subsequently seek to burden the prosecution with further searches, having failed to engage in the disclosure process previously.

KEY POINTS—DEFENCE ROLE

- Attorney General's Guidelines on Disclosure, 2011, paragraph 3(ii) provides that: 'The defence will be expected to play their part in defining the real issues in the case. In this context the defence will be invited to participate in defining the scope of the reasonable searches that may be made of digitally stored material by the investigator to identify material that might reasonably be expected to undermine the prosecution case or assist the defence.'
- The Lord Chief Justice, in the protocol dated 22 March 2005, noted: '[I]t is relevant that the defendants are likely to be intelligent people, who know their own business affairs and who (for the most part) will know what documents or categories of documents they are looking for.'

In large and complex frauds where the defendants deploy sophisticated methods in furtherance of their offences, in relation to any digital material, the respective defendants are highly likely to know:

- if there is material that supports the matters set out in their respective defence statements;
- the likely location of the material in the digital media;
- the approximate date of creation;
- the parties to records such as emails.

Keywords can often still produce too many 'hits', such that a review of the underlying material would be too onerous. To make the task manageable, the keyword hit list can be reduced by various techniques, including dip sampling.

Checklist— example standard ratios in dip sampling

- 1–100 hits—review all;
- 100–1,000 hits—review 1 in 5;

- 1,000–5,000 hits—review 1 in 10;

- 5,000–10,000 hits—review 1 in 25;

- 10,000+ hits—review 1 in 50;

- 25,000+—consider a filter sampling method (as below) to refine and manage the volume.

Another approach is to use a filtering process, for instance by searching with keywords encased within inverted commas (i.e. 'example'). Certain common terms may still provide too many hits to enable a manageable review of the underlying material to take place. A further refining of the search terms, by combining certain words, can be used as a means of further filtering the digitally stored material. This is especially useful when it is necessary to search for some very common words; for instance, an investigator would search for 'Michael' AND 'Brown', rather than just the words individually.

It should be noted that where dip sampling is employed, and if a sample examined produces relevant disclosable material, then all the material in that group will need to be reviewed and disclosed.

8.6.3 E-discovery systems for digital material in large fraud cases

Advanced tools have been used to manage digital material in civil cases for a number of years. A number of proprietary systems have been developed and are in use by different prosecution bodies such as the National Crime Agency, the Financial Conduct Authority and the Serious Fraud Office. The huge amount of material stored on computers means that in larger cases the use of such systems is becoming essential, and should be strongly considered for cases where more than a handful of devices have been seized or retained, including smartphones that are generally used more as computers than as telephones.

A principal benefit of e-discovery systems is that they can substantially reduce the amount of material to be reviewed. The traditional police approach has been to review devices one at a time in isolation, meaning that in a large case duplicate files/emails are potentially viewed many times across various devices. Also, as the task can be split between different officers, they are 'siloed' and unaware of what others have reviewed. The disclosure/evidence-gathering process is a substantial exercise, and a cumbersome issue is populating the disclosure schedules. The evidential and disclosure reviews are simplified by the e-discovery system, which unifies emails, files and images in a database covering all the seized material. Hence, an investigator can be tasked with looking at all media files at once—for instance, at all the emails concerning person 'X', or all images, or all files, with a specific keyword. Once the investigator has analysed a digital device, they still have to create and input the results manually into the disclosure schedules.

8.7 Third-party material

This is material held by organisations or people who are not part of the prosecution team. A third party has no obligation under the CPIA 1996 to reveal material to the investigator or to the prosecutor. It is of critical importance that if a third party is believed to hold material relevant to the investigation they should be requested by letter to hold that material (templates of this letter can be found in Annex B of the Disclosure Manual).

Further reading

- Annex B of the CPS Disclosure Manual, third party letter templates: www. cps.gov.uk/legal/d_to_g/disclosure_manual/annex_b_disclosure_manual/

It is essential at the outset to identify what material is relevant to the fraud investigation. Particular issues may arise where a corporate entity has already conducted an internal investigation, or where an investigation has been undertaken on behalf of a regulator. These can generate large volumes of material potentially subject to LPP, especially where the work has been contracted to one of the larger firms of solicitors or accountants.

Other agencies should be engaged with as early as possible and put on notice of the need to retain all the material in their possession. The disclosure officer needs to establish the parameters of the material held by other agencies so that it can be scheduled. In cases where third parties refuse to give up material, the disclosure officer should liaise with the case lawyer to arrange for material to be obtained either by a specific court order or by witness summons to the relevant person in the agency. In some cases prior to charge, it may be that relevant material could be covered by production orders already obtained during the course of the investigation. The material has to be of significance in relation to a real issue, being damaging to the prosecution or helpful to the defence.

8.8 Legal professional privilege (LPP) material

How LPP is to be dealt with during an investigation should be considered throughout the investigation and expert opinion sought. LPP issues can arise immediately following or even during searches, and the investigative team may have to deal with claims of LPP on digital and other material in the evidence-gathering phase. Thus, LPP material is often identified and the position clarified before the disclosure exercise takes place. Otherwise, it can be a particularly difficult issue, especially with digital material in multiple defendant cases, where there is embedded LPP material that is confidential between the various co-accused. The accepted practice is for an independent counsel to be instructed to review, identify and separate LPP material before the remainder can be examined evidentially. The disclosure officer's policy document should be used to record decision making and communication with defence solicitors.

8.9 Use of the HOLMES and other case management systems

The Home Office Large Major Enquiry System (HOLMES) is a computer database designed to aid the investigation in large-scale inquiries; it has a customised disclosure facility. For fraud cases, a reduced version of the HOLMES can be appropriate as a case management tool, as the full functionality of the system is not generally required. Comprehensive indexing is generally not necessary to use the HOLMES for disclosure purposes and for exhibit/statement management. Once the disclosure officer has made an assessment of sensitive and non-sensitive items and whether they meet the disclosure test, the HOLMES can populate and generate the items onto the relevant MG schedules. It is inappropriate to allow the defence direct access to the HOLMES because of its ability to cross-reference sensitive and non-sensitive material.

The disclosure officer must have completed training in disclosure and the specific HOLMES disclosure facility. Material in the case that is not relevant (e.g. an officer's report requesting annual leave) may be recorded. Using the 'non-relevant' button on the HOLMES will mean that these items will not be scheduled and, accordingly, the prosecutor will not see the material or be made aware of it. The HOLMES disclosure facility is designed so that the disclosure officer has to consider all the source material for disclosure purposes.

Disclosure officers can use a 'search and count' facility to inform the prosecutor of the total number of records that are being dealt with, how many have been assessed and how many are still outstanding. The HOLMES also has the facility to produce schedules in phases, and the disclosure officer can use the phases to continually reveal material to the CPS in tranches, rather than by producing one over-burdening set of schedules.

When instructed to do so, the HOLMES can remove highly sensitive material from all schedules. A separate highly sensitive schedule will need to be created by the disclosure officer. The HOLMES is automated so that if the disclosure officer selects any of the options in 7.3 of the Code of Practice, a field will appear to be completed to explain why this material meets the disclosure test and needs to be brought to the attention of the prosecutor.

8.10 **Summary**

In summary, getting disclosure right is critical to presenting a sound case in the court; the Attorney General's guidelines usefully sum up disclosure as follows:

> Disclosure must not be an open-ended trawl of unused material. A critical element to fair and proper disclosure is that the defence plays their role to ensure that the prosecution is directed to material which might reasonably be considered capable of undermining the prosecution case or assisting the case for the accused. The process is key to ensuring prosecutors make informed determinations about disclosure of unused material.

> (Attorney General's guidelines on disclosure, 2013)

Further reading

CPS Disclosure Manual: www.cps.gov.uk/legal/d_to_g/disclosure_manual/

9.1 **Introduction**

Within the police service there are a number of externally funded specialist units to investigate specific types of fraud that impact particular sectors. This chapter details the role of the:

- Police Intellectual Property Crime Unit (PIPCU)
- Insurance Fraud Enforcement Department (IFED)
- Dedicated Card and Payment Crime Unit (DCPCU)

It describes the case acceptance criteria, key legislation used and how they can support others undertaking investigations into offences of a similar type.

9.2 **Police Intellectual Property Crime Unit (PIPCU)**

The PIPCU is an operationally independent unit that was established in 2013 and is funded by the Intellectual Property Office (IPO), a part of the Department for Business, Innovation and Skills (BIS).

Technological advances and the increasing use of the internet by organisations to sell and deliver products present new challenges for government, law enforcement and industry to protect against intellectual property (IP) crime.

Protecting IP is an increasingly important means of supporting the government's economic policy of strong and sustainable growth and gives organisations the confidence to innovate and grow at home and abroad.

Since its inception, the PIPCU has worked closely with the IPO Intelligence Hub and other public sector organisations, including national and local Trading Standards, to investigate, target, disrupt and prevent online IP crime. The unit has established strong links with IP rights holders and their representative organisations, including the Alliance for Intellectual Property and a range of other stakeholders.

The PIPCU prioritises serious and organised IP crime that causes significant harm or damage to the UK economy or individual victims, with a particular focus on internet-enabled counterfeiting and digital content theft. It is not currently in the scope of the unit to investigate cases where the predominant criminal activity involves the counterfeiting of pharmaceuticals, foodstuffs, alcohol, tobacco or currency, unless exceptional circumstances apply.

9.2.1 **The PIPCU's remit and priorities**

There are a number of factors that are considered in the PIPCU's case acceptance and tasking process that are designed to identify where an appropriate balance exists between threat and harm and the likelihood of a successful outcome.

The challenges in reliably assessing the harm caused by different types of IP crime are widely recognised by the PIPCU, the IPO and other stakeholders. The PIPCU therefore considers a wide range of harm factors beyond simple financial loss. These include:

- reputational harm;
- any enabling or dependant crime, for example money laundering, forced labour or human trafficking.

Where a case has the potential to cause physical harm, the PIPCU will respond swiftly to eliminate any danger to individuals and the general public.

Referral considerations

The international nature of organised online IP crime is such that suspects are often located overseas and outside the jurisdiction of UK law enforcement; this presents a number of challenges to investigators. When assessing case referrals, the PIPCU will consider whether:

- the case falls within the PIPCU's remit;
- an organised crime group (OCG) is involved;
- there is a threat to public safety;
- there is an asset recovery opportunity;
- there are sufficient lines of inquiry to identify primary suspects;
- the suspects are within the jurisdiction of available legislation;
- there is a realistic prospect that an investigation will result in a successful prosecution.

Where a case does not meet these criteria, the PIPCU will seek to use innovative disruption strategies that are designed to disrupt and frustrate criminals and criminal enterprises.

The main sources of referrals for investigation are:

- industry;
- law enforcement;
- the IPO.

9.2.2 **Crime type—counterfeiting**

The prevalence of counterfeiting in the UK and the harm that it causes to the economy are significant. The £1.6 million worth of infringing items that were seized by the Border Force in the 12 months to June 2015 illustrates that supply often originates overseas and is frequently a result of OCGs with international structures. The PIPCU works with the IPO Intelligence Hub, the National Crime Agency (NCA), Europol and other stakeholders to develop intelligence and identify opportunities to take action against these groups.

Investigators are likely to encounter counterfeit items where they are offered for sale to the public, often from independently operated shops or markets, or where they have been purchased by individuals, either knowingly or unwittingly.

The following legislation should be considered in counterfeiting investigations:

- **Trade Marks Act 1994**: there are specific offences created by section 92 of the Trade Marks Act 1994 that investigators may find to be suitable. It should be noted that these are 'lifestyle offences' under Schedule 2 to the Proceeds of Crime Act (POCA) 2002.
- **Fraud Act 2006**: there may be circumstances in which offences of fraud by false representation and possessing, making or supplying articles for use in fraud are appropriate for consideration during the course of an investigation.

KEY POINTS—COUNTERFEITING

- **Possession of items is not necessarily an offence**: the offences relating to counterfeit goods created by the Trade Marks Act are limited to circumstances where a person acts with a view to making a gain for himself or someone else, or acts with intent to cause a loss to another person, without the consent of the owner of the trade mark. It should be noted that simple possession of a counterfeit item is not an offence unless specifically proscribed in alternative legislation, for example counterfeit notes and coins (section 16 of the Forgery and Counterfeiting Act 1981).
- **Grey market goods are not counterfeit**: grey market goods are genuine items that are bought and sold outside the manufacturer's authorised trading channels. Such markets occur as a result of either an item being ordinarily unavailable in a particular country or where the price of an item is significantly lower in one country than another. Investigators should be mindful that grey market goods are not counterfeit and, therefore, those that possess or trade in them do not commit criminal offences under the Trade Marks Act.
- **Goods advertised as replicas can still be** counterfeit: in the appeal of *CPS v Gary Robert Morgan* [2006] EWCA Crim 1742, the defendant sold watches on the internet bearing the word 'Chanel' and in one case 'Rolex'. It was made clear on the website to perspective purchasers that the items were replicas. However, the watches themselves did not identify that they were not genuine products. Morgan was acquitted at trial in the Crown Court, having successfully argued that because the watches were advertised as replicas, this did not amount to trade mark use and was not an indication of the origin of the goods. In the same trial, the defendant was, on the same basis, acquitted of possession with a view to selling three watch presentation boxes bearing signs likely to be mistaken for registered trade marks. Subsequently, the Court of Appeal ruled that advertising an item as a replica did not prevent the relevant offences from being committed and did not amount to a defence.

Case study—website disruption

As part of Operation Ashiko, the PIPCU works in close partnership with a number of rights holders to remove websites that advertise counterfeit goods for sale from the '.uk' domain tree. This tactic is utilised where the operators of identified websites cannot be identified through reasonable inquiries or where it has been established that they are in a jurisdiction beyond the reach of UK law enforcement. It has become apparent that criminals are registering websites using personal data obtained as a result of identity theft. Investigators should, therefore, be mindful that the registrant of a website that sells counterfeit goods may, in fact, be unaware of its existence. All the available information should be considered as part of an investigation strategy.

9.2.3 Crime type—copyright infringement

Computer software allows content (music, films, television and literature) to be delivered flexibly to a wide audience. There has been a corresponding shift in the way that criminal piracy is committed, with the emergence of a variety of illegal download and streaming websites and services. In some cases, these are enabled by set-top boxes that contain software designed to facilitate copyright infringement.

KEY POINTS—COPYRIGHT, DESIGNS AND PATENTS ACT 1988

There are a number of offences relating to copyright infringement that are predominantly focused upon those who infringe copyright in the course of a business or for commercial purposes, or to such an extent as to prejudicially affect the owner of the copyright:

- section 107(1): making or dealing with infringing copies of copyright works;
- section 107(2): making, dealing with or possessing an article designed or adapted to make copies of a copyright work;
- section 107(2A): infringing copyright by communicating a work to the public;
- section 198(1): making, dealing or using illicit recordings;
- section 198(1A): making a recording available to the public so that it can be viewed from a place and at a time chosen by the viewer;
- section 198(2): showing or playing a recording in public or communicating it to the public;
- section 296ZB: devices and services designed to circumvent technological protection measures;
- section 297(1): fraudulently receiving programmes;
- section 297A: unauthorised decoders;
- offences under sections 107(1), 107(2), 198(1) and 297A are 'lifestyle offences' by virtue of Schedule 2 to the POCA 2002.

Illegal content streaming

Streaming is where content is delivered to a device and viewed as it is received, rather than where a file is downloaded to a device so that it can be viewed offline. This method of copyright infringement allows unlawful access to content in real time and is used to facilitate viewing of live sporting events without payment of the relevant subscriptions. Investigators should be aware that, in addition to offences related to the manufacture and distribution of unauthorised television decoders, possession is also unlawful if it is for a commercial purpose. Criminal groups will often charge a subscription fee alongside any device or set-top box for continued access to copyrighted material.

There is a specific summary offence of dishonestly receiving a programme with intent to avoid payment where it is included in a broadcasting service provided from a place in the UK. This offence is unique in that it creates a criminal liability without any requirement for there to be a commercial or business purpose (sections 297–299 of the Copyright, Designs and Patents Act 1988).

Digital crime scenes

The nature of online copyright infringement is such that the infrastructure required to maintain websites is often located overseas and frequently in jurisdictions that do not have enforcement regimes that are as robust as those in the UK. It is therefore likely that an investigation would benefit from support from digital forensics specialists to ensure that all opportunities to maximise the recovery of evidence are fully exploited.

KEY POINTS—LICENSING BODIES

It should be noted that there are several organisations that represent rights holders and that they are often able to identify sources of further evidence and provide a global context to an investigation.

- Details can be found at: www.gov.uk/guidance/licensing-bodies-and-collective-management-organisations#other-licensing-bodies

---

Case study—Operation Creative

Online copyright infringement has the potential to generate a considerable income for OCGs through ongoing subscriptions and advertising that often appears alongside content on offending websites. One strategy used by the PIPCU is to work in partnership with rights holders and content-protection organisations to identify the most serious of websites that distribute infringing content and then restrict the income that can be derived from the criminal activity. This is primarily achieved through the maintenance of an infringing website list—shared with advertising agencies and trade groups—that allows brands to ensure that their products and services are not advertised on websites that are involved in criminal activity.

9.2.4 **Investigative considerations**

Investigators should consider the following:

- The IPO Intelligence Hub maintains a dedicated intelligence system and acts as the UK point of contact for Europol's IP crime team (see Further reading).
- There are a number of organisations that represent brands and rights holders and can provide support to an investigation, either with evidence or intelligence.
- Early referral to a financial investigator who can consider any available asset-recovery opportunities.
- Seek assistance from a digital media investigator (DMI) in relation to digital evidence, particularly copyright infringement.
- The harm caused by IP crime is not limited to financial losses to business, and investigators should seek to reflect the overall impact of an offence, particularly where safety issues arise, and should be reflected in the victim impact statement.

Further reading

- For further information on the IPO Intelligence Hub, see the Intellectual Property Office: www.gov.uk/government/organisations/intellectual-property-office
- The IPO paper of January 2016, 'Counting the Cost: The Trade in Counterfeit Goods in Manchester', contains an overview of the national issues in relation to IP crime and provides a specific focus on the Cheetham Hill area of Manchester.
- The 'Intellectual Property Crime Report 2014/15', published in September 2015, provides an annual summary of the enforcement activities that have occurred in relation to IP crime, highlights notable achievements and makes reference to a number of stakeholders and their collective initiatives to address the issues that they face.

KEY POINTS—USEFUL SOURCES OF INFORMATION

Further information about the PIPCU, and how to refer cases for investigation or advice, can be found on the City of London Police (CoLP)'s website at: www.cityoflondon.police.uk/pipcu

---

9.3 **The Insurance Fraud Enforcement Department (IFED)**

The insurance sector in the UK is the largest in Europe and the third largest in the world, employing 334,000 people and providing vital services to individuals and businesses. The Association of British Insurers (ABI) states the following statistics for insurance fraud:

> There were almost 130,000 cases of detected claims fraud in 2014 totalling over £1.3bn, a 4% increase in value compared to 2013. In addition there were 212,000 cases of application fraud.

The costs of investigating and contesting fraudulent claims directly increase the costs of all consumers' insurance, by an estimated £50 per policy. There are strong links between some insurance frauds and organised crime, movements of criminal commodities and issues that impact on local communities.

KEY POINTS—KEY DATES OF THE IFED'S DEVELOPMENT

- 2006: creation of the Insurance Fraud Bureau (IFB).
- 2012: funding through the ABI for the IFED, an operationally independent police unit run by the CoLP.
- 2013: a further part of the response is the Insurance Fraud Register (IFR), a central register of confirmed fraud risks to which insurers have access.
- 2014: Corporation of Lloyds became a further funding partner to the IFED.
- 2015: funding for the IFED extended by the ABI.

Further reading

- The ABI website's 2015 key facts guide: www.abi.org.uk
- ABI Insurance Fraud Statistics: www.abi.org.uk/Insurance-and-savings/Industry-data
- Insurance Fraud Register: www.theifr.org.uk/en/

Since its inception, the IFED has worked closely with the insurance industry, regulators, police forces and other stakeholders with regard to insurance fraud in order to:

- investigate;
- target;
- disrupt;
- prevent.

It maintains a high media profile, to raise awareness of insurance fraud and to tackle the perception that it is a low-risk crime to engage in.

KEY POINTS—IFED FACTS

Between 2012 and 2016, the IFED has:

- interviewed 1,500 suspects;
- prosecuted over 200 cases;
- recovered £1.5 million from fraudsters to return to victims.

9.3.1 The IFED's remit and priorities

The IFED deals with a broad range of insurance fraud offences, but will prioritise its resources around the following threats:

- **OCGs**: involved in motor insurance fraud (crash for cash groups);
- **professional enablers**: including doctors and solicitors;
- **serial cross-industry offenders**: defrauding multiple insurers with over-lapping or identical claims;
- **cases of high public impact**: bulk crime where a strong message can be communicated to a particular group of victims.

In addition to its investigative role, the IFED also acts as a centre of excellence for insurance fraud investigations. It provides guidance and support to other police forces and investigative bodies, sharing intelligence and increasing knowledge of insurance fraud investigation techniques.

The geographic remit of the IFED is England and Wales, and it also acts as the primary liaison conduit with law enforcement colleagues in Scotland, Europe and beyond.

The IFED also capitalises on its position to provide fast-time intelligence alerts (in relation to current threats) to industry to prevent losses and assist industry in building prevention strategies.

Referral considerations

The IFED have operational independence in case acceptance decisions. The main sources of referrals for investigation are:

- insurers;
- the IFB;
- members of the public;
- self-generated cases flowing from intelligence.

All investigations must be reported to Action Fraud to provide an audit trail and to harness the benefits of centralised reporting.

KEY POINT—USEFUL SOURCES OF INFORMATION

All referrals should be sent to ifedreferrals@cityoflondon.pnn.police.uk. For guidance or urgent cases, the unit can be contacted on 0207 164 8200.

9.3.2 **Crime type—illegal intermediaries (ghost broking)**

Vehicle insurance is a compulsory requirement of section 143 of the Road Traffic Act (RTA) 1988. Consumers can buy directly from an insurer or through a broker. Both insurers and brokers have to be authorised by the Financial Conduct Authority (FCA). Without that authorisation, an offence under section 19 of the Financial Services and Markets Act (FISMA) 2000 is made out. A ghost broker is an individual or group who sets up insurance policies for members of the public. They will either:

- take the money and provide the customer with a worthless piece of paper as an 'insurance certificate' or misrepresent the customer's details to get cheaper insurance for them;
- or use forged 'no claims' discount certificates (with varying degrees of collusion with the customer).

Research by communications consultancy Linstock (2013) found that one in five people would buy fake car insurance, and research by LexisNexis (2013) found that one in four thought that an omission or the giving of inaccurate information to reduce their premium was acceptable. In both cases, the insurance is worthless in the event of a collision, exposing the holder to prosecution, vehicle seizure and litigation.

Ghost brokers may target communities, such as foreign nationals with minimal understanding of the UK insurance market, those in financial distress and the elderly. Where there is collusion, ghost broking can be used to facilitate OCGs in high-performance vehicles that their owners wish to drive unimpeded and use to move criminal commodities.

Ghost brokers can operate with varying degrees of sophistication, sometimes using glossy websites and virtual and serviced office arrangements to project plausibility.

KEY POINTS—GHOST BROKER SCHEMES

- In some cases, the vehicles themselves will appear to be insured when checked through the police national database: a common tactic used by ghost brokers is to set up a trade policy for a company such as a car dealership, where it would be plausible for vehicles to be regularly added or removed from the policy.
- In other cases, they can operate from internet cafes or use any digitally enabled device.
- In the cases investigated by the IFED, the ghost broker will often have victims pay premiums into bank accounts used by contacts and then have the cash withdrawn from an ATM.

Checklist—ghost broking investigation

- Follow the financial trail to understand and evidence the cash arrangements.

- Obtain a statement from the FCA to prove the FISMA offence.

- Identify and interview (under caution) the ghost broker.

- Identify any additional victims and advise them as a matter of priority that they are not insured and should not drive until they obtain legitimate insurance.

- Consider liaising with the appropriate authority to seek the closure of any trade policies, websites and communication methods used in fraud.

Further reading

- LexisNexis, 'Motor Insurance Fraud Research Study', 2015: www.lexisnexis. com/risk/uk/newsroom/15-11-23-motor-insurance-fraud.aspx

---

9.3.3 Crime type—'crash for cash'

Definition of 'crash for cash':

> To stage or deliberately cause a road traffic collision solely for the purpose of financial gain.
>
> (www.insurancefraudbureau.org/insurance-fraud/crash-for-cash/)

'Crash for cash' typically consists of either a staged or induced collision:

- A staged collision involves two vehicles (both under criminal control) being deliberately crashed together. This often takes place in public, but some criminal gangs have crashed vehicles together in lock ups or other commercial premises.
- With an induced collision, the fraudster will target an innocent member of the public and typically slam the brakes on in front of them to induce a 'rear-end shunt'. Fraudsters can use decoy vehicles in front to make last-minute swerves to justify the slamming on, or use other vehicles to box in the innocent vehicle so that it has nowhere to go.

Fraudsters will target someone who appears to have a well-maintained car, so is likely to be insured, and will look for occupants who are unlikely to confront them. Collisions will sometimes be purely invented ('a paper fraud').

KEY POINTS—'CASH FOR CRASH' SCHEMES

- Repair of the damaged vehicle: values can be manipulated by clocking the vehicle back or adding extra damage with blunt force after the event.
- Physical injury: whiplash and other soft tissue damage. A further claim can be made for every extra passenger, making buses and coaches attractive targets for fraudsters. People at the periphery can be drawn in and their details added to claims (with or without their consent and knowledge), often becoming 'phantom' passengers. One in seven personal injury claims can be linked to a suspected organised 'crash for cash' (*source*: IFB 'Crash for Cash' report, 2012: www.insurancefraudbureau.org/media/1036/ifb_crash_for_cash_report_online.pdf).
- Car hire: policies may make the customer entitled to a courtesy car, and intermediaries can submit false or exaggerated invoices for cars never actually given to policy holders.
- Psychological impact: the IFED has seen an increase in claims for cognitive behavioural therapy arising from collisions.
- Loss of earnings and vehicle recovery/storage: again, invoices can be submitted for inflated charges or charges when no storage service has been provided.

The regulations allow for a claim to be submitted up to three years after the date of the incident. This makes all genuine accident data attractive to fraudsters, as they can contact the involved parties and pressure or induce them into supporting a claim through them, or just submit claims in their name without involving them. Following on from this are the issues of nuisance calls and texts, as well as bribes offered by OCGs to insurance workers to sell accident data. The IFED has issued alerts to the insurance industry to raise awareness of the number of approaches being made to insurance staff to buy data. Criminal groups are making approaches outside insurance premises: in pubs and bars, and through social media.

Checklist—'cash for crash' investigation

- The accident data is often passed through services such as digital-enabled devices, making the recovery of evidence on a subject's phone crucial. Accident management companies and claims management companies generally provide a legitimate service; however, some are established purely to carry out fraud.

- Crucial to securing payouts are professional enablers, such as storage agents, solicitors, doctors, physiotherapists and recovery agents. Many of these professions have regulators that may be able to provide specialist knowledge or intelligence to support a prosecution.

9.3.4 Crime type—employee liability and public liability claims fraud (slip and trip)

KEY POINTS—LIABILITY FRAUD TYPES

- Employee liability: in the main, incidents concern slips, trips or falls on the same level, injuries sustained while handling, lifting or carrying, and being struck by moving objects (including flying or falling objects). Approximately half of fraudulent claims are exaggerated and the other half are staged/fabricated.
- Public liability: the most prevalent incident circumstances are slips, trips or falls on the same level (mainly pothole trips), being struck by moving objects (including flying/falling objects) and falls from a height. For public liability claims, there are a higher proportion of staged/fabricated claims. It is suggested that claimants are less likely to stage an accident at work due to the presence of witnesses, and also due to the possible consequences/effects on their employment should the fraud be discovered.

There has been a recent shift in the insurance fraud landscape, with emerging organised casualty fraud rings impacting on public and employee liability policies. The new issue is driven by fraudsters latching on to new methods of making money, given the proactive law enforcement and regulations within motor insurance fraud.

The modus operandi (MO) involves an accident management company (AMC) identifying potholes and defects in car parks and then fabricating or coercing/asking claimants to make a claim for injury. Large volumes of claims can be made simultaneously.

Another MO involves criminal gangs infiltrating employers and then staging accidents in the workplace. Professional enablers, particularly AMCs and medical experts, support the OCG.

9.3.5 Crime types—fake death claims fraud

The majority of fake death claims referred to the IFED have involved deaths in developing countries in road traffic collisions. The fraudster hopes that the poor infrastructure in the country where the collision took place will make it harder for insurers to fact-check and thus make it easier to pass off forged documentation.

Checklist—fake death claim investigations

- Securing evidence from foreign jurisdictions is no different in these circumstances than in other investigations.

- Evidencing a chronology of policy inception, travel planning, actual dates of travel and any contact with family or loved ones after the event is compelling evidence in these cases.

9.3.6 Useful sources of information

- **Association of British Insurers (ABI)**: trade association for insurers and providers of long-term savings. See: www.abi.org.uk/
- **Corporation of Lloyds**: the Corporation oversees and supports the Lloyds insurance market, ensuring it operates efficiently. See: www.lloyds.com/lloyds/about-us/what-is-lloyds/the-corporation-of-lloyds
- **British Insurance Brokers Association (BIBA)**: represents insurance brokers, intermediaries and their customers. See: www.biba.org.uk/
- **National Vehicle Crime Intelligence Service (NaVCIS)**: a police unit dedicated to the prevention and detection of vehicle crime. See: https://navcis.police.uk/
- **Insurance Fraud Bureau (IFB)**: an industry-funded central hub for claims data and intelligence, using data tools and analysis to identify fraud rings for prosecution and prevention. See: www.insurancefraudbureau.org/
- **Cheatline**: a separately branded part of the Crimestoppers service. Its output is managed by the IFB. See: www.insurancefraudbureau.org/cheatline/
- **Insurance Fraud Register (IFR)**: an insurance industry-wide database of known insurance fraudsters. See: www.theifr.org.uk/en/
- **Insurance Fraud Investigators Group (IFIG)**: a members' organisation, formed of insurers, lawyers, loss adjusters and investigation agencies (it has over 320 members in total). Members can share details of tactics and suspects within the closed user group and gain responses to identify cross-industry harm. See: www.ifig.org/
- **Solicitors Regulatory Authority (SRA)**: regulating solicitors and investigating breaches of rules. See: www.sra.org.uk/home/home.page
- **Ministry of Justice (MoJ)**: owns and manages the claims portal website, which was established in 2010. All personal injury claims falling within the scope of the pre-action protocols must be processed using the claims portal. This provides for a safe and secure means of registering claims and transferring information, hence reducing bureaucracy and speeding up the claim settlement. See: www.claimsportal.org.uk/en/
- **Information Commissioner's Office (ICO)**: upholds information rights in the public interest. With regard to insurance, their interest extends to illegal marketing activity and unlawful attempts to access customer data from insurers and other companies. See: https://ico.org.uk/
- **Motor Insurers Bureau (MIB)**: established in 1946 to compensate those facing loss from uninsured and untraceable drivers, the MIB is paid for by mandatory contributions from those insurance companies that insure UK

drivers. The MIB maintains and makes available the Motor Insurance Database (MID), which allows anyone to check the insurance status of a vehicle in the UK. See: www.mib.org.uk/

9.4 Dedicated Card and Payment Crime Unit (DCPCU)

The DCPCU is a proactive police unit with a national remit. It is a partnership between:

- CoLP;
- Metropolitan Police Service (MPS);
- Home Office (HO);
- Financial Fraud Action (FFA UK).

KEY POINTS—DCPCU

- Financial Fraud Action UK (FFA UK) is responsible for leading the collective fight against fraud in the UK payments industry. Its membership includes the major banks, credit, debit and charge card issuers, and card payment acquirers. Through industry collaboration, FFA UK seeks to be the authoritative leader in defending consumers and businesses from financial fraud, by creating the most hostile environment in the world for fraudsters (FFA UK News Release, 17 March 2016).
- Scotland is not currently included in the DCPCU's national remit; however, representative(s) from Police Scotland attend the Steering Group governance meeting and work with the DCPCU on joint partnership initiatives targeting cross-border OCGs.

The unit focuses on tackling payment crime affecting the UK card and banking industry. Established in 2002, the DCPCU was the first industry-funded police unit to be created in the UK. It is fully sponsored by the UK's cards and banking industry, and comprises officers from the CoLP and MPS, working alongside banking industry fraud investigators and support staff. This model of public–private collaboration has proven very successful, and a number of other units have been established utilising the model (refer to the PIPCU and the IFED sections). The unit has achieved:

- an estimated £479 million in savings from reduced fraud;
- the recovery of over 800,000 counterfeit and compromised card numbers;
- approximately 502 convictions on fraud-related matters;
- a conviction rate of 86 per cent.

9.4.1 **The DCPCU's remit and priorities**

The primary objective of the DCPCU is to support the card and retail banking industries to reduce the levels of serious and organised crime affecting the UK payments sector. As well as the agreed Key Priority Areas (KPAs), other fraud types within the unit's remit will be considered, as long as they satisfy the following criteria:

- **Organised criminality**: the unit will target serious and organised/cross-border criminality committed by organised crime groups within the UK.
- **Ongoing criminality**: there will be a concentration on cases where criminal activity is still evident, and proactive opportunities exist. Cases where the criminality has ceased will not be accepted other than in exceptional circumstances.
- **Threat posed**: cases that pose a significant economical and/or reputational threat to the wider payment industry due to losses involved or complexity of the fraud.
- **Successful prosecution**: there must be sufficient lines of inquiry present to provide reasonable belief of a successful prosecution.
- Cases will not be accepted that are already being investigated by other law enforcement agencies, other than in exceptional circumstances.

The DCPCU operational policing plan is based upon the same framework as the serious and organised crime strategy, which is based on pursue, protect, prepare and prevent. This strategic approach is one that is now familiar with UK law enforcement and, in addition to supporting the serious and organised crime strategy, it also complements the policing plans of both the CoLP and MPS in tackling organised crime.

KEY POINTS—THE DCPCU'S OPERATIONAL STRATEGY

The operational strategy for the DCPCU is as follows:

- prosecuting and disrupting criminals engaged in payment crime (pursue);
- increasing protection against payment crime (protect);
- reducing the impact of payment crime when it happens (prepare);
- preventing people from engaging in payment crime (prevent).

While the strategic aims of the DCPCU focus on the four key component areas listed, the strength of the unit lies in the prioritisation of the critical area of pursue, focusing on the prosecution and disruption of criminals engaged in payment crime, as well as underpinning important work in the other areas of protect, prepare and prevent.

The strategy also focuses on building on existing capabilities to ensure that the unit can respond effectively to new and emerging threats, including that of e-crime (refer to online banking/card not present (CNP) fraud, see 9.4.5).

Referral considerations

Cases are primarily referred into the unit directly by the card and banking industry. However, on occasions referrals are received from other law enforcement agencies through Action Fraud. All the cases referred are assessed against the DCPCU case acceptance criteria, with key priority areas identified. The DCPCU has a clear and transparent case acceptance process, which is set out in its case acceptance guide. All decisions are recorded, along with supporting rationales.

Key Priority Areas for operational activity

Within the DCPCU, there is a governance structure comprising industry and law enforcement representatives. Consideration is given to ongoing and emerging threats against the payment industry, and key priority areas for the unit are agreed annually through the governance processes.

KEY POINTS—THE DCPCU'S KEY PRIORITY AREAS 2016

- Staff integrity;
- ATM (skimming and card trapping);
- social engineering;
- remote purchases—CNP fraud.

9.4.2 Crime type—staff integrity (insider fraud/corrupt staff)

One of the greatest priorities for the banking industry is dealing with corrupt staff who pose a serious risk to their business. Common methods of insider fraud include:

- unauthorised transactions on existing accounts;
- facilitating the opening of accounts with fraudulent identification;
- changing account details;
- simple theft of cash;
- corrupt staff placing devices to facilitate crime (keyboard, video, mouse (KVM) devices);
- software to steal large amounts of cash electronically and remotely.

....

Case study—staff integrity (insider fraud)—Operation Robo

This case related to a member of staff from a call centre at a financial institution. Their job was to deal with telephone banking inquiries. When customers called in, staff were instructed to request two digits from the customer's predetermined number. The corrupt member of staff asked certain customers for their six-digit banking number. Following receipt of the six-digit number, the staff member would correct herself, stating that she only needed two of the digits; however, she had recorded the full six-digit code.

Details of the account and the six-digit telephone banking code were then passed on to associates who made calls to the bank and transferred large amounts of money, total-ling £23,000, to accounts controlled by the associates. The money was then withdrawn in cash soon after the transfers.

Five members of the gang were arrested and charged with fraud by abuse of position and conspiracy to commit fraud by false representation. The member of staff received two years' imprisonment. The other four suspects were convicted and received cus-todial sentences.

9.4.3 Crime type—ATM fraud (skimming and card trapping)

There are a range of criminal attacks on ATMs, namely:

- skimming involves the placing of a physical device on the ATM to obtain a card's magnetic strip details and customers' provider identification numbers (PINs);
- transaction reversal fraud (TRF) involves tricking the ATM into believing that the transaction has been cancelled when, in fact, the money has been taken;
- the use of a cash claw involves placing a device on the cash drawer that pre-vents the money from being dispensed, so that it can later be retrieved by the offender. Further devices trap the actual card and are used in tandem with a camera bar that catches the PIN number;
- more recently, 'eavesdropping' devices have been placed inside the machines (by drilling a physical hole to access the card reader, which is then covered with plastic). This alters the software and allows the criminal access to the magnetic strip data from the card reader within. The device is subsequently removed from the ATM and downloaded to harvest the card data. It is then used to make cloned cards or for CNP fraud.

Case study—card skimming—Operation Hamlet

Intelligence was received that a group of criminals from Eastern Europe would travel to the UK and place skimming devices onto ATMs, with a view to harvesting bank card numbers from unsuspecting ATM users. Four suspects were arrested upon arrival in the UK, and a search warrant was executed. Various items of property were seized, including skimming equipment, computers and mobile phones. Over 8,000 bank card numbers were recovered from one of the computers that the gang had harvested; there was enough bank card data to expose banks to a potential loss risk of more than £3.4 million. The success of this particular case was due to effective European law enforcement collaboration and the sharing of intelligence.

Effective collaboration on a local, national and international level is integral to any fraud investigation. The DCPCU recognises the importance of law enforcement and industry partnership working and continues to develop initiatives and projects to enhance its ability to disrupt and tackle fraud within the card payment industry.

9.4.4 **Crime type—social engineering**

Social engineering refers to the psychological manipulation of people into performing actions or divulging confidential information. As the range of products to prevent fraud in the banking sector becomes increasingly sophisticated, the criminal has shifted the nexus of their attack directly to the customer. The general methodology in relation to banking fraud is when a customer of the bank or a member of bank staff in a call centre or branch is duped or socially engineered into doing the fraudster's bidding, which is to relieve the customer of their money. There are many varied methods of achieving this aim. Recent social engineering methods include courier fraud, where a member of the public is called over the telephone and duped into revealing their PIN and handing their payment card over to a courier. Alternatively, they can be duped into believing that there is corruption in their bank branch and that they need to move their money into another account (provided by the fraudster). When the telephone is used to deceive, this is known as vishing. Social engineering also includes fake emails requesting bank information (phishing) and text messages requesting information (smishing).

Case study—social engineering—Operation Birdcage

Operation Birdcage concerned two suspects, a husband and wife, who defrauded a financial institution of over £1 million by conducting bank account takeovers. The husband would call the bank call centre purporting to be a customer and request a change of address on an account. At a later date, he would call again, stating that he had lost his bank card and requesting a new card and PIN. The card and PIN were then dispatched to a new address (communal area), where they were collected. Fraudulent purchases were made and shipped abroad.

Phone analysis identified that the suspect (the husband) differentiated between UK and overseas call centre staff, targeting the latter as it was deemed easier to negotiate the security checks with them. He would generally terminate the call if he was put through to UK call centre staff. The suspect had also acquired sufficient knowledge of the accounts he targeted to pass security questions by using social engineering tactics. From January 2011, the bank call centre number was contacted thousands of times to effect the account takeover and approximately 120 accounts were successfully targeted, resulting in losses of over £1 million.

Voice analysis successfully identified the husband as the suspect caller. It was also identified that the wife had opened bank accounts using fraudulent identification to receive funds from the frauds. Both were subsequently convicted of the offences outlined.

9.4.5 Crime type—remote purchases/CNP

The increase of cyber-related fraud continues to be a challenge for law enforcement and industry. The use of malware (malicious software unknowingly downloaded onto a computer) or information obtained through data breaches, such as stolen credit card details that are sold online, all impact on fraud committed in the card payment industry. Most recently, the DCPCU has prioritised CNP fraud to combat online banking fraud, with remote purchases being the greatest threat of recent years. In 2015, FFA UK reported a 72 per cent rise in this area of fraud from £98.2 million to £168.6 million. Throughout the first half of 2015, the DCPCU sought to improve its knowledge and capability to tackle this crime threat through a programme of industry and business engagement, including academic and intelligence development.

Further reading

- FFA UK, 'Annual losses on UK payment cards hit £567.5m': www.essentialretail.com/security/article/56ebce390aeff-ffa-uk-annual-losses-on-uk-payment-cards-hit-£5675m

---

Case study—remote purchases/CNP—Operation Alonso

The suspect in this investigation was an employee for a payment card processing company which provided contact centre functionality for a bank. The suspect's job was to take debit card payments and customers' credit card balances over the phone.

An investigation by the bank revealed that a number of debit cards to which the employee had access had been used fraudulently. Further investigation showed that the suspect was also the beneficiary of these fraudulent transactions.

Following their arrest, the suspect admitted to making the majority of purchases on the compromised bank payment cards. Three women, with whom the suspect was in a relationship, were also unknowingly beneficiaries of fraud payments from compromised cards. As a result, all three were interviewed under caution.

The defendant also used stolen card data to pay for the balances of his partners' credit cards, holidays for him and his partners, rent on his partners' houses, food shopping, online gaming accounts and season tickets to a football club.

In total, the defendant spent £18,000 on CNP transactions. He admitted fraud by abuse of position and was sentenced to 18 months' imprisonment.

9.4.6 **Legislation used for card payment fraud**

KEY POINTS—OFFENCES UNDER THE FRAUD ACT 2006 USED BY THE DCPCU

The main offences under the Fraud Act 2006 are used to prosecute offenders concerned with payment card fraud:

- section 1(2): fraud by false representation;
- section 1(4): fraud by abuse of position of trust;
- section 1(6): possession of articles intended for use in fraud;
- section 1(7): making or supplying articles for use in fraud;
- sections 327 and 329: money laundering offences (POCA 2002).

9.4.7 **Investigative considerations**

Multi-agency working

The structure of the DCPCU lends itself to effective multi-agency working and is a prime example of the public and private sectors successfully working closely together to tackle fraud in the payment industry.

The unit also works closely with the Joint Fraud Taskforce, a collective response to disruption and investigation of organised crime comprising the CoLP, the NCA, the HO and the banking industry. The DCPCU has also forged close links internationally through collaborative working partnerships. From 2013 to 2015, the DCPCU led the European Commission-funded Project Sandpiper, working with Europol and the Romanian National Police to combat ATM fraud. See Figure 9.1.

Figure 9.1 **Project Sandpiper outcomes**

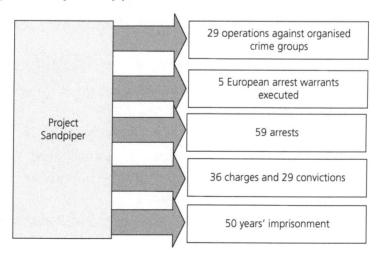

273

The DCPCU received further funding from the European Commission, as part of Project Skynet, to combat online banking fraud and develop bilateral relationships for future European joint investigation teams (JITs).

KEY POINTS—ASSISTANCE TO OTHER LAW ENFORCEMENT AGENCIES

The DCPCU has attained specialist expertise in card payment fraud and is able to provide services to other law enforcement agencies, through evidential statements and providing evidence at court in relation to:

- compromised and/or counterfeit cards;
- card-trapping devices;
- concealed ATM cameras (to obtain customers' PINs).

Although not exhaustive, the checklist below outlines factors that investigators may explore when investigating a card payment fraud, or aspects of this type of fraud that impact on any investigation.

Checklist—card payment fraud

- Identify strategy for analysis of forensic (digital) data, as card payment fraud relies on digital evidence from computers, mobile phones or other devices.

- Seek advice from force cyber units to assist following the seizure of devices.

- Seize phones from all arrested persons, analyse data to ascertain criminal association, online use, in/out calls.

- Liaise with the force's covert unit, as all four crime areas present opportunities for covert tactics.

- Early consultation with the Crown Prosecution Service (CPS) is advised, especially when covert techniques have been employed.

- Use an analyst to assist with developing trends and presenting data at court.

- Evidence the correct procedures that bank staff should adopt and the training they should receive (insider fraud).

- Obtain and evidence call data from staff or suspects to prove fraud.

- Obtain statements from account holders (although the bank is the victim) to evidence the impact of fraud or the circumstances of fraud.

- Seize CCTV, where applicable, to identify suspects.

- Preserve the items seized for forensic analysis and technical examination (ATM/ skimming).

- Consider using digital recovery specialists to retrieve data from the devices seized (ATM skimming device).

- Any compromised card data identified should be forwarded to the relevant agency to alert the banking industry (Financial Fraud Bureau).

KEY POINTS—USEFUL SOURCES OF INFORMATION

- Further information about the DCPCU and how to refer cases for investigation or advice can be found at: www.financialfraudaction.org.uk/police/advice/

10

Reviews and operational learning

10.1 **Introduction**

This chapter consists of two parts. The first part considers the benefits of conducting case reviews in fraud investigations: what they are, the various types, how they should be undertaken and by whom. The second part considers the benefits, purpose and practicalities of undertaking a structured debrief in fraud investigations.

10.2 **Fraud case reviews**

10.2.1 **Background to reviews**

In all cases of serious crime, including fraud and economic crime, it is good practice to have regular reviews of the investigation. The importance of carrying out reviews is evident across all organisations. The Byford Report, re the Yorkshire Ripper case, recognised that if regular reviews of that investigation had been carried out, Peter Sutcliffe (the Yorkshire Ripper) may have been caught earlier. Peter Sutcliffe was convicted in 1989 of murdering 13 women and carrying out seven further attacks on other women.

The Macpherson Inquiry in 1999, held after the death of Stephen Lawrence, made a recommendation in relation to reviews. It stated that, 'ACPO should devise codes of practice to govern reviews of investigations, in order to ensure that such reviews are open and thorough. Such codes should be consistently used by police services'. The National Police Chiefs' Council (NPCC), formerly known as the Association of Chief Police Officers (ACPO), has, over the intervening years, issued guidance that has been updated on a number of occasions.

Further reading

- Authorised Professional Practice guidance: www.app.college.police.uk/app-content/operations/operational-review/

In 'Reviewing the Reviewer: The Review of Homicides in the United Kingdom', 2010, Dean Jones describes reviews as: 'A constructive evaluation of the conduct of an investigation to ensure an objective and thorough investigation that has been conducted to national standards and which seeks to ensure investigative opportunities are not overlooked and that good practice is identified.'

It must be kept in mind that reviews are not re-investigations or implemented to take over the investigation. Both the review and the senior investigating officer (SIO)/investigating officer (IO) must ensure that this doesn't take place. A review has a number of purposes, but in particular it is meant to assist and support the fraud investigation by making sure that any investigative opportunities are not overlooked and are highlighted to the investigation team. Other purposes of reviewing are to ensure that both national and local investigative standards are being complied with, and any lessons, including good practice that can be learnt from an individual investigation, are being captured and appropriately disseminated.

Checklist—review types

- Management intervention reviews;
- 28-day reviews;
- thematic reviews;
- closure reviews;
- peer reviews;
- detected reviews;
- cold-case reviews;
- multi-agency reviews (which include serious case reviews for both children and vulnerable adults, domestic homicide reviews and Multi-Agency Public Protection Arrangement (MAPPA) reviews).

10.2.2 Management intervention reviews

This type of review is normally completed within the first 24 hours of the instigation of the fraud case for investigation, but can take place at seven days. Its purpose is often to ensure that nothing has been missed in the first day(s) and confirm categorisation of the inquiry, also assisting with staffing requirements.

10.2.3 28-day reviews or progress reviews

The next type of review is commonly known as a 28-day review or progress review. This is often seen as a formal review and invariably involves a full team being utilised.

10.2.4 Thematic reviews

A thematic review could look at a particular part of the investigation (e.g. prevention and disruption).

10.2.5 Closure reviews

A closure review would be conducted to ensure that an undetected fraud investigation can be closed down and all lines of inquiry are exhausted.

10.2.6 **Peer reviews**

A peer review involves a number of experienced investigators being gathered together in order to give the IO an alternative view. This type of review can be done independently or collectively.

10.2.7 **Detected reviews**

A detected review can take place at two different stages: after charge and before trial, or after conviction. If conducted before the trial, it ensures that all relevant matters have been considered. The post-conviction review considers more what has gone well and what others can learn from the particular case.

10.2.8 **Reviewing the application of the Fraud Investigation Model (FIM)**

Fraud reviews should focus on the implementation of the FIM and examine the elements contained within the model (see Chapter 1). See Figure 10.1.

Figure 10.1 FIM building blocks

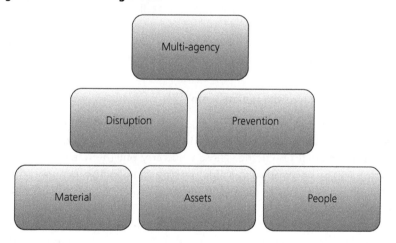

....
Case study—a review of an economic crime investigation

A police force requested a review of an economic crime investigation that they had been carrying out. This involved the theft of in excess of £1 million by the use of a cyber crime technique. The investigation was working in parallel with other agencies, as this organised crime group (OCG) had committed further crimes in other areas within the UK. The investigation had failed to identify the original offender.

The terms of reference (ToR) set were the following:

- Establish that all potential lines of inquiry have been identified and are being appropriately pursued. Ensure that there are no missed investigative opportunities. This should particularly focus on the initial offence of the theft of £1.2 million and ensure that all the inquiries necessary to identify a possible offender have taken place.
- Ensure that partnership working has been effectively conducted.
- Identify any good practice.

The review took the form of a briefing by the IO and their team, other focused interviews and the reading of all relevant materials.

The following are examples of the recommendations that were made.

- All officers that perform the role of SIO in a major fraud inquiry should have guidance and training in the completion of policy files.
- All forces should ensure that the staff within their economic crime units (ECUs) become accredited and engage in specialist national fraud courses as part of their continuous professional development (CPD).
- Forces should consider the use of the Home Office Large Major Enquiry System (HOLMES) in fraud investigations.
- Seek further expert advice to establish who manipulated the system. This should include inviting both companies' specialists to a meeting to further discuss who may have committed the initial offence.
- All major fraud investigations should consider at an early stage the use of joint protocols and information sharing with relevant partners.

....

10.2.9 **Composition of the review team**

A formal review should be led by a senior review officer (SRO) supported by review officers (ROs), who can be civilian members of staff and/or supplemented by external resourcing. Those who carry out the role need to have experience of being involved in major investigations. Some experience of economic crime would be beneficial. It is important that the team assisting both the SRO and RO have technical skills; for example, there should be an analyst or forensic accountant. It may also be appropriate to bring in relevantly qualified people from outside the force/organisation to assist (e.g. forensic experts).

10.2.10 **Terms of reference (ToR)**

The setting of the ToR for a review is probably one of the most important decision that is made, and unless it is made in a manner that is focused and specific to an individual inquiry it will hamper the prospect of having a successful review and may impede the investigation. See Figure 10.2.

The ToR are normally set by a chief officer, who will have consulted with the IO. It is also important that the SRO plays a key role in the setting of the ToR and is part of the review process from the beginning. In every review, it is

Figure 10.2 Reviewing the implementation of the FIM

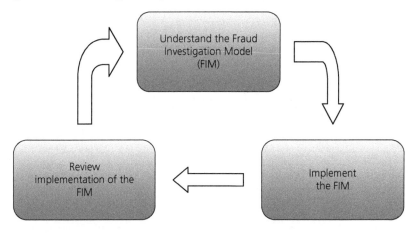

important that good practice is highlighted and investigations are improved as a result of the review.

KEY POINTS—EXAMPLE ToR

In line with the FIM, the ToR should pay particular attention to the following areas:

- disruption/prevention—parameters and strategy;
- key decision making (decision, rationale and record keeping);
- disclosure strategy—focusing on third-party material and digital examination;
- victim liaison strategy and process;
- asset recovery strategy;
- multi-agency opportunities.

The aim of the independent review is to ensure that all investigative opportunities in the above areas are conducted in a professional and ethical manner. It is also meant to identify specific actions to be carried out by the investigation, areas of good practice and procedural matters for the force/investigation team.

10.2.11 Methodology

See Figure 10.3.

As discussed earlier, the SRO needs to be appointed at the earliest opportunity so that they can be part of the writing of the ToR. In keeping with the ToR, they should appoint a person/team to identify the technical skills required for that review.

The IO must be given time to prepare the briefing, which should include:

- the current investigative situation;
- log of events;
- other important documents, in particular copies of their key decision log (KDL).

Figure 10.3 Methodology of a fraud review

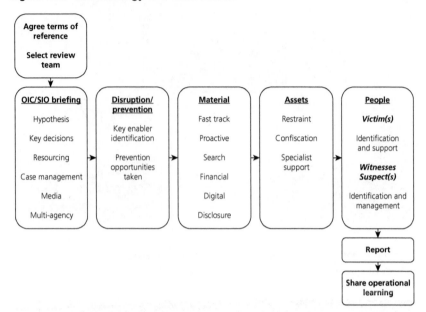

The briefing by the IO should be delivered to as many members of the review team as possible, and they should be prepared to answer questions on their part of the review to demonstrate to the investigative team their positive engagement with, encouragement of and commitment to the review.

Where applicable, the SRO and all members of the review team visit any relevant scenes in order for them to put into context what they have read and been told. Reviews always involve interviews with key members of the investigation, including the SIO/IO and their team.

The review team should hold regular meetings to share information and should also avoid duplication and excessive demands being placed upon the investigation team.

Checklist—key areas of fraud investigation to examine

- Policy file, to include hypotheses and main lines of inquiry;

- initial response;

- prevention strategy;

- disruption strategy;

- multi-agency considerations;

- forensics to include all aspects of digital forensics;

- major incident room (MIR)/HOLMES (if applicable), to include document management and actions outstanding;
- intelligence;
- covert (proactive), if applicable;
- passive data sources;
- suspect strategies;
- witness and victim strategies;
- family/business liaison;
- exhibits;
- search;
- disclosure;
- financial investigation, including restraint and confiscation;
- media and communications;
- community impact;
- management of case material.

See Appendix 7, 'Key questions for undertaking a review of a fraud investigation'.

10.2.12 **Report preparation**

When preparing reports, it is essential, if any fast-track recommendations are identified, that the IO is informed as soon as possible, so they can consider whether they need to act straight away. The report must be factually accurate, so will need checking by the SIO/IO. They should then be afforded an opportunity to meet with the SRO, so any further discrepancies can be resolved.

Checklist—report preparation

The exact format varies, but the following headings are a useful structure:

- executive summary;
- introduction (to include background to case);
- methodology;
- terms of reference;
- main lines of inquiry;

- Investigating Officer policy/decision making;

- prevention/disruption;

- multi-agency engagement;

- financial investigation;

- exhibits and disclosure;

- media;

- disclosure;

- suspects/witness/victims;

- MIR structure and action management (if applicable);

- other investigative opportunities (e.g. passive data sources or financial inquiries);

- good practice guidance;

- list of recommendations;

- appendices.

Recommendations for the report should be in three categories, ensuring that good practice and learning are captured and disseminated both locally and nationally:

1 incident specific;
2 policy/procedural;
3 organisational.

The SRO needs to be aware that all or parts of the report may be disclosed, and should take this into consideration.

Further reading

- College of Policing, 'Authorised Professional Practice—Operations: Operational Review', 2016: www.app.college.police.uk/app-content/ operations/operational-review/

10.3 **Structured debriefs**

Operational learning is an integral element of the FIM, and both IOs and SIOs should consider the benefits of identifying operational learning throughout the course of their inquiry.

This section examines the practicalities of undertaking a debrief and facilitating the workshop, ensuring all those involved in the investigation have an opportunity to give feedback on what went well, what could be improved and what advice might be given to colleagues. It considers the timing, who should be involved, question types and the practical considerations needed to successfully undertake the process. See Figure 10.4.

Figure 10.4 Initial considerations: structured debrief

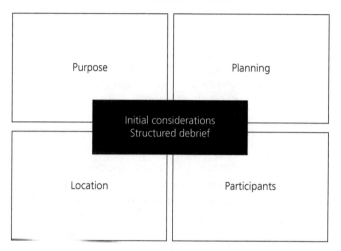

10.3.1 **Purpose**

The purpose of a structured debrief is to identify the operational learning from fraud investigations, operations and other relevant events that can be shared among stakeholders; in this chapter, these are called 'events' for ease of reference. Both the value and the mechanics involved in undertaking a structured debrief of an economic crime-related event are described.

KEY POINTS—BENEFITS OF STRUCTURED DEBRIEFS

- Improve organisational procedures.
- Develop best practice.
- Assist in personal development.
- Identify knowledge gaps.
- Identify operational strengths.
- Improve organisational resilience.

The benefit of this process is that operational learning is harvested in an efficient and structured way to the advantage of all stakeholders. It is important to consider the use of the process in events that are considered successful as well as those that are not.

KEY POINTS—WHEN TO CONSIDER UNDERTAKING A STRUCTURED DEBRIEF

- At the conclusion of an investigation;
- at the conclusion of a specific operation;
- at the conclusion of a multi-agency event;
- at the conclusion of a training event;
- following an identified phase of an event.

It should be remembered that a structured debrief is not a formal review and is based mainly on the perceptions of those taking part. The process neither reviews documentation nor involves anyone besides the attendees of the session. It is only from the perceptions of the attendees that a composite picture is established and learning is identified. For this reason, care should be taken when reporting perceptions. Though an individual may believe that what they report is factual, it may be that the reported event did not actually occur. The rationale for the report is often not explained or further explored. Individuals taking part in the process may also be emotionally charged about specific issues connected to the event, and this may dictate what they report during the process. Care should be taken not to use the structured debrief process as an alternative to a formal review or indeed a professional standards investigation.

When managed and transcribed by an experienced facilitating team, structured debriefs can be an immensely valuable process that can produce essential operational learning to be shared with a wider audience.

Organisations should consider developing and publishing a policy and process map to assist in undertaking structured debriefs; these can be developed into standard operating procedures (SOPs), which will encourage the application of the process so it becomes routine and embedded as 'business as usual'.

10.3.2 **Timing**

The timing of when a structured debrief should take place is normally decided by the investigations/operations lead. In investigations, this will normally be the SIO or the officer in charge (OIC), though it may be instigated by others who are seeking to identify operational learning. Debriefs are most frequently undertaken at the conclusion of the event. If the debrief is undertaken during an ongoing event, particularly an investigation, careful consideration should be given to the risks of undertaking the process, and attention should be given to managing both the disclosure and professional issues that such a process may reveal.

Case study—benefit of a structured debrief

In September 2011, a well-known financial institution operating in London discovered that a trader had carried out a number of high-risk and unauthorised investments (known as trades), which resulted in the bank losing $2.3 billion. The police were informed and then commenced investigations. In September 2011, the trader was charged with offences of false accounting and fraud by abuse of a position. In November 2012, the trader was found guilty of fraud-related offences and sentenced to seven years' imprisonment.

The investigation presented a number of challenges to both the investigation and prosecution teams. For example, the organisation was one of the world's largest investment banks, with 63,500 employees in 50 different countries; this caused difficulties when seeking to interview witnesses or speak with key members of staff. Additionally, the investigators and prosecutors were required to quickly understand not only the trading process with regard to complex financial investments but also a culture unfamiliar to them, together with its associated terminology.

In January 2013, a structured debrief was facilitated by members of the City of London Police (CoLP) Economic Crime Academy (ECA). The purpose of this debrief was:

- to create a forum where those involved in the inquiry could identify learning points for future, similar investigations;
- to identify both individual and organisational learning;
- to encourage and demonstrate the positive use of the learning in the organisation.

Key personnel—consisting of the SIO, members of the investigation team, subject matter experts (SMEs) who advised the inquiry team, the press officer, the Crown Prosecution Service (CPS) case worker and representatives from the CPS Central Fraud Group—attended the debrief. The process resulted in the identification of valuable operational learning concerning the investigation of complex financial crime, which was widely shared.

Examples of the learning identified from the structured debrief include the following:

- Aim to ensure the continuity of the personnel in the investigation and prosecution teams.
- Aim to develop a panel of experts who can be used in financial crime cases.
- Make use of critical incident procedures in financial crime cases.
- Develop an aide-memoire for first responders in fraud investigations.
- Maintain regular dialogue with the victim (in this case, the financial institution).
- Consider whether there is a need to seize evidence or rely on third parties to secure and produce the material.
- Have efficient protocols in place to be able to support witnesses throughout the investigation and during the subsequent court process.

10.3.3 **Who should attend?**

The value of the process will be enhanced by identifying and including repre-sentatives from all the relevant stakeholders involved in the event. It is import-ant to invite as many stakeholders as possible, particularly when debriefing following a multi-agency investigation, as this will enhance the value and scope of the learning identified. An additional consideration is to maintain an appro-priate balance of those attending to give a sufficiently holistic view of the event (relevancy over repetition).

KEY POINTS—WHO SHOULD ATTEND A DEBRIEF?

- SIO;
- OIC;
- investigators;
- financial investigators (FIs);
- digital media investigators (DMIs);
- case support staff;
- specialist support officers, for example police search adviser (POLSA);
- CPS representatives;
- victim/witness support representatives (where appropriate for that stage of the investigation).

10.3.4 **Role of the facilitator**

Once a suitable event has been identified, the person who instigates the process should appoint, wherever possible, a person who is independent of the inves-tigation who can facilitate the debrief. It is essential that the lead facilitator should be experienced in the debrief process. It is useful if the facilitator under-stands the nature and context of the event to be debriefed, but has not been involved. To maintain integrity, there should be no hidden agendas and the facilitator should guard against these. The process should at all times be fair and transparent and genuinely seek to identify operational learning. It is beneficial for the facilitator to be briefed on the event and, in particular, the start and end points, as well as any topics of interest.

10.3.5 **Timescales**

A standard debrief might last between one and two hours, though in more complex events this time can be extended. Consideration should be given to debriefs that take place over a number of days, with each session being thematic and aiding the wider agenda, i.e. the welfare of victims in particularly challeng-ing cases.

10.3.6 **Location and security**

The room where the process is to take place should be large enough to accommodate those who need to be present comfortably. Depending on the nature of the event, consideration should be given to the appropriate level of security, both in terms of the physical location and protective markings for the material generated during the process.

Further reading

- Government security classifications: www.gov.uk/government/uploads/ system/uploads/attachment_data/file/251480/Government-Security-Classifications-April-2014.pdf

---

10.3.7 **Developing the debrief questions**

The questions to be asked of those attending the debrief are key to its success. These should be discussed and agreed with those commissioning the process in advance. The two key methods for informing the attendees of the questions are to use a suitable presentation programme or a prepared briefing document. Each question should be dealt with in turn.

KEY POINTS—SAMPLE QUESTIONS

Investigation related

- Question 1—What were the three most challenging aspects of the event?
- Question 2—What were the three most positive aspects of the event?
- Question 3—What were the most significant things you learnt and how will you put them into future practice?
- Question 4—What three top tips would you give to a colleague involved in a similar event?

Investigation topic specific

Leadership/communication/surveillance

- Question 1—What were the three most challenging aspects of leadership?
- Question 2—What were the three most positive aspects of leadership?
- Question 3—What three top tips would you give to a colleague involved in leading a similar inquiry?

Inquiry resourcing

- Question 1—What were the three most challenging aspects of the resources/ staff availability (instigation and initiation of operational teams, secondment lengths and realistic expectations)?

> - Question 2—What were the three most positive aspects of resource/staff availability (instigation and initiation of operational teams, secondment lengths and realistic expectations)?
> - Question 3—What three top tips would you give to a colleague involved in a similar event regarding resources/staff availability (instigation and initiation of operational teams, secondment lengths and realistic expectations)?

The facilitator must be empowered to collect honest feedback when debriefing the event, focusing on not just the positive elements but also those that are challenging.

10.3.8 **Mechanics of the debrief**

The attendees should, where possible, be seated in a 'horseshoe' setup, enabling them to see everyone present. There has to be a board or wall big enough to allow a timeline of the event to be drawn, as this forms the 'spine' of the debrief activity. Both the note taker and facilitator should be introduced and actively engage in the process. See Figure 10.5.

Figure 10.5 **Conducting the structured debrief**

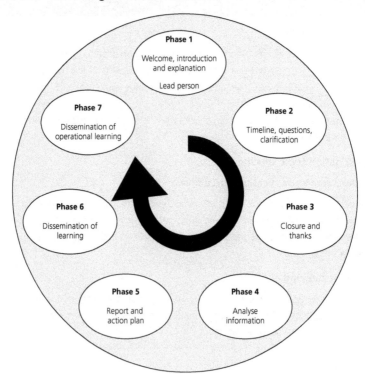

KEY POINTS—DEBRIEF CONSIDERATIONS

Include the following:

- everyone should get a proportional say;
- comments should not be attributable to specific individuals, but might be attributable to roles, for example POLSA;
- it should not be a blame forum or a debating platform;
- the process should inform the basis of an action plan to improve operational practice.

Once all the attendees are present, it should be explained that everyone has an equal voice and that this is not an opportunity to apportion blame where things didn't go so well. It is important to emphasise that any comments made will not be attributable to any particular attendee.

A timeline should be drawn up and significant events added; for example, these may be the initial inquiry instigation, searches, interviews, charges, court proceedings and confiscation hearings. Each attendee is then given a collection of sticky notes and asked to consider the agreed questions. The attendees should then write their comments on the sticky notes and add these to the timeline. The questions should be colour-coded. It is beneficial to use the following colour-coding:

- green: positive;
- red: developmental;
- orange: most significant learning;
- blue: top tips.

It is best to do one set of questions in turn, with the opportunity to ask for explanations of the rationale behind the comments made. The facilitator should then ask questions to clarify the comments made on the notes and to add detail where necessary. The attendees' comments should be recorded by a note taker.

The use of colour-coded sticky notes will provide a visual narrative relative to the questions asked. The groupings of the sticky notes will be very indicative of where the attendees have focused their attentions.

The attendees should be thanked for sharing their thoughts and informed that the final report will be circulated to them.

Where possible, the sticky notes should be secured on the flip chart. It is also recommended that a photograph be taken of the timeline and sticky notes. This will assist in writing the final report.

10.3.9 **Conflict resolution**

During the debrief, it is not unusual for attendees to express views that can cause conflict between those attending. It is important for the facilitator to focus on de-escalating any conflict that does occur. This should be done by paying close attention to the attendees and what is being written and said. The facilitator should remind them that this is not the forum for personal blame or criticism, and all the views expressed should be constructive, evidenced and relevant. Any conflict that cannot be satisfactorily resolved during the debrief session should be dealt with after the session has ended.

10.3.10 **Final report**

At the conclusion of the structured debrief, the facilitator of the session compiles a structured debrief report. Depending on the complexity of the debrief, the report can be produced using either the standard format below or a more bespoke template. The use of standard formats assists in the consistency of the presentation of outcomes, learning and recommendations.

KEY POINTS—DEBRIEF REPORT FORMATS

Standard debrief report format headings

- Event
- Author
- Owner
- Introduction
- Methodology
- Logistics
- Challenging aspects
- Positive aspects
- Key learning points
- Tips to colleagues
- Recommendations.

Complex debrief report format

- Foreword
- Executive summary
- Introduction
- Key recommendations
- In-depth findings
- Specific topic areas:
  - future investigative considerations;
  - positive aspects;
  - challenging aspects;
  - tips to colleagues.

The report should be circulated to the identified stakeholders and those who attended the debrief session. It should be made accessible to the widest audience and, where possible, should be available through an operational learning portal. It is important to share the learning with those preparing educational material, so that any developments in best practice can be incorporated into training products. Consideration should be given to presenting the findings to the relevant parties.

10.3.11 **Action plan**

There may be a number of points that require further action, and these should be placed into an action plan. Each element should be separately identified and an action manager allocated. Regular meetings should be arranged to ensure that progress is made on the action points and that the action plan is met. Again, stakeholders and attendees should be updated on both the progress and final outcomes of the action plan.

10.3.12 **Conclusion**

Structured debriefs are an essential component of effective event management and are an important element of the FIM. The SIO/IO should actively seek opportunities to engage with the debrief process. The process relies on an effective, empowered facilitator who can encourage the attendees to share their thoughts in an open and constructive manner, which will enable the identification of good practice that should be shared with a wide audience; this has been proved to be invaluable in economic crime investigation.

Checklist—structured debriefs

- Risks considered and mitigation plan in place.
- Facilitator and note taker identified and briefed.
- Stakeholder groups identified.
- Physical and material security considered.
- A sufficiently large room arranged for the debrief.
- Provision of a wall or board to draw a timeline ensured.
- Refreshments arranged (if applicable).
- Attendees invited.
- Debrief held.
- Briefing note prepared.

293

- Timescale/topics and questions agreed.

- Sufficient stationary obtained (sticky notes, sticky tape, clipboards and pens).

- Chairs placed in a horseshoe setup facing the location of the timeline.

- Report and action plan prepared.

- Action plan and/or report circulated.

Appendix 1

CPS template for memorandum of understanding

CPS template in Annex F of the Disclosure Manual with the following headings:

Operational Memorandum of Understanding

- Header
- Section 1—Urgent response and initial contact record
- Section 2—Strategic proposals
  - Aims and objectives of joint or parallel operations
  - Agency roles incl. lead status (where appropriate)
  - Criminal activity under investigation
  - Offences and relevant legislation (including foreign statutes, jurisdiction, prosecution and extradition issues)
- Section 3—Tactical proposals
  - Tasking and coordination
  - Disclosure
  - Dissemination of intelligence
  - Forensic strategy
  - Exhibit management
  - Firearms support
  - Financial investigation
  - Authorities
  - Arrest, interview, prosecution and exchange of evidence
  - Source handling
  - Undercover operatives
  - Operational security
  - Technical support
  - Surveillance
  - Military aid to the civil power
  - Media strategy
  - Health and safety
  - Fiscal and administrative
  - Other relevant issues
- Agreement:
  - Signatures
- Review periods.

See: www.cps.gov.uk/legal/d_to_g/disclosure_manual/annex_f_disclosure_manual/

Appendix 2
Fraud investigation planning—aide-memoire

This fraud investigation aide-memoire lists a number of general considerations, regardless of fraud type, for the investigator to consider following the report of a fraud. The suggested headings below could be included in the investigation plan.

Checklist—first responders

- In all circumstances, sufficient details should be obtained to establish whether a crime has been committed and allow an assessment to be conducted.

- Information regarding the vulnerability of any victim should be noted and any observations made as to whether the victim is likely to become a repeat victim.

- Time-critical evidence, such as closed-circuit television (CCTV), should be secured at the earliest opportunity.

- Documentation, including letters, envelopes, brochures, literature, victims' bank statements, emails, telephone records, handwritten notes, receipts of cash transactions, deposits and postal receipts, should be preserved for forensic examination and as evidence of the offence.

- These crimes are often perpetrated remotely, with no physical contact between the victim and the fraudster. That said, the usual investigatory principles still apply. Has the victim met with the suspect, and if so are there any other potential witness statements that need to be obtained? If not, how have they communicated with the fraudster?

- Phone numbers, email addresses, Internet Protocol (IP) addresses and screenshots should be obtained at an early stage. The capture of this information will help to progress any inquiry.

- Consideration should be given to trying to prevent further losses to the victim. Where bank cards or accounts have potentially been compromised, suggest that early contact with the bank be made to minimise any financial loss. Does a computer need to be cleaned/seized? What other devices are linked/potentially compromised?

- Consideration should be given to whether the victim requires support from partner agencies and/or family.

- A witness statement is required from the victim, and consideration as to how and when this is obtained needs to take into account the victim's state of mind.

- Conduct due diligence background checks to evaluate the allegation and to look for other evidence of fraud or corruption.

Checklist—initial investigation considerations

Identify offences

- Identify offences: for example, fraud by false representation or money laundering.

- From this, identify what the points to prove for each individual offence are.

- This will assist in identifying the lines of inquiry.

Victims/witnesses

Consider elements such as:

- particular demographic;

- vulnerabilities;

- business or person;

- category of witness, i.e. significant;

- record statement, or consider visually recorded interview if vulnerable or intimidated;

- whether the Youth Justice and Criminal Evidence Act (YJCE) 1999 applies;

- victim support services;

- give fraud prevention advice to prevent further loss or becoming a repeat victim;

- media strategy, press releases, etc;

- the number and location of victims and develop a victim management strategy;

- manage the victim's expectation of recovering their losses.

Suspects

Elements for consideration if the suspect is known or unknown.

- Unknown: name, nickname, photographs, distinctive marks and features, CCTV, Police National Computer (PNC), Police National Database (PND), intelligence checks, vehicles—Automated Number Plate Recognition (ANPR), photo ID, e-fit, similar offences that might be linked, IP addresses, phone numbers, billing data.

- Known: Companies House, National Insurance, Department for Work and Pensions (DWP) checks, Special Branch, UK Visas and Immigration, covert tactics, camera deployments, social media, phone inquiries (billing, International Mobile Station Equipment Identity (IMEI), cell site analysis), computers (IP addresses, internet history, documents, keyword searches), finance-related checks (Experian etc).

Scene

The scene may be different in fraud offences to more traditional crime, but the same concepts apply; it can even be a digital scene. Considerations include:

- company accounts;

- digital devices;

- computers;

- tax returns;

- mobile phones;

- trading records;

- invoices;

- personal bank accounts;

- internet browsing history.

These can all yield highly relevant evidence required in fraud investigations.
Consider the use of the following:

- section 18 searches;

- section 32 searches;

- section 8 PACE warrants (magistrates' court);

- Schedule 1 warrants (Crown Court);

- police search adviser (POLSA) searches;

- cash dogs (searches);

- video/photographs of lifestyle;

- cash seizure and restraints if funds are known (take advice from the financial investigation unit).

Lines of inquiry

Generally, these should be targeted around the points to prove. What makes fraud investigations different is more of a focus upon the financial strand, and often there will be a seemingly legitimate front for the suspects to operate behind. An extensive investigation will sometimes be required to identify whether a criminal offence has taken place, whether the act falls within the remit of Trading Standards and civil enforcement or whether there is a civil dispute over the purchase.
It may be helpful to consider the lines of inquiry suggested below.

Financial checks

- Credit reference checks: these can reveal useful information about the suspect's bank accounts, debts, property, home addresses and former addresses.

- Her Majesty's Revenue and Customs (HMRC) (via Anti-terrorism Crime and Security Act (ATCSA) request)—HMRC can reveal declared income for previous financial years, benefits and other earnings declared to HMRC. This is useful, as it can show wide variations between actual and declared income and uncover other potential offences.

- Companies House: this is a public record that will show the directors, company secretaries and accounts of companies. Directors can be directors of many companies and this can uncover a network of companies (held by one suspect) being used to launder money. It will also have the director's home address, or contact address.

- Insolvency Service: this is a public record that can be useful for lifestyle offences where the suspect has declared themselves bankrupt. They will have had to make a declaration of assets and will have had restrictions placed upon their access to credit.

- PACE order: granted at the Crown Court, this will grant access to the bank accounts of a company or suspect. This will show income and outgoings, but the account opening documents may uncover information about earnings, or false declarations made to the bank when the account was opened.

- Think wider: retail loyalty cards can reveal substantial detail about shopping and lifestyle habits. A suspect may live a cash-rich lifestyle, which is difficult to evidence, but the club card can show exactly what was bought, as well as where and when.

- Receipts: seizing receipts, as well as expensive assets, can also assist the investigation. These give times, dates and locations, which can then be evidenced through the store to identify further accounts, cash purchases and (through CCTV) who purchased the goods.

Victim communication methods

The victim will have been contacted in one of a number of ways: face to face, by phone or by some other communication method (email, letter). Otherwise, there may have been no personal contact (card cloning, skimming, etc).

- Face to face: consider photo ID, video ID, e-fit, CCTV, forensics at the scene. Were they a cold caller, or was there previous contact to arrange a meeting?

- Phone/email: billing data can be used to establish the suspect's number, who that number is registered to, the IP addresses of emails sent and to whom those IP addresses are registered.

- Remote: CCTV can be used to establish where a card was used (if at an ATM), if it was used online, what was purchased and to where it was sent (delivery address).

Flow of money

- The element in a fraud investigation is showing a gain for a person, or showing that a loss/ exposure to loss has been experienced by another person. The flow of money is vital in identifying who has benefited from the dishonest act.

- A forensic accountant can be considered for more complex cases, but in simpler ones spreadsheet summaries to show transactions from the victim to accounts controlled by a suspect are usually sufficient for court when backed up with the exhibited bank account statements.

Wider assistance

- If the investigation proves complex, early liaison with specialist investigators and the Crown Prosecution Service is advisable and may prevent wastage of resources.

- Other agencies can assist with and/or complement a police criminal inquiry with their own legislative or regulatory powers and sanctions. As examples, HMRC; the Insolvency Service; Trading Standards; the Department for Business, Innovation and Skills (BIS); and the Financial Conduct Authority can generate further lines of inquiry or provide other routes to tackling offenders. Potential offences under the Companies Act 2006 or the Data Protection Act 1998, or offences of tax evasion, may be uncovered.

Professional enablers

- Accountants, solicitors, independent financial advisers and similar roles are covered by their own industry codes of conduct. There may be disciplinary offences that can be tackled internally by their supervisory bodies.

Inquire into beneficiary accounts

- Who is the keeper of the account?

- Is the beneficiary account based in the UK?

- Did they supply a date of birth, address or any phone numbers when opening the account?

- What identification was used to open the account?

- Can you obtain a copy of the documentation used to open the account?

- What other transactions have been occurring in and out of the beneficiary account?

- When/where was money withdrawn? Is there CCTV evidence?

- Consider whether the beneficiary account is being used as a 'mule account'.

- PNC any personal details provided to open the beneficiary account.

- Consider completing a production order on the beneficiary account.

- Consider conducting a Suspicious Activity Reports (SARs) check through a financial investigator.

Inquiries with an online platform

- Establish if your organisation/force has a Single Point of Contact (SPoC) for the online platform. If they do, make contact with them to recover relevant material.

- Try to establish what details they provided when opening the account.

- Do they have other adverts under their control?

- Are the other adverts still running?

- What is their transaction history?

- Does this identify other potential victims?

Inquiries into businesses' names/addresses

- If the business is UK registered, conduct a check via Companies House.

- Use the information provided via Companies House to make further inquiries around the address provided and the directors of the company.

- Complete local inquires on the address using intelligence systems.

- Visit or speak to the owners of the address to establish how and when the premises were rented. How often did people attend? What background checks were conducted? What identification was provided? Is there CCTV at the premises? How do they pay for the business address?

- If the address provided is a 'serviced office' or virtual office, liaise with the providers to establish what information and identification were provided in order to rent the space.

Other inquiries

- Consider an intelligence request to the National Fraud Investigation Bureau (NFIB) to establish links to other reported crimes or inquires.

- Consider sending out appropriate alerts to other parts of the force area or beyond where a crime type is targeting a specific category of victim or activity indicates the emergence or resurgence of a particular trend.

- Consider whether your investigation is targeting the main organiser or just money mules.

Identify key enablers

- Internet;

- financial;

- communications;

- consider disruption tactics.

Prevention

- What were the principle enablers that allowed this fraud to be perpetrated?

- Who else could be at risk from this or a similar fraud?

- What could have been done to remove or reduce the risk from this fraud?

- How can the lessons learned be used to prevent others from becoming a victim of a similar fraud?

Appendix 3

Frequently asked questions regarding the reporting, assessment and investigation process of fraud or cyber crime

I'm not sure if I have been a victim of fraud or cyber crime, how can I get some advice?

Use the online chat service on the Action Fraud website or call 0300 123 2040, where an adviser will give you advice on what you can do next.

You may also find the following websites helpful:

www.actionfraud.police.uk/
www.citizensadvice.org.uk/consumer/scams/scams/
www.moneyadviceservice.org.uk/en/articles/beginners-guide-to-scams

How can I make a report to Action Fraud?

- Using the online reporting tool on the Action Fraud website www.actionfraud. co.uk. You may find this a quicker service which you can use from your own home or using a mobile device whilst you're on the go.
- Call 0300 123 2040. This call centre is open Monday–Friday, 9 am–5 pm but may take longer than using the Action Fraud website.

Since making a report to Action Fraud I haven't heard anything, what can I do now?

Action Fraud will send you a letter within 28 days of reporting a crime to update you on what has happened to your report. This may be via email if that is your preferred method of contact. If you have made an information report rather than a crime report then you will not receive this letter.

If you have not received an update and believe you should have, then please contact Action Fraud via email on contact@actionfraud.police.uk or by writing to PO Box 36451, 182 Bishopsgate, London EC2M 4WN.

Someone is using my identity, why are Action Fraud not doing anything?

The misuse of someone's identity is a complex area; a fraud is only committed when a person uses your details to make a gain, for example to open bank accounts, credit accounts or loans in your name without your knowledge or permission.

In these circumstances, it is the company that has supplied the loan or account that has been defrauded and therefore they must be recorded as the victim of the crime and not you. This can be frustrating; however, police services across England and Wales are governed by a set of rules called 'The Counting Rules', set by the government, which determine when and how to record crimes.

Action Fraud will record all of the information about how and where your details have been used in an information report rather than a crime report, which may be used to support other investigations.

If you have discovered accounts opened in your name, we suggest you get a copy of their credit report. You can contact any one of the three credit reference agencies and receive support in resolving credit problems caused by identity-related fraud:

www.callcredit.co.uk/; www.equifax.co.uk/; http://experian.co.uk

If you do find further fraudulent activity, we would advise you to report this information to Action Fraud.

I don't agree with the decision not to investigate my crime, can I appeal it?

The process used by the National Fraud Intelligence Bureau (NFIB) ensures that all reports are reviewed using a consistent criteria and then progressed accordingly.

If you have more information that you believe may change the outcome of the NFIB's assessment, you should add this to your report. You can do this by logging on to the Action Fraud website with your National Fraud Reporting Centre (NFRC) reference (which starts NFRC followed by 12 numbers) and password or, if you no longer have these details, by making a further report to Action Fraud. This will not guarantee a change in the outcome but the information will be assessed again.

If you are still not satisfied with the way your report has been dealt with, you can contact Action Fraud which may be able to provide further information on what has happened to your report. They will advise you of any further options that you may have if you are still dissatisfied. This team can be contacted via email at contact@actionfraud.police.uk or by writing to PO Box 36451, 182 Bishopsgate, London EC2M 4WN.

I have provided details for the suspect, why are the NFIB not taking any action?

The NFIB use consistent criteria to assess reports, and will take action to disrupt or develop information for a police force where possible. Criminals, however, often use fake details when committing fraud, so although you may feel you have provided clear suspect details the NFIB may identify these as fake through further checks and therefore will not be able to use them to identify a suspect.

It is also not usually possible for the NFIB to take action if the details you have provided identify a suspect or suspect account overseas as the NFIB only have powers to act in England and Wales. This can happen with international bank accounts or websites that are hosted by companies based overseas.

Why has my report been sent to a police force that is not local to me?

If your report has been sent to a police force that is not your local force, this can be frustrating but is decided by where the crime is likely to have been committed or where the suspect may be located. The process used to decide where a report is sent to is set out by the government, which you can find on the www.gov.uk website.

Can I get my money back?

Action Fraud are a crime reporting bureau which, where possible, provides intelligence packages to local police forces to consider investigating and are not in a position to recovery money. If your report is sent to a police force, they will consider whether money can be recovered from the criminals; this is something you can discuss with the investigating officer.

If this is not possible or there is no criminal investigation, there are methods of seeking recompense through the civil courts which you may wish to consider.

Citizens Advice offer advice on their website www.citizensadvice.org.uk about bringing claims generally and also what your rights are in certain instances, such as when buying a used car or in other consumer situations.

I have been the victim of fraud or cyber crime and am now struggling to cope, what support is there for me?

We understand that being a victim of fraud can have a huge impact on you and the way you feel and we would like to remind you of services available to you by these agencies.

- Victim Support: gives free and confidential help to victims of crime, witnesses, their family, friends and anyone affected across England and Wales (www.victim-support.org.uk).
- Counselling Directory: a free, confidential and easy-to-use network giving information on counselling as well as listing counsellors in areas across the UK with their contact details, fees and the areas they cover (www.counselling-directory.org.uk).
- Samaritans: free, impartial helpline available to talk to at any time in confidence (www.samaritans.org).
- National debt line: gives free, impartial advice to people about debt and related matters (www.nationaldebtline.org).

You can also find information about other agencies on the Action Fraud website or through the Victims' Information Service.

How can I find out about the latest scams?

You can sign up to receive the latest alerts affecting your area and nationwide. You can find more information on the Action Fraud alert website: www.actionfraudalert.co.uk

You can also sign up to scam alerts from the Trading Standards e-crime team on their website: www.tradingstandardsecrime.org.uk

Appendix 4
Available support services

Victim Support
National charity giving free and confidential help to victims of crime, witnesses, their families, friends and anyone else affected in England and Wales.

Tel: 0845 303 0900 (9 am–9 pm, Monday to Friday; 9 am–7 pm, weekends; 9 am–5 pm, bank holidays)

Website: www.victimsupport.org.uk

Think Jessica
Think Jessica is invaluable for people who are either family of or friends with someone who is being bombarded with scam mails or is a victim/recipient of scam mail themselves.

Website: www.thinkjessica.com/

Address: Think Jessica, PO Box 44 42, Chesterfield S44 9AS

Email: advice@thinkjessica.com

Get Safe Online
Website providing free, independent, user-friendly advice on a wide range of topics, including: how to protect your PC, how to avoid online scams, advice for small businesses, and how to stop identity theft.

Website: www.getsafeonline.org

Mailing Preference Service
The Mailing Preference Service (MPS) will prevent the receipt of unsolicited direct mailings sent from member companies of the Direct Marketing Association (DMA) and will take steps to prevent the receipt of unsolicited direct mailings from companies that are non-DMA members.

Website: www.mpsonline.org.uk/mpsr/

National Debtline
Free, impartial helpline and website that gives advice to people about debt and related matters. Their website has a range of factsheets, a debt self-help pack and sample letters for dealing with a range of debt problems.

Tel: 0808 808 4000

Website: www.nationaldebtline.co.uk

Samaritans
Free, impartial helpline staffed 24/7 by volunteers. They are available to talk to at any time confidentially. The caller doesn't have to be suicidal.

Tel: 116 123 (UK)

Email: jo@samaritans.org

Credit Industry Fraud Avoidance Service (CIFAS)

The CIFAS Protective Registration Service enables victims of identity theft to place a protective warning on their credit file. The CIFAS Protective Registration Service will undertake additional checks to ensure that the applicant is genuine and not a fraudster trying to use your details to commit identity theft.

Website: www.cifas.org.uk

Tel: 0330 100 0180 (8 am–6 pm, Monday to Friday)

Financial Conduct Authority (FCA)

The FCA is the regulator of the financial services market in the UK. Organisations providing financial services should be FCA-registered (not including solicitors and accountants). A register of FCA-registered organisations is available via the FCA website.

Website: www.fca.org.uk

Tel (Freephone): 0800 111 6768 (8 am–6 pm, Monday to Friday (except public holidays); 9 am–1 pm, Saturday)

Money Advice Service

Independent service offering free and impartial advice on all money matters. The Money Advice Service does not solve complaints; however, it can advise on how to complain to a financial services provider and what to do if things go wrong.

Website: www.moneyadviceservice.org.uk

Tel: 0300 500 5000 (8 am–8 pm, Monday to Friday; 9 am–1 pm, Saturday)

Appendix 5
Example victim management strategy

Introduction

This document is designed to provide direction and clarification in respect of the victims identified and should be read in conjunction with the investigative strategy *[insert date]*.

Throughout this investigation, victims have been targeted by means of *[insert details]; for example, cold-calling by the offenders, who have offered non-existent invest-ment opportunities. UK-based investors have been contacted by suspected offenders from within the UK. The suspected criminality dates back to . . . .*

This operation has now been separated to focus on the following companies:

1.

2.

3.

Initial contact, method and analysis of information

Suspected victims identified through bank accounts or by other means will be contacted by officers from the investigation team to establish if they have been defrauded, and to what extent. The following steps will then be taken.

- A questionnaire (which can be typed onto a section 9 statement form, if required) will be sent out to identified persons asking them to record the extent of any losses (if they experienced any at all). *Part of the questionnaire should include asking questions to aid in identifying vulnerable/intimidated witnesses.*

- Personal details of the victim should be recorded on the rear of the front page of the MG11. Upon receipt of the questionnaire, the officer in the case (OIC) will make an assessment as to whether a further comprehensive statement is required. The OIC should allow a period *of at least six weeks* for the return of said questionnaires to be able to make a full assessment of the potential evidence available. Furthermore, the OIC can then select 20 per cent of victims from the varying degrees of losses, to include time frames spanning from the beginning to the end of the offending.

- Should a further comprehensive statement be required, it might be the case that the OIC or other members of the team are not in a position to obtain the statement. Should further assistance be required, a request (via the Detective Sergeant (DS)) for assistance from the major investigation team or agency staff can be made to visit the victim and obtain a further comprehensive witness statement, seizing exhibits as appropriate.

- Details of all victims and commodities will be recorded onto a spreadsheet and saved in the victim folder.
- All evidential correspondence received from victims will be submitted into the HOLMES to be registered accordingly. Care will be taken at registration to prevent any duplication where some victims may share the same identity. It should also be noted that some victims may have invested in multiple commodities.
- Any letters sent to victims need not be individually registered. These should be saved on individual officers' drives and a sample letter submitted to the major incident room (MIR) and registered accordingly.

COMMUNICATION AND VICTIM UPDATES

- Victims will be updated every month as per the Victims' Code of Practice.
- Investigation records and local force systems will need to be updated accordingly when the OIC has dispatched victim letters and spoken to victims.
- As referred to above, individual letters need not be registered but should be saved in the OIC's file; this includes all subsequent monthly update letters.
- Template letters are also to be saved.
- Current victim spreadsheets will be saved.
- The persons identified initially will be asked to supply a current email address; *this will be the preferred means of contact.*

For victims who do not possess an email address, consideration will be given to the following means of contact:

- prerecorded telephone messages;
- personal updates via letter.

Victims will be updated either by email or by post in accordance with senior investigating officer (SIO) policy, and all contact will be recorded in their investigation records. The OIC will then update the investigation record on a monthly basis so that the victim updates are confirmed to be taking place and up to date.

The update letter initially created will be reviewed after the first roll out and a suitably worded update letter, tailored to each investigation strand, will be devised.

Furthermore, another update letter will be sent to those potential victims who were contacted initially but did not respond, as well as newly identified victims (either through bank statements or by other means).

REPEAT VICTIMS

Officers should bear in mind that some of the victims they come into contact with may be victims of other investment frauds. Should these be from the same force, then the victim(s) should be referred to the relevant OIC dealing with the case. Officers should also consider that their victim may have invested in multiple commodities from the same fraudulent company.

Should victims wish to report offences of fraud or the officer suspects that new offences are being/have been committed, then the victim should be encouraged to report the matter to Action Fraud on 0300 123 2040.

Repeat victims should also be encouraged to contact Victim Support on 0808 168 9111 or via www.victimsupport.org.uk and/or any of the partnership agencies recorded below.

Depending on the circumstances of the victim, consideration should be given to contacting the social services team for their local area, to assist with care and well-being, if appropriate.

Should any vulnerable adults be identified, relevant forms are to be submitted. This covers any adults you have concerns for, due to their appearance, demeanour and communication, or based on your professional judgement. The public protection unit will refer the person to their respective local authority, and then monitor this.

Should any 'follow-on frauds' or other linked frauds be identified, then this should be highlighted to the victim in a letter. In any case, victims should be warned to look out for these offences.

Should other fraudulent activity be identified, then consideration should be given to asking the National Fraud Intelligence Bureau (NFIB) to circulate an alert to the general public.

VULNERABLE PERSONS

In 2012, the Association of Chief Police Officers (ACPO) definition of a vulnerable person was: 'A person may be vulnerable by reason of age and/or their circumstances. Or, who suffers from mental or physical disabilities, illness, or other such special feature which renders them either permanently or temporarily unable to care or protect themselves against harm or exploitation.'

When recording victims on the master spreadsheet, a traffic-light system is to be employed in order to highlight vulnerable persons and witnesses. This is as follows:

Red = vulnerable; Green = no issues identified.

Vulnerability should encompass the definitions of both 'vulnerable' and 'intimidated'.

When contacting new victims, either by telephone or questionnaire, officers should seek to identify vulnerability and in doing so incorporate a vulnerability assessment in their dealings.

A record should also be logged on the spreadsheet of any support services offered or measures put in place to reduce any identified risk.

VULNERABLE AND INTIMIDATED VICTIMS

As many of the victims identified during this investigation are elderly, including numerous individuals with disabilities, consideration should be given to the following:

- If the victim is identified as vulnerable or intimidated, then an Achieving Best Evidence (ABE) interview should be conducted at the earliest opportunity, in order to obtain the best evidence in accordance with the Ministry of Justice (2011) publication *Achieving Best Evidence in Criminal Proceedings: Guidance on interviewing victims and witnesses, and using special measures.*

- In addition to a witness who is under the age of 18 at the time of the court hearing, three other types of vulnerable witness are identified by virtue of section 16(2) of the Youth Justice and Criminal Evidence Act 1999. These are:
  1. witnesses who have a mental disorder as defined by the Mental Health Act 1983 (as amended by the Mental Health Act 2007);
  2. witnesses significantly impaired in relation to intelligence and social functioning (witnesses who have a learning disability);
  3. witnesses who have a physical disability.

Vulnerable witnesses in this category are only eligible if the quality of the evidence that is given by them is likely to be diminished by reason of their disorder or disability (section 16(1)(b)).

Intimidated witnesses are defined by section 17 of the Act as those whose quality of evidence is likely to be diminished by reason of fear or distress. In determining whether a witness falls into this category, the court should take account of:

- the nature and alleged circumstances of the offence;
- the age of the witness.

And where relevant:

- the social and cultural background and ethnic origins of the witness;
- the domestic and employment circumstances of the witness;
- any religious beliefs or political opinions of the witness.

Any behaviour towards the witness by:

- the accused;
- members of the accused person's family or associates;
- any other person who is likely to be either an accused person or a witness in the proceedings.

Vulnerable and Intimidated Witnesses: A Police Service Guide (Ministry of Justice, 2011) suggests that victims of and witnesses to domestic violence, racially motivated crime, crime motivated by reasons relating to religion, homophobic crime, gang-related violence and repeat victimisation, as well as those who are elderly and frail, also fall into this category.

Research suggests that the intimidation of witnesses is likely to arise in sexual offences, assaults and those offences where the victim knew the offender, as well as in *crimes that involve repeat victimisation*, such as stalking and racial harassment. *In addition, some witnesses to other crimes may be suffering from fear and distress and may require safeguarding and support in order to give their best evidence.* While the legislation distinguishes between vulnerable and intimidated witnesses, in respect of the criteria for their eligibility for special measures, it is important to recognise that:

- some witnesses may be vulnerable as well as intimidated (e.g. an elderly victim of vandalism who has dementia on an inner-city estate);
- others may be vulnerable but not subject to intimidation (e.g. a child who witnesses a robbery in the street);
- others may not be vulnerable but may be subject to possible intimidation (e.g. a young woman who fears violence from her current or former partner or someone who has been the subject of a racial attack).

While these examples provide illustrations of the application of the legislation, *it is important not to attempt to categorise witnesses too rigidly.*

Special measures

The special measures that are available to vulnerable and intimidated witnesses, with the agreement of the court, are:

- the use of screens (section 23);
- the use of a live TV link (section 24);
- giving evidence in private (section 25) (limited to sexual offences and those involving intimidation);
- the removal of wigs and gowns (section 26);
- the use of video-recorded interviews as evidence-in-chief (section 27).

Vulnerable witnesses are also eligible for the following special measures:

- communication through intermediaries (section 29);
- the use of special communication aids (section 30).

Access to special measures is very much a matter for the court and is contingent on the application of three 'tests'. These 'tests' are set out in section 19 as follows:

- whether the witness is 'vulnerable' or 'intimidated', as defined by sections 16 and 17 respectively;
- whether any of the special measures/any combination of them is likely to improve the quality of the witness's evidence;
- which of the available special measures are most likely to maximise the quality of the witness's evidence.

Vulnerable or intimidated witnesses can also receive social support at all stages of the investigation. Three distinct roles for witness support have been identified, and it is unlikely to be appropriate for the same person to be involved in all three. These roles are the following:

- Interview support provided by someone independent of the police, who is not a party to the case being investigated and who sits in on the original investigative interview. They may be a friend or relative, but not necessarily so.
- Pre-trial support provided to the witness in the period between the interview and the start of any trial.
- Court witness support from a person who may be known to the witness, but who is not a party to the proceedings, has no detailed knowledge of the case and may have assisted in preparing the witness for their court appearance. A direction for evidence to be given via live link under section 24 of the Youth Justice and Criminal Evidence Act 1999 (as amended by the Coroners and Justice Act 2009) may also provide for a supporter.

Significant witnesses (not eligible for special measures)

Significant witnesses, sometimes referred to as 'key' witnesses, are those who:

- have or claim to have witnessed, visually or otherwise, an indictable offence, part of such an offence or events closely connected with it (including any incriminating comments made by the suspected offender either before or after the offence);
- have a particular relationship to the victim or have a central position in an investigation into an indictable offence.

While significant witnesses are usually defined with reference to indictable-only offences, investigating officers may consider designating witnesses as significant in any other serious case where it might be helpful.

Interviews with significant witnesses should usually be video recorded because they are likely to:

- increase the amount and quality of information gained from the witness;
- increase the amount of information reported by the witness being recorded.

Video-recorded interviews with significant witnesses can also have the additional benefits of:

- safeguarding the integrity of the interviewer and the interview process;
- increasing the opportunities for monitoring and for the development of interview skills.

There is no statutory provision for video recordings of interviews with significant witnesses to be played as evidence-in-chief, although interviewers should be aware that the defence might ask the court for permission to play some or all of the recording in support of their case.

Should a witness be willing to attend court, an MG2 should be completed highlighting what special measures are required. Additionally, a separate statement should be obtained *specifically detailing why having those special measures in place (it could be a combination of reasons) would enhance the quality of their evidence.*

Should any vulnerable adult be identified, the relevant forms are to be submitted. This covers any adults you have concerns for, due to their appearance, demeanour and communication, or based on your professional judgement. The public protection unit, which will refer the said person to their respective local authority, will then monitor this.

Victim compensation

To ensure that all victims of crime receive a fair and professional service from the force, the following matters are to be taken into consideration for this investigative strand in relation to compensation.

- *All* suspected victims should be recorded on the master victim spreadsheet, *irrespective of no response being received from a questionnaire.* They should also still *continue* to receive regular updates.
- *All* suspected victims again should be included and recorded on the master victim spreadsheet, *irrespective of them having provided a witness statement or not.* Again, they should also still *continue* to receive regular updates.
- As already referred to, regular Action Fraud checks are to be conducted to ensure that new victims are added to the ongoing spreadsheet. This should continue during and until the conclusion of any court trial(s).
- Should victims subsequently move outside England and Wales, they should *still be scheduled and kept updated* in accordance with the above direction.

Every effort will be made to identify and approach potential victims for a questionnaire/statement to include them in any future repatriation of funds. If victims' details are not recorded on the master victim spreadsheet, then they will not be included in the compensation orders granted by any court.

Future consideration will be required in respect of 'cut off' points for victim compensation. At the point of any future conviction(s), a media campaign will take place to capture any further victims who have not yet contacted the police. An agreed deadline will then be set and a policy decision recorded accordingly.

A spreadsheet of assets will be maintained by the financial investigator and confiscation will be considered from an early stage.

Any suspected victim who has not cooperated with the investigation team will receive a suitably worded letter upon any future convictions to ensure that they are included on the spreadsheet.

A victim loss schedule will be kept in the master victim spreadsheets for each strand of the investigation.

Appendix 6
Developing an overarching fraud interview strategy

The following should be considered before a suspect is interviewed in a fraud investigation:

1 **Selection of interviewers:**
   - Training: are the interviewing officers trained to the appropriate level;
   - experience;
   - suitability;
   - number of interview teams required;
   - use of subject matter experts.

2 **Managing the interview:**
   - Coordination;
   - PACE officer;
   - disclosure;
   - suspect support and welfare;
   - continual review;
   - expert support;
   - link with major incident room.

3 **Planning:**
   - Briefing—requirements—objectives;
   - interview team not to undertake other roles;
   - research evidence;
   - formulate interview structure;
   - disclosure—format—package—method (consider tape recording with solicitor);
   - venue;
   - expert support;
   - remote monitoring—guidelines—equipment;
   - back-up team;
   - preparation for suspect response:
     - admission;
     - explanation;
     - denial;
     - memory loss;
     - no comment;
     - prepared statement;
     - requirement for an appropriate adult.

Appendix 7
Key questions for undertaking a review of a fraud investigation

Agree terms of reference	• Who draws up the terms of reference?
	• What should they include (i.e. key decisions/investigation strategies/current operation infrastructure/risks/case management/budget/fraud investigation model/recommendations)?
	• What are the parameters/third-party investigations/time scales?
Select review team	• What skills does the senior reviewing officer need and what experience should they have?
	• What skills and knowledge are required within the review team?
	• Are any specialist skills required?
	• Are they available for the duration of the review?
	• Is it a sensitive investigation? Should an external review team be used?
	• Does it need to be independent (e.g. due to political/media pressures)?
	• Arrange a pre-meeting of the review team before the SIO/OIC briefing, which should explain the methodology and who will do what; allocate tasks according to expertise.
	• Set up daily team meetings to share information.
SIO/OIC briefing	• Who should attend (e.g. SIO, management team, all review team members)?
	• What should be discussed? Consider the application of the Fraud Investigation Model, the main lines of inquiry, strategies, policy decisions, key witnesses, suspects, intelligence, media, prevention, disruption, multi-agency working, victim management, confiscation and restraint, disclosure, case-specific issues and case management.
	• Establish the facts, investigation theories/hypotheses, major lines of inquiry, significant scenes.
	• Establish a single point of contact to obtain documentation.
	• What is the criminality? When was it reported, by whom and why? Was it identified correctly in the initial investigation? How did they originally investigate it?
	• Who needs to be investigated? Are the correct people identified in the investigation?

- How are the different suspects to be managed? What staffing is required in order to successfully manage the suspects?

- Is there a need to establish an understanding of the number of scenes in the investigation? What are they? How are they to be managed?

- What staffing was originally allocated to the investigation and was it sufficient for the complexity and scale of the fraud?

Where can it go wrong?

SIO review as a 'threat'.

Review conducted as a 'disciplinary' inquiry.

No credit given to what has been achieved.

Terms of reference not drawn up correctly or adhered to.

Conduct review

The commencement of the review can take a number of different streams from:

- reading as much of the investigation documentation as possible;

- reading/researching documents specifically relevant to their tasks;

- reading personal interviews of those with key roles in the investigation;

- investigating desktop evaluation.

Arrange for the review team to attend the MIR daily briefings (if applicable) and introduce themselves and explain the role of the review team.

The areas to cover are: initial action; intelligence; SIO policy file content; and stand-alone strategies. Planned method of investigation: MIR.

As a minimum, the desktop investigative evaluation should include:

- initial hypotheses of what has happened;

- identification and location of suspect(s)/person(s) of interest;

- location of potential material/evidence;

- involvement of professional enablers;

- involvement of organised crime groups;

- assessment of jurisdictional issues.

But could also include:

- MO—how the fraud was perpetrated;

- identifiable investigative leads;

- estimate and impact of harm caused;

- scale and location of known victims;

- opportunities to assess recovery;

- prognosis of future harm or loss;

- how the crime maps against strategic/operational priorities;

- issues and potential complexities of an investigation;

- likelihood of bringing a case to a successful conclusion;
- whether the crime has a significant impact on victims (particularly vulnerable victims), giving rise to significant public concern;
- whether the fraud was committed, or knowingly facilitated, by professional advisers.

Analyse

findings

Recommendations should be sorted into three categories, ensuring that good practice in learning is captured and disseminated:

- incident specific (these should be considered by the SIO and acted upon accordingly);
- policy/procedural;
- organisational.

Prepare

report

- Need to be aware of the parts of the report that may be disclosed.
- The report's content should be non-judgemental, succinct, factual, fair and balanced.
- The fast-track recommendations identified should be brought to the SIO's attention ASAP.
- The SIO should be afforded the opportunity to meet with the reviewing officer to resolve discrepancies and ensure factual accuracy.

The suggested report structure should include the following:

- executive summary;
- introduction and terms of reference;
- methodology;
- structured approach to areas of review (in accordance with terms of reference, to include recommendations and evidence of good practice and lessons learnt);
- conclusion (to give an overall view of the investigations);
- list of risks;
- list of recommendations;
- conclusion;
- list of appendices;
- list of reviewing officers.

As part of the process, the SIO/OIC should be given a draft of the report and allowed time for reading.

The head of review should meet the SIO/OIC to discuss any factual inaccuracies.

Submit report

- Findings agreed and allocation of recommendations;
- creation of recommendations matrix;
- creation of good-practice matrix and consider circulating nationally;
- creation of lessons-learnt matrix.

Bibliography

Books and reports

Alighieri, D, 2012. *The Divine Comedy: Inferno, Purgatorio, Paradiso*: Penguin.

Association of Chief Police Officers Crime Committee, 1999. *Revised Guidelines for the Use of Policy Files.*

Attorney General and Chief Secretary, 2006. *Fraud Review—Final Report.*

Attorney General's Office, 2013. *Guidelines on Disclosure.*

BDO LLP, 2016. *FraudTrack Report—February 2016.*

Byford, L, 2006. *Report into the police handling of the Yorkshire Ripper case*: Home Office.

Chartered Institute of Management Accountants (CIMA), 2009. *Fraud Risk Management—A guide to good practice.*

Chianese, J, Haimoff, I, McSwain, J and Wiseman, M, 2012. *Red flags of fraud*: Deloitte Financial Advisory Services LLP.

CMS Cameron McKenna LLP, 2010. *A guide to existing bribery and corruption offences in England and Wales.*

Cook, T, 2016. *Blackstone's Senior Investigating Officers' Handbook.* Fourth edn: Oxford University Press.

Cook, T, Hibbitt, S and Hill, M, 2013. *Blackstone's Crime Investigators' Handbook*: Oxford University Press.

Crawford & Co, 2009. *Fraud Investigation: A practical guide to the key issues and current law.*

Department for Business, Energy and Industrial Strategy, 2015. *Cyber essentials scheme: overview.*

DiNapoli, T P, 2007. *Red Flags for Fraud*: State of New York Office of the State Comptroller.

Diog, A, 2012. *Fraud: The Counter Fraud Practitioner's Handbook*: Gower.

Drew, J M and Drew, M E of Griffith Business School, 2010. *Ponzimonium: Madoff and the Red Flags of Fraud.*

European Union Agency for Network and Information Security, 2013. *The Directive on attacks against information systems*, Version 1.5, October 2013.

Experian, PKF Littlejohn and the University of Portsmouth's Centre for Counter Fraud Studies, 2016. *Annual Fraud Indicator 2016.*

Farrell, S, 2007. *Blackstones Guide to the Fraud Act 2006*: Oxford University Press.

Financial Fraud Action UK Ltd, 2015. *Fraud the Facts 2015—The definitive overview of payment industry fraud and measures to prevent it.*

Financial Fraud Research Centre, 2015. *Framework for a Taxonomy of Fraud.*

Fraud Advisory Panel, 2011. 'An introduction to fraud indicators', *Fraud Facts*, Issue 14.

Graham, W and Financial Conduct Authority, n.d. *A quantitative analysis of victims of investment crime.*

Griffiths, S, 2013. *Investigative Interviewing: The Conversation Management Approach.* Second edn: Oxford University Press.

HM Government, 2013. *Serious and Organised Crime Strategy 2011/2012.*

HM Revenue and Customs, 2012. *Crime and fraud prevention for businesses in international trade.*

HM Treasury and Home Office, 2015. *UK national risk assessment of money laundering and terrorist financing.*

Home Office, 2015. *Serious and Organised Crime Protection: Public Interventions Model.*

Intellectual Property Office, 2015. *IP Crime Report 2014/2015.*

Intellectual Property Office, 2016. *Counting the Cost—The Trade in Counterfeit Goods in Manchester.*

Jones, D, Grieve, J and Milne, B, 2010. 'Reviewing the Reviewers: The Review of Homicides in the United Kingdom.' *Investigative Sciences Journal*, 2(1): 1–31.

Kassem, R and Higson, A, 2012. 'The New Fraud Triangle Model.' *Journal of Emerging Trends in Economics and Management Sciences*, 3(3), 191–195.

Lord Chief Justice of England and Wales, 2005. *Control and Management of Heavy Fraud and Other Complex Cases*: Crown Prosecution Service.

Metropolitan Police Service, 2013. *Operation Sterling—Personal Prevention Toolkit.*

Ministry of Justice, 2013. *The Witness Charter: Standards of care for witnesses in the criminal justice system.*

Ministry of Justice, 2015. *Code of Practice for Victims of Crime.*

Ministry of Justice, 2015. *Civil Rules and Practice Directions.*

Ministry of Justice, 2015. *Criminal Rules and Practice Directions.*

National Centre for Policing Excellence, 2006. *Murder Investigation Manual.*

National Crime Agency, 2015. *JMLIT Amber Alert—Trade Based Money Laundering.*

National Crime Agency, 2015. *JMLIT Red Alert—Cuckoo Smurfing.*

National Fraud Intelligence Bureau, 2015. *Victimology Report.*

National Fraud Intelligence Bureau, 2016. *Fraud Force Profile.*

National Policing Improvement Agency, 2009. *Briefing Paper, National Investigative Interviewing Strategy.*

Office of Surveillance Commissioners, 2014. *Oversight arrangements for covert surveillance and property interference conducted by public authorities and to the activities of relevant sources.*

PKF Littlejohn LLP, 2015. *The Financial Cost of Fraud 2015.*

Ponzi, C, 2001. *The Rise of Mr Ponzi*: Inkwell Publishers.

Raphael, M, 2010. *Blackstone's Guide to the Bribery Act 2010*: Oxford University Press.

Rees, F T, 2015. *Blackstone's Guide to the Proceeds of Crime Act 2002.* Fifth edn: Oxford University Press.

Serious Organised Crime Agency, 2008. *The National Intelligence Requirement for Serious Organised Crime.*

Sir William Macpherson of Cluny, 1999. *The Stephen Lawrence Inquiry.*

Tunley, W G B, 2015. *The Accredited Counter Fraud Specialist Handbook*: Wiley.

West London Mental Health NHS Trust, 2013. *Joint Operational Policy for the Reception and Care of Service Users Admitted Under Section 136 Mental Health Act 1983.*

Web resources

Action Fraud, 2016. 'Action Fraud.' Available at: www.actionfraud.police.uk/

Association of Chief Police Officers in England, Wales and Scotland, 2005. *Guidance on Major Incident Room Standardised Administrative Procedures (MIRSAP)*. Available at: http://library.college.police.uk/docs/APPREF/MIRSAP.pdf

Association of Chief Police Officers in England, Wales and Scotland, 2005. 'Practice Advice on Core Investigative Doctrine.' Available at http://library.college.police.uk/docs/acpo/Core-Investigative-Doctrine.pdf

Association of Chief Police Officers, 2012. 'ACPO Good Practice Guide for Digital Evidence.' Available at: http://library.college.police.uk/docs/acpo/digital-evidence-2012.pdf

Attorney General's Office, 2012. 'Guidelines on Disclosure 2005 and 2011.' Available at: www.gov.uk/guidance/attorney-general-s-guidelines-on-disclosure-2005-and-2011

Attorney General's Office, 2012. 'Use of the common law offence of conspiracy to defraud.' Available at: www.gov.uk/guidance/use-of-the-common-law-offence-of-conspiracy-to-defraud--6

Australian Competition and Consumer Commission, 2016. 'Scamwatch—Nigerian Scams.' Available at: www.scamwatch.gov.au/types-of-scams/unexpected-money/nigerian-scams

Bank of England, 2016. 'Bank of England Home Page.' Available at: www.bankofengland.co.uk/Pages/home.aspx

BBC News, 2004. 'PA Convicted of £4.3m Bank Fraud.' Available at: http://news.bbc.co.uk/1/hi/england/london/3564533.stm

Bereavement Register, 2016. 'Helping to stop unwanted direct mail to the deceased.' Available at: www.thebereavementregister.org.uk/

Bindel, J., 2005. 'The High Price of Robbing the Rich': The Guardian. Available at: www.theguardian.com/theguardian/2005/sep/17/weekend7.weekend

British Insurance Brokers' Association & Insurance Fraud Bureau, 2013. '"Get A Real Deal" Campaign Led by the Insurance Fraud Bureau.' Available at: www.biba.org.uk/technical-updates/motor/get-a-real-deal-campaign-led-by-the-insurance-fraud-bureau/

Cabinet Office, 2014. *Government Security Classifications*. Available at: www.gov.uk/government/uploads/system/uploads/attachment_data/file/251480/Government-Security-Classifications-April-2014.pdf

Centre for the Protection of National Infrastructure, 2016. 'Centre for the Protection of National Infrastructure Home Page.' Available at: www.cpni.gov.uk

Charity Commission, 2016. 'Charity Commission Register of Charities.' Available at: http://apps.charitycommission.gov.uk/showcharity/registerofcharities/registerhomepage.aspx

Charity Finance Group, 2016. 'Charity Finance Group Publications.' Available at: www.cfg.org.uk/resources/Publications/cfg-publications.aspx

Chartered Institute of Management Accounts via Fraud Edge, 2016. 'Famous Frauds: Joyti De-Laurey.' Available at: www.fraudedge.ie/famous-frauds/famous-frauds-joyti-de-laurey/

Chavez, J, 2015. 'Top 10 Red Flag Warnings of Fraud.' Available at: www.accountingweb.com/aa/auditing/top-10-red-flag-warnings-of-fraud

Christie, S, 2013. 'Most common fraud scams to watch out for': The Telegraph. Available at: www.telegraph.co.uk/finance/personalfinance/money-saving-tips/10173262/Most-common-fraud-scams-to-watch-out-for.html

City of London Police—Action Fraud, 2016. 'Action Fraud Alert.' Available at: www.actionfraudalert.co.uk

Coenen, T, 2010. 'Fraud Files: With Madoff, There Were Many Red Flags': Daily Finance. Available at: www.aol.com/article/2010/04/13/fraud-files-with-madoff-there-were-many-red-flags/19432502/?gen=1

College of Policing, 2016. 'Authorised Professional Practice.' Available at: www.app.college.police.uk/app-content

Companies House, 2016. Service providing public digital data held on the UK register of companies. Available at: http://direct.companieshouse.gov.uk/

Court of Appeal, 2010. 'Disclosure: A Protocol for the Control and Management of Unused Material in the Crown Court'. Available at: www.judiciary.gov.uk/wp-content/uploads/JCO/Documents/Protocols/crown_courts_disclosure.pdf

Crown Prosecution Service, 2016. 'Legal Guidance: Bail.' Available at: www.cps.gov.uk/legal/a_to_c/bail/

Crown Prosecution Service, 2016. 'Proceeds of Crime Act 2002 Part 7—Money Laundering Offences.' Available at: www.cps.gov.uk/legal/p_to_r/proceeds_of_crime_money_laundering/

Crown Prosecution Service, 2016. 'The Fraud Act 2006.' Available at: www.cps.gov.uk/legal/d_to_g/fraud_act/

Cyber Aware, 2016. 'Cyber Aware Home Page.' Available at: www.cyberaware.gov.uk

Deceased Preference Service, 2016. Stopping direct mail and protecting the identity of the deceased. Available at: www.deceasedpreferenceservice.co.uk

Durham Police, 1829. 'Sir Robert Peel's Principles of Law Enforcement.' Available at: www.durham.police.uk/About-Us/Documents/Peels_Principles_Of_Law_Enforcement.pdf

Europol, 2016. 'European Cybercrime Centre—Combating crime in a digital age.' Available at: www.europol.europa.eu/ec3

Financial Action Task Force (FATF), 2016. 'Financial Action Task Force Home Page.' Available at: www.fatf-gafi.org/

Financial Conduct Authority, 2016. 'Consumer Credit Register.' Available at: www.fca.org.uk/firms/consumer-credit-register

Financial Conduct Authority, 2016. 'Financial Conduct Authority Home Page.' Available at: www.fca.org.uk

Financial Conduct Authority, 2016. 'Warnings.' Available at: www.fca.org.uk/news/search-results?n_search_term=&start=1&np_category=warnings

Financial Fraud Action UK, 2016. 'FFA UK Home Page.' Available at: www.financialfraudaction.org.uk/

Financial Fraud Action UK, 2016. Businesses. Available at: www.financialfraudaction.org.uk/businesses/

Get Safe Online, 2016. 'Get Safe Online Home Page.' Available at: www.getsafeonline.org

Hexillion, 2016. 'Advanced online Internet utilities.' Available at: http://centralops.net/co/

HM Government, 2015. 'Fact Sheet: Part 2—Computer misuse.' Available at: www.gov.uk/government/uploads/system/uploads/attachment_data/file/415953/Factsheet_-_Computer_Misuse_-_Act.pdf

HM Government, 2015. 'Small businesses: What you need to know about cyber security.' Available at: www.gov.uk/government/uploads/system/uploads/attachment_data/file/412017/BIS-15-147-small-businesses-cyber-guide-March-2015.pdf

HM Government, 2016. 'Companies House.' Available at: www.gov.uk/government/organisations/companies-house

HM Government, 2016. 'Company Director Disqualification.' Available at: www.gov.uk/company-director-disqualification

HM Government, 2016. 'Competition and Markets Authority.' Available at: www.gov.uk/government/organisations/competition-and-markets-authority

HM Government, 2016. 'UK Legislation.' Available at: www.legislation.gov.uk

HM Government, 2016. 'The Insolvency Service.' Available at: www.gov.uk/government/organisations/insolvency-service

HM Passport Office, 2016. 'The General Register Office.' Available at: www.gro.gov.uk/gro/content/

Home Office, 2014. 'Covert surveillance and covert human intelligence sources codes of practice'. Available at: www.gov.uk/government/publications/covert-surveillance-and-covert-human-intelligence-sources-codes-of-practice

Home Office, 2016. 'Counting Rules for Recorded Crime—Fraud.' Available at: www.gov.uk/government/uploads/system/uploads/attachment_data/file/515640/count-fraud-april-2016.pdf

Information Commissioner's Office, 2011. 'Data sharing code of practice.' Available at: https://ico.org.uk/media/1068/data_sharing_code_of_practice.pdf

Institute of Chartered Accountants in England and Wales (ICAEW), 2016. 'ICAEW Home Page'. Available at: www.icaew.com

Insurance Fraud Bureau, 2016. 'Crash for Cash.' Available at: www.insurancefraud-bureau.org/insurance-fraud/crash-for-cash/

Intellectual Property Office, 2016. 'Licensing bodies and collective management organisations.' Available at: www.gov.uk/guidance/licensing-bodies-and-collec-tive-management-organisations#other-licensing-bodies.com

Joint Money Laundering Steering Group, 2016. *Joint Money Laundering Steering Group Guidance*. Available at: www.jmlsg.org.uk

KPMG, 2016. 'Profile of a Fraudster.' Available at: https://home.kpmg.com/ch/en/home/media/press-releases/2016/06/profile-of-a-fraudster.html

Law Society, 2013. 'Anti-Money Laundering Practice Note.' Available at: www.lawso-ciety.org.uk/support-services/advice/practice-notes/aml/

LexisNexis, 2015. 'Motor Insurance Fraud Research Study.' Available at: www.lexis-nexis.com/risk/uk/newsroom/15-11-23-motor-insurance-fraud.aspx

Magenta Systems Ltd, 2016. 'Magenta Dialling Code Lookup.' Available at: www.telecom-tariffs.co.uk/codelook.htm

Mailing Preference Service, 2016. 'Mailing Preference Service.' Available at: www.mpsonline.org.uk

Metropolitan Police Service, 2015. *The Little Book of Big Scams*. Third edn. Available at: www.met.police.uk/docs/little_book_scam.pdf

Metropolitan Police Service, 2016. 'Fraud Alert.' Available at: http://content.met.police.uk/Site/fraudalert

Ministry of Justice, 2011. *Achieving Best Evidence in Criminal Proceedings: Guidance on interviewing victims and witnesses, and guidance on using special measures*. Available at: www.cps.gov.uk/publications/docs/best_evidence_in_criminal_proceedings.pdf

Ministry of Justice, 2011. 'The Bribery Act 2010: Guidance.' Available at: www.jus-tice.gov.uk/downloads/legislation/bribery-act-2010-guidance.pdf

National Association of Business Crime Partnerships, 2016. 'National Association of Business Crime Partnerships Home Page.' Available at: www.businesscrime.org.uk/

National Crime Agency, 2016. 'Crime Threats—Money Laundering.' Available at: www.nationalcrimeagency.gov.uk/crime-threats/money-laundering

National Crime Agency, 2016. 'National Cyber Crime Unit—What we do.' Available at: www.nationalcrimeagency.gov.uk/about-us/what-we-do/national-cyber-crime-unit

National Cyber Security Centre, 2016. 'The National Cyber Security Centre Home Page.' Available at: www.ncsc.gov.uk

National Trading Standards eCrime Team, 2016. 'Latest Scams.' Available at: www.tradingstandardsecrime.org.uk/alerts/

Office for National Statistics, 2016. 'Office for National Statistics.' Available at: www.ons.gov.uk/

Office for National Statistics, 2015. 'Improving Crime Statistics in England and Wales—Developments in the coverage of Fraud.' Available at: http://webarchive.nationalarchives.gov.uk/20160105160709/www.ons.gov.uk/ons/rel/crime-stats/crime-statistics/year-ending-june-2015/sty-fraud.html

Phone-paid Services Authority, 2016. 'Guidance on premium rate service regulation.' Available at: www.psauthority.org.uk

PricewaterhouseCoopers, 2016. 'Global Economic Crime Survey 2016: UK Report.' Available at: www.pwc.co.uk/forensic-services/assets/gecs/gecs-uk-brochure-2016.pdf

Sentencing Council, 2014. 'Fraud, Bribery and Money Laundering Offences—Definitive Guideline.' Available at: www.sentencingcouncil.org.uk/wp-content/uploads/Fraud_ bribery_and_money_laundering_offences_-_Definitive_guideline.pdf

Telephone Preference Service, 2015. 'Telephone Preference Service Home Page.' Available at: www.tpsonline.org.uk/tps/index.html

UK Cards Association, 2016. 'Financial Fraud Bureau (FFB).' Available at: www.theukcardsassociation.org.uk/what_we_do/ffb.asp

US Securities and Exchange Commission, 2013. 'Fast Answers: Ponzi Schemes.' Available at: www.sec.gov/answers/ponzi.htm

Who.Is, 2016. 'WHOIS Search, Domain Name, Website, and IP Tools.' Available at: https://who.is

Index